Contents

Preface

What's the secret to regularly killing mature bucks in pressured areas? The answer is easy and is absolutely no secret: work very hard and hunt extremely smart. Bowhunting for mature bucks anywhere is difficult, but if you hunt in areas with extreme hunting pressure, like most of us do, the amount of work needed to enjoy regular success is much different than the work necessary in lightly hunted areas. A few late-summer scouting trips to hang a few stands is just not enough, and this is your first mistake. Hunting for mature pressured bucks is a passion that takes a great deal of time and hard work, twelve months a year. For us, hunting never really ends. It is a cycle that reaches its high point in the early spring and its climax in the fall, and then starts all over again.

We have designed this book to provide a clear path through every month of the year. The first part follows a month-by-month format that allows you to pinpoint the best time for each step in the chronological process. Starting after the last season ends, it begins with the month of January and works through the following season. We explain how we go about hunting pressured whitetails, relating each step as clearly and concisely as possible and illustrating how critical the right timing is to regular success. Each chapter is designed to stand alone, so there is some overlap in information when important aspects of hunting span more than one time frame. The second part of the book covers some special situations you might encounter that may be critical to your hunting success. The book ends with a discussion of perhaps the most important aspect of success: the bowhunter's attitude.

Join us as we take you through our hunting year. Our hunting system has taken us decades to develop and is based on long years of trial and error. We hope that our experience and insight help you along the long, bumpy road to becoming a better, more successful hunter.

INTRODUCTION

UNDER PRESSURE

Hunting pressure is one of the most important aspects influencing bowhunting success and failure. Deer react severely to heavy pressure, which is natural for them, considering that they are a prey species. Heavy pressure also means more deer killed, particularly more bucks, leaving fewer of them to live to maturity. It logically follows that areas with extremely heavy hunting pressure produce far fewer mature bucks than areas with light hunting pressure, and that it is far more difficult to kill mature bucks in these hard-hunted areas on a regular basis than in areas with little pressure. In some heavily hunted areas, up to 90 percent of the bucks are killed as yearlings. This means that two-and-a-half-year-olds are already few and far between, and some estimates place the survival rate of bucks to real maturity, three and a half years old and above, at less than 1 percent.

Not only is it statistically less probable that a hunter will kill a mature buck in pressured areas, but pressured bucks act differently than their brethren in lightly hunted areas. They have to, or they would not live to maturity. Nearly every mature buck living in a pressured area is severely nocturnal, even during the rut phases. And with fewer mature bucks in a local deer population, there is less rutting competition, creating a rut situation very much different from that in a herd with a more balanced sex ratio. These differences, among others, are a big deal and require special hunting tactics. A serious bowhunter simply cannot afford to ignore the effects of hunting pressure.

But the fact that hunting pressure is absolutely critical to bowhunting success on mature bucks in most areas has been largely ignored by the well-known whitetail "experts." The reason for this is simple: Recognition as a whitetail expert in the hunting community usually depends on the number of large bucks a hunter has killed or a career as a wildlife biologist. Killing the number and quality of bucks required to be considered an expert is easiest in areas with light hunting pressure, and the vast majority of well-known whitetail hunters hunt in those areas. They do not have to deal with hunting pressure and therefore have no idea how to hunt in such circumstances. Their advice is usually as follows: If you want to kill mature bucks, travel to the places where big bucks are easy to kill. This is realistic advice, but it is impossible to follow for most bowhunters. We are not in any way suggesting that the experts lack the desire and dedication to take big bucks in the areas they hunt; we are simply saying that those same practices will not produce big bucks with any regularity in pressured areas.

Whitetail biologists generally are experts in the behavior of deer held in captive environments. Their knowledge can be helpful, providing insight into biological processes, but there is a distinct difference between watching deer behind a high fence or in a severely controlled environment and actually hunting deer that are in an unbalanced herd and live in areas with tremendous hunting pressure. Most deer biologists who hunt do so in areas with little or no hunting pressure, in which deer react similarly to the deer they study in enclosures. Hunting nonpressured areas then lends credibility to their studies in enclosures. Although those studies are beneficial for the small percentage of hunters who hunt in similar circumstances, they are often of little use to those who hunt pressured deer. One recent study examined bucks of different ages in a large enclosure to see how many does they bred with during a specific breeding season. The bucks were from one and a half to six and a half years old, with multiple bucks in each age bracket. The question is, how could a study such as this shed any light on breeding habits in a pressured area where most of these age brackets do not exist?

We often encounter bowhunters from heavily hunted areas, with perhaps one or two 100-inch bucks to their credit, who have a skill level far above that of many of these whitetail experts but will never kill the huge bucks so prevalent in the hunting literature and videos. They are simply in the wrong location to do so. This location problem is the reason why so few well-known whitetail hunters hunt in the really pressured states, such as Pennsylvania, West Virginia, Michigan, and New York, even though some of them hail from these areas. And it is the same reason that an abundance of big-name hunters are from Minnesota, Iowa, Illinois, and Kansas. The playing field is simply not level. Having hunted in both types of areas, we are speaking from direct experience. A hunter of average ability in pressured areas will more than likely be able to kill mature bucks regularly in some lightly hunted areas. That same hunter will have severe difficulty killing any two-and-a-half-year-old in other areas with more pressure. Many of the techniques presented in most modern hunting videos would be unthinkable in a pressured area.

A hunter's expectations are tightly bound to the region in which he hunts. In some areas, bucks that score 100 inches are far more rare than 160-class bucks in other areas. Heavy hunting pressure is a major reason for this discrepancy, though habitat has huge implications as well. In some of the big-woods areas we hunt in northern Michigan, it usually takes a buck three and a half years to grow antlers that measure just over 100 inches. The slow growth rate coupled with heavy hunting pressure makes larger antlered bucks absolute rarities. Considering that 80 to 90 percent of the bucks are killed as yearlings, you can imagine how few make it to three and a half. A quick look at the Commemorative Bucks of Michigan records for Clare County will prove our point (see the table below, printed with permission from CBM). That county always has had, and still has, as much hunting pressure as any other county in the state. Here, bucks that score in the 120s make the top-ten list of all time, and not a single buck has measured more than 151. On the other hand, we have hunted agricultural areas in less pressured states where the average two-and-a-half-year-old buck has antlers that approach, or even exceed, the Pope and Young minimum, and most three-and-a-half-year-olds measure around 140 or higher.

TOP BUCKS TAKEN WITH ARCHERY EQUIPMENT, CLARE COUNTY, MICHIGAN

Rank	Score	Year Taken
1	150.4	2000
2	147.7	1999
3	146.2	1983
4	135.5	1999
5	134.3	1990
6	133.0	1990
7	129.2	1991
8	126.1	1997
9	126.0	1999
10	125.7	1980
11	125.2	2000

Listed here are the eleven all-time top bucks taken with archery equipment in Clare County, Michigan. This list includes all the bucks that make the Pope & Young minimum score. Clare County is year for year one of the heaviest hunted counties in Michigan. (Scores taken from the Commemorative Bucks of Michigan record book 2001 edition.)

John's son Jon took this two-and-a-half-year-old eight-point on state land while it was feeding on acorns.

It is obvious that hunter expectations will differ from area to area, and the antlers on the head of equally mature bucks can vary widely. A buck with a rack that a hunter from a big-buck state might nail onto his barn, or not even shoot at in the first place, may be taxidermist material in pressured areas. In relatively poor habitat, we have taken mature bucks of four and a half to five and a half years that gross scored only in the mid-120s, and when we hunt these areas, we target any buck with a rack in excess of 100 inches. Despite their smaller size, these bucks are the ones we are the most proud of. It follows that the number of big racks a hunter has is not always an indication of his or her skill level.

Chris took this buck in northern Michigan. Two and a half years old, it scored less than 100 inches, proof positive of the differences in antler growth from area to area. Chris has taken two bucks the same age in other states that have scored over 120 inches.

To reinforce our claims, we have done some research and come up with some interesting statistics. Like all statistics, they should be taken with a grain of salt, and there are always some exceptions. We calculated bowhunter density per square mile in most of the whitetail states. Our results, shown in the table and map on the following pages, reveal an interesting pattern of hunter density. Whereas a bowhunter in Pennsylvania has to share each square mile with at least three others, a bowhunter in Kansas has about eight square miles to himself. Hunter density, though, is not so interesting until it is coupled with the number of mature bucks entered in the record books. To complement hunter density, we calculated the absolute number of bucks entered in the 2000 Pope and Young record book from a few representative states at both ends of the pressure spectrum, and then took an average score of the bucks entered. There is an almost direct inverse relationship between hunter density and the number of record-class bucks produced: the more hunters, the lower the chances that a hunter will take a mature buck. Not only are more bucks entered from the states with light hunting pressure, but also the average score of those bucks is much higher than in states with high hunter density (see the table on page xx). This leaves us with the suspicion that the rates of buck entry in the record books are lower in states with light hunting pressure than in those with heavy hunting pressure. It simply takes a bigger buck to attract attention in states where mature bucks are almost commonplace, whereas a 125-inch buck in a heavy hunted state is often considered the buck of a lifetime.

BOWHUNTER DENSITY BY REGION, 2001

State	Bowhunter Density Per Square Mile
North Central	
1. West Virginia	5.81
2. Michigan	5.39
3. Wisconsin	4.74
4. Kentucky	4.63
5. Ohio	3.90
6. Indiana	3.06
7. Illinois	1.97
Northeast	
1. Pennsylvania	6.03
2. New Jersey	5.48
3. Rhode Island	4.18
4. Vermont	3.89
5. Maryland	3.78
6. New York	3.76
7. Delaware	3.58
8. Massachusetts	2.93
9. Connecticut	2.83
10. New Hampshire	2.50
11. Virginia	1.50
12. Maine	.51
West of the Mississippi (North)	
1. Missouri	1.42
2. Minnesota	.90
3. Iowa	.71
4. Kansas	.24
5. Nebraska	.19
6. North Dakota	.19
7. Montana	.17
8. South Dakota	.17
9. Wyoming	.11
West of the Mississippi (South)	
1. Louisiana	.73
2. Arkansas	.57
3. Oklahoma	.33
4. Texas	.28

continued on next page

State	Bowhunter Density Per Square Mile
Southeast	
1. Tennessee	2.18
2. Georgia	1.67
3. Alabama	1.37
4. Mississippi	1.37
5. South Carolina	1.32
6. North Carolina	1.12
7. Florida	.51

Densities calculated by dividing the number of licenses sold per state by the square miles of each state. For instance, in 2001 Connecticut sold 13,715 bowhunting licenses and has a total area of 4,845 square miles, giving us 2.83 licenses sold per square mile. This number is not the same as the actual number of hunters per square mile—in most cases the actual number is much higher, but it is a good indication of the general amount of hunting pressure a state receives.

Bowhunting license sales taken from *Archery Business Magazine*, September 2002. State sizes from *Almanac*, U.S. Department of Commerce, Bureau of the Census.

We are aware of the limitations of these statistics. We are not able to account for many variables, such as developed land, human population density, varying habitat quality, areas devoid of whitetails, exclusive hunting areas in generally pressured states, or fluctuations in hunter density within states. Michigan provides good examples of all of these. Hunter density, like general human population density, is far lower in the Upper Peninsula than in the Lower Peninsula. This fact distorts the hunter density average for the entire state. The Lower Peninsula is hunted very heavily, particularly the northern end, which has an abundance of public land and is within an hour's drive of some big cities. With a human population of about 10 million and the cities themselves taking up large amounts of space, hunter density is increased on the remaining land. States with fewer large cities and people have more space for hunters to spread out.

Habitat quality also varies dramatically in Michigan. The southern half of the Lower Peninsula is rich agricultural country. This area supports relatively high deer densities and produces more quality bucks than other areas of the state, despite heavy hunting pressure. The northern half of the Lower Peninsula is a mixture of sandy woodland and swamp, with far less agriculture. The habitat is just not as productive as in the southern half for large deer. The Upper Peninsula, particularly along Lake Superior, has low deer densities and somewhat regular deer die-offs due to severe winters. After these die-offs, some areas are almost devoid of deer for several years. Deer densities vary considerably in the Upper Peninsula, from high deer densities in the southwest to very low deer densities in the north. Though big mature bucks are always taken in the Upper Peninsula, few are found in the big swamps that dominate that part of the state. There are also exclusive areas in Michigan, mostly private hunt clubs, where big mature bucks are commonplace, just as there are heavily hunted zones even in the most lightly hunted states.

United States Bowhunter Density, 2001

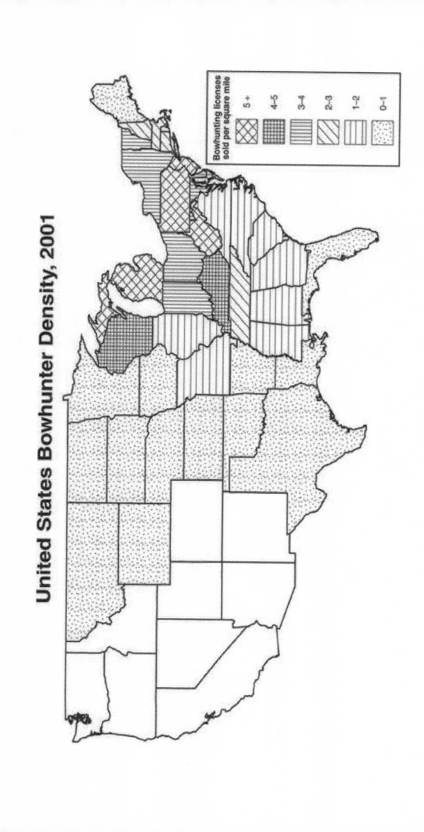

Bowhunting licenses
sold per square mile

5 +

4-5

3-4

2-3

1-2

0-1

Ratios of P & Y Bucks to Hunters, 2001

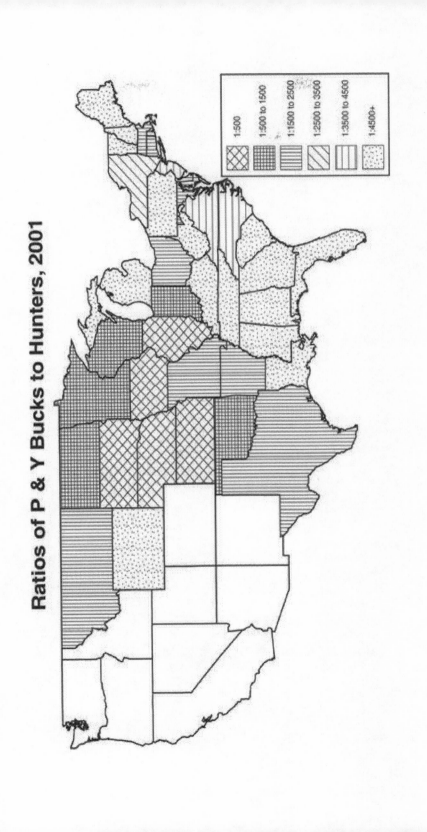

POPE & YOUNG STATISTICS BY STATE, 2001

State	160+	150+	140+	125+	NT	Total
1. Iowa	4	17	47	80	22	170
2. Kansas	8	13	7	43	7	78
3. Nebraska	1	6	5	19	6	37
4. Illinois	26	34	54	118	31	263
5. South Dakota	2	-	9	18	3	32
6. Wisconsin	8	22	71	239	18	358
7. North Dakota	-	1	-	12	1	14
8. Minnesota	2	5	16	38	3	64
9. Oklahoma	2	1	3	10	3	19
10. Indiana	9	6	19	44	9	87
11. Maryland	-	4	6	13	1	24
12. Ohio	6	8	15	57	11	97
13. Texas	1	2	6	31	4	44
14. Massachusetts	-	-	2	11	-	13
15. Montana	-	-	6	8	-	14
16. Missouri	4	4	11	31	3	53
17. Connecticut	-	1	3	2	-	6
18. Arkansas	-	-	2	10	-	12
19. New York	-	6	16	36	2	60
20. Delaware	-	1	-	1	-	2
21. Virginia	-	-	2	14	-	16
22. New Jersey	-	-	2	8	-	10
23. North Carolina	-	2	-	9	2	13
24. Rhode Island	-	1	-	-	-	1
25. Georgia	-	2	3	16	-	21
26. Pennsylvania	2	2	8	40	6	58
27. West Virginia	2	1	3	23	1	30
28. Kentucky	4	10	6	15	4	39
29. Wyoming	-	-	2	-	-	2
30. Mississippi	-	-	3	7	1	11
31. Louisiana	-	-	-	4	-	4
32. Michigan	1	1	2	28	4	36
33. Tennessee	-	-	-	5	2	7
34. Alabama	-	-	-	5	-	5
35. Maine	-	1	-	-	-	1
36. New Hampshire	-	-	-	1	-	1
37. Florida	-	-	-	1	-	1
38. South Carolina	-	-	-	1	-	1

NT = nontypical
Taken from Pope & Young record book 2001 recording period

RATIO OF POPE & YOUNG BUCKS ENTERED TO
BOWHUNTING LICENSES SOLD, 2001

State	Licenses Sold	P&Y Bucks Entered	Ratio	Comments
1. Iowa	40072	170	1 – 235	
2. Kansas	19913	78	1 – 255	2
3. Nebraska	15105	37	1 – 408	2
4. Illinois	110000	263	1 – 418	
5. South Dakota	13740	32	1 – 429	2
6. Wisconsin	257571	358	1 – 719	
7. North Dakota	13228	14	1 – 944	2
8. Minnesota	72000	64	1 – 1125	
9. Oklahoma	23000	19	1 – 1210	
10. Indiana	110000	87	1 – 1264	
11. Maryland	37000	24	1 – 1540	
12. Ohio	160000	97	1 – 1649	
13. Texas	75000	44	1 – 1704	
14. Massachusetts	23000	13	1 – 1769	
15. Montana	25000	14	1 – 1785	2
16. Missouri	97883	53	1 – 1846	
17. Connecticut	13715	6	1 – 2285	
18. Arkansas	30000	12	1 – 2500	
19. New York	177900	60	1 – 2965	
20. Delaware	7000	2	1 – 3500	
21. Virginia	59720	16	1 – 3732	
22. New Jersey	40719	10	1 – 4071	
23. North Carolina	55000	13	1 – 4230	
24. Rhode Island	4371	1	1 – 4371	
25. Georgia	96721	21	1 – 4605	1
26. Pennsylvania	270529	58	1 – 4664	
27. West Virginia	140000	30	1 – 4666	
28. Kentucky	184214	39	1 – 4723	
29. Wyoming	11339	2	1 – 5669	2
30. Mississippi	64500	11	1 – 5863	1
31. Louisiana	32000	4	1 – 8000	1
32. Michigan	306266	36	1 – 8507	
33. Tennessee	90000	7	1 – 12857	1
34. Alabama	69600	5	1 – 13920	1
35. Maine	15852	1	1 – 15852	
36. New Hampshire	22500	1	1 – 22500	

continued on next page

RATIO OF POPE & YOUNG BUCKS ENTERED TO
BOWHUNTING LICENSES SOLD, 2001 *continued*

State	Licenses Sold	P&Y Bucks Entered	Ratio	Comments
37. Florida	27878	1	1 – 27878	1
38. South Carolina	40000	1	1 – 40000	1

Comments

1. The states in the Southeast represent an exception to the typical relation between mature buck harvest and bowhunter density. Despite low overall bowhunter density, there are relatively few bucks entered in the Pope & Young record books. We surmise there are several factors contributing to this. Some of the factors include liberal hunting seasons and bag limits, special hunting methods (such as hunting with hounds), a unique hunting culture that places less emphasis on the entry of bucks in the record books, and simply a smaller subspecies of deer.

2. These states' bowhunting license sales include other species, such as mule deer, making the actual ratio even lower.

License sales from *Archery Business Magazine*, September 2002.

Pope & Young entries from Pope & Young 2001 recording period.

Interesting, too, are the exceptions, particularly Wisconsin and Ohio. Both of these states produce high numbers of big, mature bucks despite relatively high hunter densities. We suspect that this is due to a combination of terrain features, state and private deer management practices, and regulations. Wisconsin and Ohio both have excellent deer habitat throughout their entirety, a situation that seldom occurs. In most states, habitat quality varies dramatically from areas with deer overpopulation to areas devoid of deer. Ohio, with its single-buck rule, allows more bucks to live to maturity than otherwise. Michigan, on the other hand, with its multiple-buck rule and lack of a checking system, has more bucks killed and less departmental control over herd composition. It is common for hunters to shoot the first buck they see, and then wait for a larger one. Or conversely, a hunter may shoot a mature buck, and then shoot a smaller buck later. States with mandatory deer checks also tend to produce more mature bucks than states with no such system. Wisconsin and Ohio both have mandatory check systems for all deer killed. Perhaps these systems keep some hunters from cheating.

Now that we have established the relationship between hunting pressure and number of mature bucks, it is clear that if you happen to live and hunt in a pressured area, you should be severely depressed. Just kidding! There is still hope. It is possible to kill mature bucks on a fairly regular basis, without having to move to Kansas, even in pressured areas. This endeavor, however, takes a lot of hard work, dedication, patience, sacrifice, and a passion to hunt.

If any of these elements are missing, you might be better off redefining your hunting goals and simply enjoy recreational hunting, rather than seriously pursuing mature pressured bucks. False expectations can be detrimental to simply enjoying the hunting experience.

The real "secret" to hunting mature bucks in a pressured environment consists of hard work and paying very close attention to your surroundings throughout the entire year. There are no shortcuts, and we are not talking about hard work implementing a Quality Deer Management (QDM) program or working extra hard at your job to be able to pay for a guided hunt on managed property, though guides definitely have their place in hunting, and QDM, like any other habitat improvement, can be commendable in some situations. Unfortunately, QDM and some other recent trends tend to mutate into shortcuts for hunters who are not prepared to do the work necessary to succeed in real hunting conditions. These trends take the form of trophy buck management, extremely limited access, astronomical leasing rates, and high fences, all of which can represent, in varying degrees, the ugly side of hunting. Then there's the recent emphasis on "upper end" deer management in books and videos these days, which seems to approach the gray zone between deer hunting and deer farming. Exactly how wild is a free-ranging buck that has been named, whose sheds have been collected by the deer manager since its first set, and that has been allowed to reach full maturity before being "harvested"? This is a question you have to answer for yourself. Ethics is always a gray zone.

Don't misunderstand what we are attempting to say. There is absolutely nothing wrong with spending time and money doing what you love. We spend probably far more money on hunting than we should, or than is healthy for our budgets. Everything costs money, including bowhunting. If you have the money and desire to hunt exclusive areas, set up extensive management, and hire guides, by all means do so. The best thing about hunting, though, is that it could possibly be considered the last best deal and one of the last bastions of equality remaining. Hunters come from all social and economic classes. In most states, a resident hunting license costs less than dinner and a movie. Nonresident licenses are available in numerous states for less than it costs for a round of golf on a decent course. This is a pretty good deal, considering that most hunting seasons last for at least three months, and you get to keep the meat! There are equipment and travel costs involved in hunting as well. Such costs are part of any outdoor endeavor, from jogging to scuba diving. The low price tag of hunting is a golden opportunity for bowhunters. It is still possible to be an excellent bowhunter and take mature bucks without paying outrageous sums to do so. Bowhunting also allows you to take part in the natural environment, which is valuable in itself.

In 2000, John took this five-and-a-half-year-old eight-point in a section that has well over forty bowhunters hunting in it.

We prefer to bowhunt where we are able to take all the steps involved without any shortcuts. Perhaps we are old-fashioned, but to us, hunting is more than just showing up and shooting. It's a way of life that goes beyond spending a few days in the woods each fall. It means constant effort and lots of time logged outdoors, all year long. We cherish the challenge that mature pressured bucks provide and the opportunity to spend as much time in the woods as possible. Guides, large expensive leases, and private QDM efforts are as out of reach for us as they are for most hunters. Like most other hunters, we have neither the money, property, or desire for that kind of luxury. We are left to make the best of the ever-diminishing hunting opportunities that are close at hand and affordable, which involves gaining permission on private land, hunting on state land, and dealing with hordes of other hunters, not to mention nonhunters and antihunters. This situation has forced us to refine our hunting practices to reach even a moderate level of success. With fewer and warier mature bucks around, in order to be successful, you have to work harder and more precisely, and depart from the ways of average bowhunters. With the right attitude, though, success is within grasp. In this book, we share with you our hunting technique, step by step, which has proven itself successful on truly pressured whitetail bucks. And for those of you fortunate enough to live and hunt in one of the lightly hunted big-buck areas, any technique that works well in pressured areas will work even better in less pressured areas.

PART I

A BOWHUNTER'S YEAR

CHAPTER 1

January and February

Depending on where you live and hunt, January and February can be two of the most important months of the year, as far as scouting and preparation are concerned. In most states, the hunting season has just ended. After three to four months of hunting, you're probably worn out, and the last thing you want to think about is scouting. This is a common way to feel, but in order to take full advantage of last fall's sign, while it is still visible, it is an excellent idea to spend some time scouting in January and February. You are not the only one who does not want to get up and move in the cold winter months. In northern states, winter can also bring hardship for deer. Short days, cold temperatures, and snow cause the deer to enter a sort of walking hibernation. The deer conserve as much energy as they can by moving as little as possible, just to stay alive. In the North, deer die-offs during winters with heavy snow are not uncommon. With the deer in mind, get your winter scouting done as expediently as possible, and then leave them alone. Their toughest month of the year is February. For the late fawns and mature bucks, which have been known to lose up to 25 percent of their body weight during the rut, this is a critical time. In severe conditions, the less they are disturbed, the better they will come through the winter.

January is also the time to begin anew your fitness routine that you discontinued just prior to hunting season. We all know how easy it is to gain weight during the winter, so don't put your fitness program off until spring. Being fit not only makes hunting easier, but also increases your chances at tagging a good buck. The mental toughness it takes to hunt on long, cold, uncomfortable days is directly related to physical fitness. As in any sport, the better tuned your body is, the better you will be able to react to stress situations and the more successful you will be. An automobile analogy makes this clear. Let's say you were about to drive across country. Would you rather drive a car that is in good running shape or a beat-up old clunker? The old clunker might make the trip but will cost you a great deal of anxiety and will clearly be less efficient, all in all reducing the quality of the experience. The hunting experience is similar. Even the most unfit person can hunt and may experience some success. A hunter who is fit, though, will simply be better able to withstand the stresses of the season and recover more quickly, thus increasing the overall quality of the experience and the chances for success.

EARLY SCOUTING FOR THE LATE SEASON

If you are serious about hunting white-tailed deer, particularly in areas with heavy hunting pressure, you have to start your postseason preparation as soon as possible after the just completed season. This usually means January in most areas. You can begin even earlier if you have tagged out for the year. In areas that receive snow, the earliest scouting in the calendar year is primarily for the latest hunting period the following fall and winter.

Weather conditions can vary dramatically in the winter, and depending on the situation, there are different factors to be aware of. The first and most obvious thing to look for is winter deer activity, particularly if there is snow or extremely cold temperatures. Try to find areas of intense activity. Food is the major factor in winter scouting: Find the main food source and you will find the deer. Other than a few southern states that have their main rut in mid to late December, deer in the rest of the country will be heavily feeding by this time, with the food sources becoming less prevalent and nutritious than during the rest of the year. The deer must feed more before their metabolism slows for the late-winter months. This should clue you in to where to attempt to pinpoint stand locations for December hunting next season. Travel routes between protected bedding areas—those that are mainly protected from the wind—are the best locations to ambush a postrut buck.

A protected bedding area might be found on a south slope that is more exposed to the sun or in thick cedars or conifers that provide thermal cover. If you are in the North, finding a deeryard can be the key to late-season success in following years. In future seasons, if the mercury takes a drastic fall or a heavy snow comes early, you will know where the deer are headed and will be able to adjust your hunting accordingly. Mentally note all the winter deer holding locations for future reference and add them to your hunting notebook. You might even clear out a tree or two. Generally, the weather conditions necessary for hunting such locations only come about every few years. If, during the late bow season, the proper weather conditions arise for hunting such a location, setting up a tree at that time, after gun season, would be very detrimental to success in that spot. Cutting lanes, trimming trees, making noise, leaving scent, and spending time in one location will all cause heavily pressured deer to alter their routine immediately.

Here's an example of the importance of scouting for this kind of deer movement. An area that we hunted for several years had deer in abundance. As soon as the mercury dropped below freezing for a few days and snow hit the ground, the deer simply vanished, despite some good bedding areas and leftover crops. It took us a while, but eventually we figured out where all the deer had gone. About two miles from the area we hunted was a fair-size, extremely thick cedar swamp. As soon as the weather turned frigid, nearly all of the deer from the surrounding sections made a migration to that swamp, some moving more than five miles. Considering the area, mainly farmland with interspersed woods and some decent bedding areas, a deer migration was unusual. In most of the surrounding country, deer yarding and migration very seldom took place, usually only in cases of very severe winters. The local deer, though, moved every year, even during light winters.

What did this minimigration mean to our hunting? It meant that we had to refine our hunting plan in our initial area. We concentrated our hunting during the early season and rut, and as soon as the snow and cold arrived, because we did not have permission to hunt the swamp, we hunted other areas with deer activity. This adjustment may seem obvious, but we regularly encounter hunters who continue to pound areas, even after the deer have departed as a result of a change in the weather. Being able to react and, better yet, predict deer movement is very important to successful whitetail hunting. Scouting in January and February can provide you with the insight necessary to react when the weather turns cold in the coming seasons.

The second element of this winter scouting is to learn how the deer react to hunting pressure, particularly gun-hunting pressure. After the onslaught of gun season, deer behavior changes. Deer automatically alter their movement patterns in various ways. Their initial reaction to sudden intense pressure is to find secure zones within the pressured areas and seek refuge there. These can be small areas of tight cover that most hunters overlook or areas that are difficult for hunters to access. The deer will reside there until long after the pressure subsides. Along with this initial reaction of refuge seeking, the deer, particularly the mature bucks, immediately become extremely nocturnal, even though the rut may still be in full swing.

Knowing how the deer react to extreme pressure in your hunting spots is a big step toward future success. Your window of opportunity to find these safety zones is quite short. During the gun season and for a few short weeks thereafter, the deer will continue to use these spots. Afterward, the deer will resume their activity with more normal early-winter patterns. Therefore, if you want to be able to take advantage of this situation in future seasons, you have to be in the woods while the deer are still in a disturbed state. As soon as you are sure the hunting is completed in an area, get out in the woods and note any concentrations in deer activity. If you find good deer activity, you can be sure that the deer are there because they feel safe. Clear out a tree or two for the next late season.

Take note of any deer you spook at this time of year. Carefully observe the escape routes these deer use and inspect them thoroughly. Return after the snow is gone to see if the deer were using the same escape routes earlier in the season. Escape routes are good places to hunt when the pressure is on, as long as they offer good cover. A tree along an escape route can be an excellent spot at certain times, such as the opening days of bow season, or pheasant season in agricultural areas. Spooking deer during the postseason will not affect next fall's deer movement whatsoever, so do not be shy about acquiring in-depth, detailed knowledge of your hunting property.

The third, and by far most important, element of winter scouting is pinpointing last fall's rut activity. To be able to do this, however, the ground must be free of snow. Because Michigan almost always has snow during January and February, we discuss this type of scouting for March and April. If, however, you hunt in an area where snow is seldom or are experiencing a mild winter without snow, do the majority of your scouting the first two months of the year.

Under normal winter conditions, you are scouting for a few weeks in the late season for future years. Each part of the hunting season has to be hunted differently and with a plan. Your scouting is the basis for this plan, and every spot has to be incorporated into this plan for a short time frame during the season. Your scouting at this time has to be precise for hunting the few short weeks after gun season.

FITNESS

If you've hunted hard, your body is worn out by January, so it is important to give yourself a couple weeks to recuperate from the stresses of a long, hard season. Other than scouting, take a couple weeks and relax. By about mid-January, you should resume your fitness routine.

It is true that sitting in a tree stand for a few hours does not require much fitness. Viewed individually, the steps required to be a successful bowhunter do not require a great deal of fitness; viewed as a whole, however, hunting can be grueling. Scouting is a never-ending process, in which you easily can walk up to five miles in an outing, and involves clearing out trees, which requires both upper-body strength and balance. Actual hunting can last up to four months, during which you are constantly on the go, outside in the elements, and often get too little sleep. It is easy to see that keeping fit can make hunting easier and more enjoyable.

Staying in good physical condition will enable you to endure a long season of hard work.

Although you do not have to be a marathon runner to bowhunt, endurance is the most important aspect of a bowhunting training regimen. We accomplish this with regular cardiovascular workouts three or four times a week. Your workout does not have to be anything fancy, just something that raises your pulse rate for at least twenty minutes. This can be done by jogging, biking, using a treadmill, or walking vigorously. The important thing is that you do it and get in shape. The second aspect of your fitness program should be upper-body strength training. We like to do light weight training combined with stomach exercises, but this can also be accomplished without any equipment. A program of sit-ups and push-ups can be sufficient. The third part of your training program should consist of light stretching. Flexibility is important for climbing trees and moving smoothly. It is also the first thing that is lost with age. The important thing is to find a level of fitness where you are comfortable and in decent shape. Again, it is not as important how you train as that you do train.

Yet another element of hunting fitness that is often neglected at this time of year is regular practice with your bow. It is very important to keep your shooting muscles in shape the entire year. There are several items on the market that replicate the drawing of a bow to keep these muscles strong. This not only will help your shooting consistency, but also will help your confidence at the moment of truth. And on top of that, with regular practice throughout the entire year, you can be certain that you will be able to draw your bow on those cold November and December mornings.

CHAPTER 2

March, April, and May

Although deer behavior in the spring is of little importance to your fall hunting, paying attention to what is happening in the deer woods should always interest hunters. Too many hunters act as if deer exist only in the fall. As the days lengthen, the deer's metabolism begins to increase, meaning that the deer need more food. This increase in food consumption coincides with the spring greenup. Last year's fawns experience a growth spurt at this time. The mature does have to feed heavily to nourish the fawns they will bear in June, and the bucks begin growing their new antlers. Getting enough food to match growth demands is what spring is all about to deer.

Other than actual hunting, the majority of work required during the entire hunting year in pressured areas should be completed between March and May. While hunting pressured areas, you cannot just walk into the woods in the fall and expect to arrow a mature buck. Though this sometimes happens, it is an exception. Consistent success requires consistent hard work, particularly in the spring. A good bowhunting year begins with spring scouting and tree preparation. In heavily hunted locales, the majority of your scouting involves finding adequate property to hunt, which should be one of your principal tasks during the spring. Most actual in-the-woods scouting should take place between snowmelt and the growth of new foliage; in northern areas, this is between March and May.

The first line of business in the spring is finding places to hunt. If you already have ample property to hunt, you are lucky. For most hunters in heavily hunted areas, this is one of the biggest barriers to consistently arrowing mature bucks. The simple reality is that there is more competition for diminishing hunting land than there was ten, or even five, years ago. In heavily hunted areas, many hunters spend the entire season hunting a single small parcel of land less than forty acres in size, sometimes as small as ten acres. The problem that arises from this circumstance is that hunters usually overhunt their properties. With so little property to hunt on, this is an almost unavoidable situation. Excessive hunting pressure is extremely detrimental in the pursuit of mature bucks.

There are two ways to counter this problem: either wait until the hunting situation is perfect to hunt your property or find more places to hunt. The second option is the one we recommend. You can never have enough property to hunt when seriously pursuing mature bucks in pressured areas. Between the two of us, we usually start the season each year with about ten properties to hunt, on which we prepare or retrim up to eighty trees, most of which will not get hunted. Ten properties may sound like a lot, but mere numbers do not always reveal the truth of the situation. Here in Michigan, hunting pressure is intense, mature bucks are somewhat uncommon, and most property parcels are small. Of the ten or so properties, we will have a decent chance at a mature buck on only a couple. Because of the lack of mature bucks in some of the areas we hunt, several of the properties may be home to such a buck only every few years. We try to retain permission on all of these properties so that when a mature buck shows up, we can attempt to capitalize on the situation. The quality varies considerably on these properties, which consist of both private and a great deal of public land. Some are excellent, others are good, still others offer only an outside chance at a mature buck, and some are doe-hunting spots with virtually no chance at a good buck. The point is to try to have as much land to hunt as possible, to open up as many hunting options as possible.

OBTAINING PERMISSION FOR NEW HUNTING PROPERTIES

Gaining permission for a new hunting property can be very difficult and time-consuming. This is particularly true if you cannot afford a large lease. The best time to ask for permission to hunt is during late winter and spring. Timing is important. In the spring, the previous hunting season is already a few months behind us, and the coming season is still quite a ways in the future. Most people, landowners included, are not thinking much about hunting. This means that a request to hunt a property will probably be unexpected, increasing the likelihood of receiving a positive response.

There are numerous ways to go about getting hunting permission. The easiest and best way is by networking. Most of the permission we have was acquired through networking. The concept is simple: Let friends, relatives, and acquaintances know that you are a bowhunter and are looking for a place to hunt. You never know where hunting permission will come from. Some of the best property that Chris has to hunt came through friends he met while in college. People you know are far more likely to grant permission than total strangers. This is a simple fact. Get the word out and you might be surprised at the new hunting properties you have this fall.

John asking for permission to hunt a property. If you don't ask, you won't get it.

The more difficult option to finding new land to hunt is simply asking landowners in places you would like to hunt. In areas with numerous hunters, this can be challenging and full of disappointment. Overwhelmingly, your request for hunting permission will be turned down. Probably the worst way to attempt to gain permission is by a mere phone call. People have grown wary of telephone calls from unknown people and are accustomed to saying no over the telephone. The problem is similar with simply knocking on doors.

Landowners are approached regularly door to door by salesmen and others for various reasons and are usually quite suspect of such activity. With a good plan, however, you can dramatically increase your chances for success. It is a good idea to know the names of the people you will be asking for permission. The best tool for this is a plat book, in which you can find the names of the owners of properties you're interested in hunting. Plat books can usually be purchased for a nominal fee (between $12 and $20) from the county seat. We simply call and have the books mailed to us. You can also find this information on county property appraisers' websites on the Internet. Once you have a name, you can use a telephone book to find the person's address and telephone number. In some states, the plat book gives this information.

Sit down and write a letter to the landowner. The letter should contain some basic personal information and a request for a short visit. The letter could be constructed similarly to the following example:

Dear Mr. Landowner,

My name is Joe Bowhunter, and I work at Johnson's excavating in Lapeer. My family and I have lived in the area for ten years. I am an avid ethical bowhunter seeking permission (for me only) to bowhunt on your property this year. As a member of the local chapter of Whitetails Unlimited, a nonprofit organization, I am committed to conservation, fair-chase hunting, and landowner rights. I, of course, would respect any wishes that you might have regarding where you prefer me to hunt and during which times. It would also be my pleasure, if successful, to share a portion of my good fortune with you and your family as a way of saying thank you.

I will stop by on Tuesday, March 25, around 7 P.M. to discuss my request and any issues that you may have concerns about. If that is not convenient, or you do not wish to grant me permission, please feel free to contact me at 555-5555. If I am not home, please leave a message. I look forward to speaking with you and hope to meet you in the near future.

Sincerely,
Joe Bowhunter

Make sure to include your telephone number and address, as well as a request to meet on a certain date and time. Such an approach conveys an air of seriousness and will separate you from the majority of hunters, who do not ask for permission until a few weeks before the season. It also gives landowners forewarning of your intentions and an easy out.

Also be sure to visit at the time you promised. Being punctual shows that you are serious and responsible. Dress casually but nicely. Your appearance has an immediate impact on your chances. Look at this appointment as if it were a job interview. The only reason you are there is because your chances of getting permission are decent.

Introduce yourself, and ask the landowner if he received your letter. If he says he did not receive your letter, briefly explain what it said and your intent to ask for hunting permission. If the landowner says he has received your letter but immediately refuses permission, thank him politely for his time and ask why he denied your request. Often the answer will be that he and his family hunt the property. Sometimes the landowner will have had a bad experience with allowing people to hunt his land. Others are simply antihunting. That quick question will perhaps lead to a pleasant conversation, which in turn could open doors. A follow-up question might be whether the landowner knows anyone else who might grant permission. This could lead to inside information on new hunting property.

At every turn, be very respectful, even if the outcome is negative. Remember that you are representing all hunters, and hunting in general. Your actions can have repercussions on the future of hunting. If you are granted permission, establish in detail where, when, and how you may hunt. Whether your request is granted or denied, thank the landowner for his time and be as polite as possible. Never try to hard sell a landowner into giving you permission. This is both impolite and inappropriate. Take a negative response as part of the game and move on.

Although knocking on doors is not as good a method for obtaining permission, we use it for random situations where networking or letter writing is not possible or for spur-of-the-moment attempts. While working, we travel quite a lot and spend a great deal of time in certain areas away from home. In such situations, you may want to hunt in the general area where you work. The problem is that time is short for both seeking permission and hunting. When we see an area that looks promising along our route, we stop and ask for permission to hunt. Expressly for this purpose, we carry several copies of a letter similar to the one above, accompanied by a short general résumé that states, among other things, our jobs, family status, and other hobbies. We give these directly to the landowner at the time of request. These requests are tough, because you never know what you might encounter. Sometimes you are met with a resounding no in the first few seconds. Other times the landowner will hear you out. And sometimes you will be granted permission. Thirty years ago, this method worked like a charm, particularly for permission to bowhunt, which was relatively uncommon in those days. Times have changed, and these days we receive permission only sporadically and usually after many requests. Again, it is imperative to remain polite and respectful, no matter what kind of response you receive.

Yet another possibility is attempting to gain permission through the backdoor. With landowners whom we know are wary of allowing hunting permission, we attempt to gain permission to do something else. One possibility is predator hunting. Farmers are generally not all that fond of coyotes, for example, and will often allow hunting for them, although they would deny deer-hunting permission. A farmer might even think you are doing him a favor by going after predators that frequently kill young livestock and poultry. This opens up the possibility of establishing a trusting relationship with a wary landowner, or at least proving that you are considerate and responsible. Predator hunting is primarily practiced in the dead of winter, and this may cause the landowner to respect your dedication. After you have opened up a dialogue with a landowner, your chances of getting permission to hunt deer in the future increase dramatically.

Predator hunting is only one of almost endless possibilities. Some others that we have used are turkey hunting, wildlife photography, or looking for mushrooms. The nonhunting options are particularly attractive in semirural areas with a high percentage of nonhunting population. Some people who would be appalled at a cold request for hunting permission will think that photography is great, shows a real interest in nature, and, contrary to the negative stereotype of most hunters, that you are out for far more than just killing. After you prove to these people that you are truly interested in deer and nature, and have developed a courteous dialogue, they will be more likely to grant you hunting permission.

Gaining hunting permission for land that can potentially hold a mature buck is a huge part of the equation to killing mature bucks on a regular basis. Fortunately, this is still possible without having to pay to hunt. You must, however, be willing to get out there and find places to hunt. This is not easy, and as time goes on, it is going to become even more difficult. Always evaluate the situation and attempt to land permission the best way possible.

RECONFIRMING PERMISSION FOR PRESENT HUNTING PROPERTIES

This is also the time of year to reconfirm permission on properties you are presently hunting. Usually we pay landowners a short visit, with a small gift as a sign of our appreciation. The gift does not have to be extravagant. If we know they have small children or grandchildren, we usually bring something for them. If the landowners happen to enjoy venison, we will bring them a few steaks. Whatever the circumstance, we try to give something inexpensive that will be appreciated.

Owning property does not come cheaply, so it is always best to make it very clear that you are appreciative of the opportunity to hunt private property. Our main goal during our visit is to reconfirm, or solidify, our hunting permission for the coming hunting season. If you don't remind a landowner that you are hunting, or if he has not seen you for a while, he may forget you are there or assume that you no longer hunt his land and grant someone else permission. It is tough to find hunting property in the first place, so it is really disappointing when hunting property slips away or you suddenly have to share. Our visit is a small reminder to the landowner that we are indeed continuing to hunt his land.

The meeting also provides the landowner an opportunity to discuss any concerns he may have and engage in friendly conversation. Perhaps the landowner found some trash on his land or a hole in a fence somewhere. This is your opportunity to clarify any problem that may have been attributed to you and could become the source of difficulties in the future. Take any concerns the landowner has very seriously. Most of the time, however, the conversation will be more focused on the deer you have seen or taken and more general matters. Through simple interest and conversation, we always try to establish a trusting relationship with landowners. This trusting relationship and general familiarity mean a lot as far as hunting permission is concerned. The better the landowner knows you and respects you, the more difficult it will be for him to deny you permission in the future. This kind of relationship takes time to establish and is based on following any wishes the landowner may have. This includes respecting the property, closing gates, picking up trash, offering to keep other unwanted hunters off the property, and perhaps lending a helping hand when the landowner needs something. An occasional short, friendly visit can ensure your hunting permission for many future seasons.

EXPLORATORY SCOUTING ON PUBLIC LAND

The search for new places to hunt is not limited to private property. Public land can provide excellent hunting, if you can find out-of-the-way or overlooked spots. In fact, some of John's largest bucks were taken on public land, and his brother, David, has also taken several very big bucks from state land. Finding public land that holds mature bucks is even more challenging than gaining permission to hunt private property. In states with high hunter numbers, you can be sure that all the obvious state land areas will be hunted. The trick is to find state land that is overlooked or difficult to access.

There are two steps to the process. The first is to locate areas of public land. You can do this with a map and plat book. The plat book will give you an indication of the ownership of the surrounding properties. It may be possible to find a public parcel surrounded by large tracts of property where hunting is not allowed, or a landlocked piece of public land. One parcel of state land that we sometimes hunt is completely surrounded by patrolled private property and is accessible only by canoe. The landowners of the surrounding property even attempted to kick us off the state land, insisting that we were trespassing. After we produced a copy of the applicable plat book page and offered to call the conservation officer ourselves, the private property suddenly became public after all. The Internet is also a good source of information on public land. Numerous websites list all public land hunting opportunities in each state. A quick search on your computer can save you some time in the search for public land in your hunting area.

After you have found potential hunting properties, the next step is to get out in the woods and explore the new areas. This initial exploration is to check the property for hunting potential. Most of your exploratory scouting will be far less than spectacular. Usually you will discover that the area you had in mind is already hunted. But with persistence, you may find some overlooked or out-of-the-way hot spots that are worth the effort. Check particularly in places where access is limited, such as tracts reached only by boat or canoe or where motorized vehicles are not allowed.

Hunters, like the majority of people, tend to be lazy. Most hunters will not walk very far, with half a mile being the usual maximum—even less where there are no trails to walk on. If you can find a place back in the woods more than half a mile, the chances that such an area is being hunted diminish greatly. The extra walk can mean undisturbed animals.

For getting back into the woods, a mountain bike can be an excellent tool. In areas where there are trails and motorized vehicles are forbidden, a bike will get you away from the masses with relative ease and speed. The work necessary to get back in the woods could put you in a hunting area virtually untouched by other hunters, particularly during bow season.

Another way to open up new hunting areas is to carry a pair of waders. Simply crossing small rivers flowing through state property will usually mean less hunting pressure. Water is a large barrier to most bowhunters. We hunt a couple places where we cross small rivers with waders. The hunting pressure diminishes drastically on the other side of the water. We simply carry our waders on our backs until we arrive at our crossing point, and then pull them on. After crossing, we change back into our rubber boots and hide the waders. After we are done hunting, we return to our crossing point and hidden waders. This little trick can open up some good hunting.

Exploring state land must be completed in the early spring for the same reasons that your scouting in general must be done in the spring. You will be able to get a clear indication of what the fall deer activity is, and you will not disturb the area with your presence. Particularly important while scouting state land is to look for sign left by other hunters. This will often be quite obvious in the spring, and you will not be messing up someone else's hunting, as you would by scouting in the fall. If you hunt in a state where baiting is legal, the sign left behind will be very obvious by the bare spots on the ground.

On heavily hunted state land, hunter movement has greater impact on deer activity than just about any other factor. Look for gaps in hunter activity. This might take the form of a large swamp, a spot so far back in the woods that no one has gone to the trouble to hunt there, or a strip of land close to a major road or highway. The converse of hunters not venturing too far back in the woods is hunters not hunting the first hundred yards of land next to a major road. This often overlooked area can be a big-buck hot spot. In 2001, John took a big buck within 100 yards of a major highway on state land.

In pressured areas, the majority of places you inspect will already have been hunted very heavily. They may have great habitat, thick bedding areas, and an abundance of deer sign, but mature bucks will likely be rarities. When your exploratory scouting reveals a good out-of-the-way or overlooked spot, mark the area on your topographical map and include it in your scouting rotation. Unlike most private property, where access is controlled, on heavily hunted public land, it can often take you several years of both hunting and scouting to properly figure out subtle nuances in deer movement. Until you actually hunt there, there is no way of really telling where the deer feel comfortable moving during daylight.

SCOUTING NEW PROPERTY

The principal reasons to get your scouting done in the early spring are simple. Before the new foliage arrives, the sign from last fall's deer activity is still obvious, particularly the sign left by mature bucks. Getting a clear idea of the land and the subtleties of fall deer patterns is much easier before new growth limits vision, makes old scrapes and rubs unnoticeable, and creates a situation where jaunts through the woods become a great deal more difficult. You will also be able to explore your entire hunting area without fear of spooking the deer, including the bedding areas, which are taboo in the late summer and fall. You will definitely spook deer in the spring, but they have plenty of time to resume natural behavior by fall. Another very important factor is the comfortable spring weather, which makes it easier to get out in the woods and work before the heat of summer arrives.

BOWHUNTING IN THE 1960s AND '70s

B owhunting has evolved tremendously during my forty-plus bow seasons. In the sixties and seventies, there was virtually no information out there about how to bowhunt. What little information existed was poor at best. The only way to become a decent bowhunter was to get out in the woods and figure things out for yourself. Most hunters were gun hunters in those days, and other than upgrades in shotgun and muzzleloader technology and the advent of permanent heated blinds, hunting in Michigan then was not much different than it is today. Gun-hunting success in Michigan, in most cases, simply revolves around how good a piece of property is and luck, with deer frantically attempting to get out of harm's way on opening day, which is probably when upward of 80 percent of the bucks are taken. Therefore, looking to gun hunters for advice on bowhunting was rather useless.

John took this eight-point in 1972. The buck had been feeding on acorns.

Equipment was also a major problem in the sixties and seventies. The only camouflage patterns available were of the military variety, until Jim Crumley came out with the first hunting camouflage, called Treebark. Most of the time I hunted in olive drab cotton coveralls, which were available at stores that provided work clothing. Even more of a problem was stands. In the mid to late seventies, the only commercial stand available was the Baker Climbing Stand, which, to say the least, was a death trap. Some other major items that were not available back in the sixties and early seventies were sights, release aids, detachable quivers, compound bows, rangefinders, screw-in tree steps, ladder sticks, and a host of other accessories that we take for granted these days. In those days, most hunters either used large oak, beech, or maple trees that provided a natural place to sit or nailed boards into crotches of trees to sit on. This type of stand hunting severely limited what areas could be hunted from trees and the ability to adjust to changing deer movement.

The deer herds across the now big-buck-rich Midwest and in most agricultural areas across southern Michigan were much smaller than they are today. This was partly because farms then were being tilled and groomed. Now we have CRP set-aside weed fields that the federal government pays farmers not to plant, old overgrown orchards and old fencerows, and lots of property owned by anti- and nonhunters. All of these factors make for higher deer densities and great deer habitat, though it is not as easily accessible as it used to be. Back then, in most states, the majority of the deer herds were found in the big-timber areas, and Michigan was no exception. The deer population in southern Michigan, where I did most of my hunting in the sixties and early seventies, was much lower than today. At that time, at least 90 percent of the gun hunters migrated to the big woods of northern Michigan, where the deer population was very high. You had either very few deer to hunt in agricultural areas or lots of deer to hunt in big-timber areas, with few bucks ever living beyond one and a half years old. The general hunting situation and equipment limitations made bowhunting really tough. Therefore, killing any deer with a bow was regarded as a major accomplishment.

There were, however, some positive aspects to hunting in those days. In the late seventies, bowhunting was just beginning to become popular in Michigan. With far less bowhunting pressure than there is today, it was more common for bucks to move during daylight throughout the season. Fewer bowhunters also meant that landing permission to hunt was far easier than it is today. The majority of farmers and property owners would allow you to bowhunt their land. Large leases and concern about liability weren't even thought of in those days. This also meant that there were large tracts of land where no bowhunting was taking place at all.

With a little luck and some cold weather on his side, John recovered this eleven-point in a short hayfield after pushing him out of his bedding area the previous day. John's daughter Traci helped with the photo.

Despite access to good hunting land, I rarely saw a two-and-a-half-year-old buck. The vast majority of bucks were cropped off as one-and-a-half-year-olds during gun season, which was normal in the bucks-only days. In fact, from 1964 through 1978, I can remember seeing only five bucks while on stand that were over two and a half years old, and I hunted a lot. I was still in the early phases of my hunting learning process, my seasonal timing was poor at best, and even though I spent much more time in the woods throughout the entire season than I do now, I saw fewer bucks. I was not hunting smart; I was just hunting. By 1978, I had been bowhunting for more than a decade and had managed to kill a couple of bucks that were decent by Michigan standards, though luck was the biggest factor in those kills. I was considered a veteran bowhunter by most of my friends, who were just starting with bowhunting. In mid-October that year, my friend Dave asked me to help him set up on a big ten-point that he had been seeing but always remained out of range. Dave had been bowhunting only a few years. I agreed to help him, on the condition that he get me permission to hunt the property he was hunting. This was one of the best pieces of property to hunt in the whole area. Dave managed to land me permission to hunt for about two weeks. The landowner allowed bowhunting only until the end of October, so that the deer would not be spooked for the traditional gun opener on November 15, when he and his family took to the woods. Though we were probably the only bowhunters within a mile, the area was hit hard during gun season.

Dave had been hunting from a giant white oak tree that was located in a small opening about one hundred yards from the edge of a huge swamp. The swamp was about a mile long and half a mile wide; it consisted of tall marsh grass, cattails, and brush, with a lot of water interspersed with small, dry mounds throughout. The deer in the area bedded on these dry mounds. The land Dave had to hunt on had a lot going for it. It was the only property bordering that swamp containing a good number of mature red and white oaks. The rest of the property surrounding the swamp was primarily fallow fields on sandy soil, containing little more than short grass and mature stands of planted pines, which provided very little quality browse. The nearest crops were more than five miles away and had virtually no effect on the hunting in this spot. Inspecting Dave's tree, I could see why he had chosen this spot. The giant oak was full of acorns, was easy to climb into, and had a natural place to sit with good cover at about fifteen feet. Though there were other good trees within sight of this one, it was clear that Dave had simply chosen the tree that was easiest to hunt from.

About seventy yards to the west of Dave's tree was a block of woods that was about a quarter mile wide. This woodlot butted up to the swamp on the south side and bordered a road to the north. The swamp and the road were about half a mile apart. Across the road was a big block of mature timber —pines, oaks, and maples—that extended for more than a mile, with no low or thick ground that could serve as a bedding area. Almost all the deer that moved in that block of woods bedded in the big swamp and crossed through the patch of woods next to Dave's tree, though at the time, I was not yet completely aware of this movement pattern.

Along the east edge of the woods was a row of mature white oaks. A quick inspection revealed that most of the feeding took place under these trees. We selected the largest white oak for Dave to hunt from. This oak had several rubs around it and a lot of droppings, some very large, indicating that bucks were feeding there. We nailed a couple boards in a crotch about twenty feet up for Dave to sit on and cleared a few saplings to open up some shooting lanes. This was the best huntable tree in the woods. Now that Dave's tree was completed, we set out to find a tree for me to hunt from. Our main goal was to get Dave a shot at the big ten-point he had been seeing, but I also wanted a chance at one of the other decent bucks that he had seen.

I chose a smaller white oak that was farther in the woods, closer to the swamp, and in thick cover. After nailing a couple boards in a crotch about twenty-five feet up and trimming some lanes, my tree was ready. This was a typical hunting setup for me those days. Most of my bowhunting consisted of finding acorn-bearing oaks and sitting in those trees, with far less consideration about travel routes or destination points. I was still learning. Since the area was best suited for evening hunting, Dave and I agreed to hunt together the following evening.

Dave had been seeing deer as early as 3:30 P.M. on previous hunts, so we were in our new trees by 2:00. We were far enough apart from one another that we could not hear if the other shot. It was a clear sunny evening, yet cool, with the temperature hovering around the 50-degree mark. It was still early when a spike and some does fed under Dave's tree. This was a tough situation for Dave. He had killed only a couple deer with his bow up to that point, and ordinarily he would have shot the spike, but because of the bigger bucks he had seen, he decided to pass on the shot. In the seventies, there was really no such thing as a whitetail trophy hunter, particularly with archery equipment. His decision to hold off turned out to be a good decision. The next deer he saw was the big ten-point. The buck casually moved down the edge of the woods toward his tree. At a distance of only fifteen yards, the big buck presented a perfect broadside shot. According to Dave, he was overtaken by a case of buck fever and shook so badly that he had a hard time drawing his bow, not to mention holding his pin on the buck's chest. His arrow flew over the buck's back, causing the buck to promptly disappear in the direction from which it came. Dave never saw that buck again until gun season, in the back of a pickup after another hunter had killed it.

I also had some action that night. At about 5:30, a single deer suddenly appeared in the woods, right out of the big swamp. This was the first deer of the evening, and to my surprise, it was a nice buck. The buck browsed contentedly in my direction. It was feeding on acorns at just over ten yards when I drew my Bear Polar II. At full draw, I blatted to stop him, then released. Like Dave, I too had a small case of buck fever. Through the shakes, however, I managed to hold my pin on the buck, but my arrow hit a little farther back than where I had aimed. In a blur of action, it appeared as if the arrow passed through the rear end of the rib cage as the buck sped back to the swamp. After darkness fell, I climbed down and inspected my arrow, which was lying on the ground. A glance confirmed my reservations about the shot. Brown, gritty matter covered the arrow, but there was also a strong blood trail. This meant that I had probably hit the liver and paunch.

Dave and I met up a few minutes later and exchanged stories. I could not tell Dave how many points the buck carried or any other details. I had seen only that it had a good rack, and then concentrated on the shot. Together we decided to wait until the next morning to track the buck. Although there were numerous coyotes in the area, we did not want to push the buck deep into the swamp, which would make recovery nearly impossible. Dave wound up having to work the next morning, so another friend helped me track the buck. The blood trail was relatively easy to follow, and we found the buck just inside the swamp, about two hundred yards from my tree. The beautiful eight-point had expired in a bedded position, facing his back track, which confirmed our decision to wait with the tracking. The buck was my fourth biggest up to that point.

John waited until the next morning to recover this eight-point.

Though a lot of luck had been involved in killing this buck, this hunt opened my eyes to a couple of bowhunting fundamentals that had not been so clear to me previously and changed the way I hunt. I began to concentrate more on the big picture, rather than hunt individual sign and random oak trees. Travel routes between bedding and feeding areas became some of my main areas of focus. Another thing this buck taught me is that isolated mast trees close to cover are excellent spots. These are the first spots to which deer head in the evening before moving into more open terrain farther from bedding areas. Both of these realizations may seem simple and self-evident today, but in the seventies, they were for me a big step forward in hunting knowledge that opened the door for quicker learning the next few years.

The first step in March or April, depending on the weather, is to scout. The snow must be gone before you begin. If you hunt in an area where there is little or no snow, you may begin your postseason scouting as soon as the previous season is over. Any property where you hunted during the previous season for the first time needs to be rescouted thoroughly in the spring. During the season, you likely noticed deer activity that differed from your previous scouting notes, and if you did not react to it then, now is the time to scrutinize that activity.

Spring scouting is time-consuming and a lot of work. It is important to approach it with the right attitude. This scouting is what will make or break your upcoming hunting season. In fact, this is the most important aspect of hunting for the entire year, apart from the actual shot. It is what you do now that will actually put yourself in position for that shot in the fall. Proper preparation and planning are key to killing mature pressured bucks on a regular basis. Once you begin to consider scouting a very important part, if not the most important part, of hunting, it almost takes on the feel and urgency of hunting. We are nearly as excited to scout new property as we are to hunt new property. Scouting is somewhat like a treasure hunt; you never know what you might find. That pot of gold could be just over the next ridge in the form of an excellent primary scrape area or staging area. Every new scouting trip could reveal that dream funnel, where it is possible to get a crack at a mature buck every year. The only way to know what is out there is to check it out. So feel privileged to be in the woods, take your time, and do the work necessary for success.

Before we scout a new property, we check its shape and size in a plat book, and then compare this to aerial photos and topographical maps, which are available on the Internet and various computer software. We then print each and include them in our scouting notebook. These photos and maps can be excellent tools to pinpoint areas on property where deer are concentrated. The aerial photos are an excellent source of information about the deer travel corridors on neighboring property, where you are not allowed to enter. The thorough overview can be helpful in pinpointing where deer enter and exit your hunting property. A funnel or bedding area on a neighboring property might cause bucks to enter your property at a point that is not so obvious from your side of the fence. The maps are only a very general guideline, however. They tend to be a couple years old, and sometimes cuttings or new houses have altered the situation quite dramatically. Use them only as a reference. After the homework is done, it is time to begin the actual legwork.

When we scout a new property, we usually begin by walking the perimeter. With your notebook in hand, note obvious funnels, travel routes, feeding areas, bedding areas, food sources, and any other noteworthy sign. Before it was easy to get topo maps and aerial photos, we used to draw maps by hand. Now we usually mark interesting areas on the downloaded map that we have printed out. This saves some time and eliminates the unavoidable hand-drawn map distortion. Also label the makeup of the various woods and funnels on the topo map, which you can discover only by actually taking a look. For instance, looking at an aerial photo can reveal a mature stand of woods but not the makeup of the woods below the canopy. Note on your map the details of the terrain, including anything relevant to your future hunting, such as whether the woods are open under the canopy or have pockets of underbrush suitable for deer cover. Maybe the area was timbered off years ago and the loggers left the tops, which can make for excellent bedding areas if the surrounding area is devoid of better bedding areas. Getting to know the true makeup of a given piece of property can be done only on foot.

After you have an overview of the property, which might take a couple outings to achieve, you will have a general idea of where the feeding and bedding areas are located and some points of interest, such as obvious travel routes or funnels. Now return to the most productive-looking spots for a closer look. Never assume that you know what is in an area without actually having a look. Some of our best hunting spots are so unlikely in appearance that other hunters simply overlooked them. One of these spots is a low island surrounded by a water-filled marsh. The grassy island is impossible to see until you step on it. If we had not taken the time to explore that marsh fully in the spring, we still would not know that there is an island in the middle of it, which is a center of buck activity in that area.

Usually we gain permission to hunt smaller properties that encompass only a very small portion of a buck's home territory. This means that it is impossible to follow all the sign to the best spot for a single buck. We are forced to find the best spots on the property we have available. The best spot on some marginal properties might be a single runway or even a single oak or apple tree. On each new property, we look for the best available sign to develop a hunting plan particular to that spot. Every property varies considerably and requires individual planning. The more peripheral a property is in relation to a buck's core area, the more difficult it is to pinpoint that buck's movements through the property. Throughout the years, we have developed a hierarchy of sign we look for to help us select sites for hunting stands and lookout stands. Descriptions follow in order of importance.

Primary Scrape Areas

In the areas we hunt, the main sign we focus on finding is primary scrape areas. Generally speaking, a primary scrape area can be defined and recognized as a group of scrapes in a small area or around a single tree. A scrape is an area of ground from one to six feet across that has been scraped free of everything except dirt; no leaves or branches are left in a freshly made scrape. A scrape looks as if someone raked the spot until only dirt remained, although we have occasionally seen some well-rooted grass. By spring, the scrapes will likely have some clutter of leaves and small branches that were blown in after the scrapes were abandoned when the rut ended. Another key element of a scrape is at least one overhanging licking branch; most have several. The licking branches are the most important sign left at a scrape. The more licking branches used, the more the scrape was being revisited.

Although it is extremely rare, we have seen as many as fifteen scrapes in areas as small as thirty yards across; however, most primary scrape areas consist of just three to six scrapes. Primary scrape areas are found only in areas with concentrated deer activity, usually in or close to thick cover, but still open enough to allow visual contact among deer for quite some distance.

Hunted correctly, primary scrape areas will provide you with your best opportunities at mature bucks, especially in pressured areas. Despite their importance and sometimes obvious appearance, hunters often have problems finding them. They can vary in appearance and do not exist on all parcels. In agricultural areas, there are usually only one to three primary scrape areas per section. Their main locations are in funnels between bedding areas, funnels between bedding and feeding areas, around apple trees, on oak ridges, and at the tips of wooded or brushy fingers protruding into preferred cropfields. You may also find them at inside corners of cropfields and at the bases of ridges that drop off into marshy areas or swamps. A common mistake is to think that a group of scrapes along the edge of a picked or short cropfield is a primary scrape area. Although such scrapes may become very active during the season, they are almost always used exclusively after dark, whereas primary scrape areas are used in daylight as well.

Primary scrape areas are started by mature bucks with at least one breeding season behind them. They are made in an attempt to mark or lay claim to a specific heavy-traffic location. By the time the mature doe come into estrus, they know of these areas, because they have traveled through or close to them, and frequent them in search of a mature buck. These areas become stomping grounds for other mature and subordinate bucks as well. Like all other animals when it comes to breeding, bucks are opportunists and will take advantage of a primary scrape area during the rut phases when the dominant buck is not in the area.

As with any other hunting location, if primary scrape areas are disturbed or overhunted, the bucks, and deer in general, will stop using them during daylight. They also are less permanent than bedding areas or food sources. This deer flexibility can be maddening for hunters and causes many of them to give up on scrape hunting.

When you find a primary scrape area, mark it with a big X on your map or topo photo. This will usually be your most important spot, and you should consider yourself fortunate to have found it. Then continue scouting.

Staging Areas

Staging areas are next in order of priority. They receive far less attention than they should, because they too can be difficult to recognize and to hunt. In modern hunting literature, there is some disagreement about what exactly a staging area is. Staging areas are commonly defined as areas where bucks enter cover near the edges of cropfields or other food sources before nightfall, waiting for the security of darkness to head for the food source. And indeed, this is a form of staging area. This sort of staging area will be recognized as some sort of cover within close proximity to an open, short cropfield, with the exception of standing corn. This type of staging area is used most often before any rut phases. These staging areas usually have rubs and possibly an occasional scrape on the runway or runways leading to them. They also are likely to have some rubs and possibly a scrape or two where the buck actually stages. In pressured areas, the effective hunting time frame of this sort of staging area is usually very short, just a couple days, before hunting pressure pushes mature bucks into a totally nocturnal routine.

We concentrate on a different form of staging area that serves another, more important function and offers a much better opportunity to intercept deer during daytime activity in pressured areas. We refer to them as "rut staging areas." These are areas that bucks use extensively during the rut phases, particularly in pressured agricultural areas. On morning hunts, mature bucks enter a rut staging area well before daylight and bed down. Here they stage, waiting for any passing does returning from a night of feeding. If a doe passes through, the waiting buck is there to intercept her and check her for receptiveness. This saves the buck a great deal of energy by reducing the amount of seeking he has to do in order to find a hot doe, and it also makes the buck less vulnerable to hunters, as he doesn't remain in open cropfields after daybreak. This behavior is generally demonstrated only by mature bucks; yearlings tend not to use staging areas. Their breeding experience simply is not advanced enough for this type of behavior.

A rut staging area may or may not be the same as a feeding staging area. It may look very similar to, and sometimes also serves as, one of the dominant buck's primary scrape areas. If this is the case, the area will likely be littered with rubs, have a few scrapes, and have several runways leading to it.

Rut staging areas are almost always found near a break or change in terrain and have a couple usual components. The staging area will provide the buck good perimeter cover for an expedient and undetected exit if a predator approaches, usually a hunter. In pressured areas, in order for a staging area to consistently hold a buck beyond daybreak, it also must have perimeter cover between it and the nearby food source—that is, in the direction from which the does and predators approach. This prevents detection from the more open food source after daylight. Without perimeter cover, a buck will likely leave the staging area just before daybreak.

The main problems hunters have with rut staging areas are, again, recognition and faulty hunting. Improperly hunting these areas causes the disturbed bucks to quit using them altogether. The use of rut staging areas also depends on the current preferred food source the does are using, so it is vital to know where the does are feeding and bedding. Crop rotation and food mast trees also have a major influence on where staging areas will be found. If the does alter their travel route, the bucks will alter their staging areas as well. Thus buck use of a staging area can change overnight.

An example of a rut staging area is one that Chris recently began hunting. The staging area is located at the end of a relatively long, wide, weedy and brushy point that extends into a cornfield. The point meets a swath of mature hardwoods about fifty yards wide, bordered by a brushy ravine, which drops into a huge bedding area. This spot is a classic rut staging area. It has all the elements for bucks to stage: access to a feeding area, a brushy border between the feeding area and open woods, open hardwoods that provide good visibility, and quick access to thick cover in the event of danger. Quite often, a rut staging area will be a mature buck's summer bedding location, but in pressured areas the buck will likely be pushed back into heavier cover when most hunters start their preseason scouting.

Rut staging areas are also found in big woods, though they are far less prevalent and not used as consistently as those found in agricultural regions. Big-woods areas tend to have lower deer densities and less distinct food sources. This creates a situation where deer movement is far more random than in agricultural areas. The does will wander from food source to food source. Without distinct travel routes, as found in agricultural areas, the bucks are forced more to their feet in an effort to intercept estrous does, which is why rut staging areas are far less common. A buck could theoretically wait for days in a big-woods staging area before a receptive doe showed up. Big-woods areas also tend to have more cover everywhere, giving mature bucks more security for daytime movement during the rut phases. In big woods, staging areas will likely be located along travel routes, usually at the narrowest point or at terrain changes between food sources and bedding areas, such as oak ridges, saddles, or swamp edges. Like agricultural staging areas, big-woods staging areas must provide the buck with escape cover. A major difference is that because of the less defined food sources, there generally is no buffer of cover between the feeding zone and the staging area.

When you find a feeding or rut staging area, mark it with a big X on your map, and continue scouting.

Funnels

Funnels are the next sign of interest. A funnel is simply the narrowest area of cover between two larger areas. This is the route a mature deer would most likely take to get from one area to the other. A funnel can appear in just about any type of terrain, from a tall, weedy fencerow to a classic narrow neck of cover between two larger woodlots. It is important to be able to recognize the vast variance in what can constitute a funnel. For instance, in one area we hunt, the funnel between two bedding areas is a row of mature oaks. The does in the area filter out of some large hardwoods and nearby cropfields to these oaks, which lead to a big, thick, almost impenetrable bedding area. The tightest funnel is the point where the oaks and the hardwoods come together. Any deer coming through the hardwoods also pass through this point. It is here that we have a tree cleared out. Bucks cruise this row of oaks during the prerut and rut, searching for estrous does that passed into the bedding area.

Another example, this one not so obvious, is a spring drainage that cuts through the center of an open stand of hardwood for about four hundred yards. At the north end of the depression is a thick cedar swamp; at the south end is a willow and cattail marsh. During the prerut and rut, bucks moving in midday follow this barely noticeable funnel. This is also a good example of an excellent spot that cannot be seen from an aerial photo.

The hand-drawn marks on this photo indicate four defined funnels that enable deer to move from cover to cover with the least amount of exposure.

The important thing is to find travel routes between bedding areas and other high-traffic locations that cause deer to move through some narrow point. Spots like these are excellent and should be considered among your best. Mark the narrowest place along a funnel on your map with yet another big X.

Funnels between separate bedding areas are the first type of funnel to look for, and the most important for mature pressured bucks. These funnels can be excellent spots from which to ambush a good buck during the prerut and rut. During the rut phases, mature bucks cruise from bedding area to bedding area in their core area searching for estrous does, and the tightest funnel of cover available is likely where they will travel through. Depending on the size and makeup of a particular bedding area, mature bucks will often just scent-check the perimeter. During this time frame, they also check primary scrape areas and staging areas for receptive does. And most important, this happens quite often during the middle of the day. If a mature buck does not find a doe in one area, he will make his way to the next. On his way, he will almost always use the best cover available to get there, particularly where hunting pressure is heavy. Bucks may also use this type of funnel as a staging area. During the prerut and rut, they will bed down in the funnels and wait to intercept does passing through in the morning or in the evening.

John took this fourteen-point in 1997 while traveling through a tight funnel between bedding areas.

Funnels between bedding areas and food sources are what to look for next. Locate all obvious bedding areas and food sources on your property. Food sources vary throughout the season and from year to year, and bedding area use can also change with the season, usually in relation to the current preferred food source, but also with the loss of foliage. This constant change has to be considered while scouting. A sudden shift in the preferred food source in the area, such as the harvesting of a cropfield or a sudden abundance of acorns, can alter deer movement drastically. For example, deer will bed in a standing cornfield, but after it is cut, they have to move to another bedding area. With this in mind, it is a good idea to mark all relevant food sources on your scouting map. As the season progresses, you have to know where, and on what, the deer are feeding.

Don't limit yourself to knowing what food sources are present only on the property you hunt. For deer to travel up to a mile while feeding at night is not uncommon. If such a migration is taking place in your hunting area, it is good to know about it. In one area we hunt, the deer we shoot always have bellies full of corn. Interestingly, the nearest cornfield is over a mile to the north. This has important implications for our hunting situation in that spot, which is one of the major bedding areas in the area. It takes the deer quite some time to cover the distance from the corn back to the bedding area in the morning. This means we have a great deal of deer movement later in the morning than usual, with a peak coming at around 10:00 A.M., even in the early season. Knowing that the deer are on the way makes early mornings with few deer sightings pass quickly and with a sense of optimism.

If you are hunting small parcels, it is also a common situation that within the boundaries of the property parcels there are either bedding areas or food sources, but not both. You have to know what the food source situation is for the entire area, which can usually be determined by driving around the section. By knowing this, you will be able to speculate when and where the deer should be feeding during the entire season. For instance, the deer may feed heavily on beans until frost arrives, at which point they turn brown and deer may move to another food source. When white oaks have a good crop of acorns, these will be the preferred food source during the period in which they are falling. The implications this has on your spring scouting are obvious.

You have to prepare for any likely possibilities. That means choosing trees to hunt from between any bedding area and any possible feeding area. Accordingly, you need to have numerous trees prepared for different times of the season in order to adjust to changing feeding habits. Search along travel routes for trees that are much closer to the bedding areas than to the feeding areas. Your trees must be far enough from the bedding areas, however, for you to enter and exit without being detected by any deer that may be bedded there. Keep in mind that early in the season before any hunting pressure, a mature buck or other deer may be bedded on the outer fringes of the bedding area. Spooking any deer in that situation will be detrimental to your hunt, especially if it is an evening hunt. You also must have a way to get in and out of the woods without spooking deer feeding in the fields.

Don't set your stands on field edges. This is a mistake that many hunters make. In spots like this, you will usually see numerous deer, at least the first couple times you hunt there, but then comes the difficulty. You cannot hunt field edges without spooking deer, either on the way to your tree in the morning or while departing in the evening. You may continue to see deer throughout the entire season, but mature bucks will become wise to your hunting and avoid that spot, at least until after dark. On a couple occasions, from a distance, we have patterned a mature buck coming out into a short cropfield prior to the season, and then successfully set up on the field edge for the first and possibly second evening hunt. If we are not successful after two hunts, we change our plan of attack and do not hunt the field edge again. While hunting for mature bucks between bedding and feeding areas, you simply have to stay off the food source after it has been pressured.

At the tightest funnels possible, mark your selected trees with Xs on your scouting map. Such stands are usually decent producers where you will see a lot of deer. You will hunt these spots throughout the season on a regular rotation. They are not your best spots, but there is always a chance a decent buck will pass through in the early season, on his way to or from feeding, or during the rut stages, while chasing or looking for estrous does.

Rub and Scrape Lines

Rub and scrape lines are the next priority. A rub line is a series of buck rubs along a runway, and a scrape line is a series of scrapes along a runway. Scrape lines will usually have rubs along them, but the reverse isn't always true. A runway that only has rubs is often used exclusively by a single mature buck, and it would be difficult to see if not for the rubs. Runways that have both scrapes and rubs will almost always be used by other bucks and does, but mature bucks will most likely use them only during the rut phases; these runways are usually easier to identify, since more deer use them.

If you have already found primary scrape areas, staging areas, and various funnels, you more than likely will have found runways with rub and scrape lines along them. Rub lines without scrapes along them are likely preseason and early-season rub lines, or they were made by subordinate bucks. Mature bucks rarely hang out with year-and-a-half-old bucks or does. After they start shedding their velvet, they have survived a hunting season and know that using the same runways as the other deer during daylight makes them vulnerable.

In pressured areas, bucks that reach maturity do so because they take a different route than other bucks. Sometimes a rub or scrape line will cut off through the middle of the woods for no apparent reason. We once found a rub line that gave away the whereabouts of a buck that followed a tiny row of brush across a fallow grassy field, to bed in a tiny swale. This was a mature buck living in an area with extreme hunting pressure. Although more than one buck may frequent a well-traveled rub and scrape line, rub lines in unusual locations are usually the work of a single buck and will rarely have scrapes along them. It is imperative to follow any rub line that you find in both directions on the property you have available. Discovering where a rub line enters a bedding area is an excellent situation, and it is even better when you know exactly where the buck is headed. If left undisturbed and nothing changes—acorn mast or crop rotation—and if the buck survived the previous hunting season, he will likely follow the same route next fall.

If the buck that made this rub line survived, he will most likely use the same area next fall.

Clusters of rubs will also be revisited the following fall if a buck survives and no major change in the food sources occurs.

We found this huge scrape in late April. Note the perimeter cover, which is needed for daytime activity.

Set up a stand along any rub line or scrape line. If the rub line shows signs of activity just prior to the season, you will already have a tree prepared to take advantage of the situation during the first couple days after the opener. There is a possibility that the buck already may have been killed, and clearing out a tree along his route will be futile. This is the chance a hunter has to take. When bowhunting pressured property, the margin between success and failure is sometimes minuscule.

Recently, the hunting media have shown a great deal of interest in hunting rub lines, catapulting them almost to wonder status. Rub lines are naturally good bets in some situations, but they are not magic, particularly in pressured areas. Other than the first few days of the season, when a mature buck may still be in a summer daytime routine, we usually consider them secondary spots.

John killed this eight-point on a rub line leading to a tall weed field; Chris had hit him between the spine and lungs not five minutes earlier. The buck was using the rub line as an exit route to his bedding area.

Other Sign Combinations

With the main sign covered on your property, it is time to look for various other sign and combinations that might produce an opportunity at a mature buck. Always look for soft mast trees or plants, such as apple or pear trees, wild grapevines, or whatever grows in your region. Individual soft mast trees bearing fruit located in the right places attract deer like magnets. Hunting near these trees at the right time can mean some great hunting. In many of the areas we hunt, apple trees play a major role. Old overgrown apple orchards are somewhat common in Michigan, and there are single apple-producing trees in most areas. If an apple tree is in some cover, it will be the first place deer go before entering fields to feed in the evening, and it will also be the last stop before bedding down in the morning. Fruit-bearing trees work on a first-come, first-served basis; only a few apples fall each day, and the first deer there get the lion's share. Mark any fruit-bearing trees on your map and find a tree within bow range to hunt from. Revisit them once during the summer. Any trees that have fruit must be included in your early-season hunting rotation.

Some great spots are often overlooked by hunters, such as single mature oaks in the middle of cornfields or bedding areas. Imagine how secure a buck must feel feeding under a mature oak surrounded by acres and acres of standing corn. We have several such trees ready to go. In years when there are no acorns, these trees do not get hunted. In years with acorns, we hunt them occasionally until the acorns are gone. They are great options to have during the slow period in mid-October. Or imagine the amount of deer activity a single mature acorn-bearing oak in the middle of a bedding area must attract. This type of stand has to be hunted very carefully in order to enjoy success. You cannot expect to just march to your stand in the middle of a bedding area in the afternoon and not spook the deer. With a careful morning hunting plan and exit strategy, however, these trees can only be described with superlatives. Prepare any such trees you find to hunt from.

Small swales in the middle of open fields are often overlooked, but if there are no suitable trees nearby, these can be outstanding spots to use a pop-up blind to ambush an otherwise unkillable buck. Mature bucks in pressured areas have figured out that it is sometimes dangerous in the woods, and a small swale surrounded by crops or tall weeds can provide safety from an onslaught of hunters. Any patch of cover that could provide bedding must be checked over for buck sign.

Note the two lone oaks mixed into the heavy brush. This is an outstanding food mast location.

Other things to look for are weedy fencerows, deep brushy ditches, and grassy points in fields. Bucks like to use this sort of terrain, especially if it is far from the woods, to evade hunters. Also inspect any woods or cover near houses or developments inhabited by elderly owners without children. These areas receive little if any activity beyond grass mowing, and quite often a mature buck will be bedding in the closest available cover. Hunters often avoid these spots because they assume they are too close to human activity to hold deer. This is especially true in semirural areas. Many mature bucks reach old age by living and bedding virtually in someone's backyard. Every interesting spot should be clearly marked on your map, even if there is no sign from the previous season. This type of location needs to be checked every postseason and preseason for sign.

This is also the time of year when you need to thoroughly inspect every bedding area on every new hunting property. Large bedding areas almost always have some terrain aspects that are impossible to recognize at first glance from the edge. Any small rise in an otherwise thick bedding area will possibly be a center of buck activity. These are all-day hunting spots that you will hunt only a few times during a season, usually during the rut phases, when bucks are more likely to be moving. Hunting bedding areas is a touchy business. We hunt such areas only when conditions are perfect or as a last resort as the season is coming to a close. Perfect conditions include a light evening rain or a windy afternoon, which will allow entry with minimal noise. All that is needed for a morning or all-day hunt is an extremely early arrival, at least an hour and a half before first light. When hunting pressured mature bucks in a bedding area, you will need to arrive even earlier to achieve consistent success.

Water holes are another thing to watch for in areas without much available water. Early in the season or during hot spells, knowing where the water is can be a definite key to finding a good buck.

Our sign hierarchy is not set in stone. Every property is different, and the best sign on each property will be unique to that spot. This is what makes scouting so enjoyable. Each time you set foot on a new property, you will find a set of circumstances found nowhere else. Sometimes the combination is perfect for a mature buck; other times a property that looked good at first glance will turn out to be a dud. Getting out in the woods and finding areas where mature bucks live is half the battle. Indeed, mature bucks have been killed in all types of habitat; your job in the spring is to find those areas where mature bucks feel comfortable. For the most part, we tend to hunt particular areas as opposed to individual bucks. In pressured areas, bucks come and go, but if an area was held a mature buck and that buck was killed, others will likely follow—he was there for a reason. By hunting areas instead of individual bucks, you increase your chances of success dramatically.

Now, if you take a look at your map, you should notice that it is covered with Xs, each of which represents a potential stand. Every X means more work that you have to do.

Lookout Stands

Once you have selected all of your hunting stand sites, you may want to set up lookout stands. These are trees, or spots, from which you can observe deer movement. Their situation must be such that you can view the deer from a distance and can enter and exit without spooking them. On properties that warrant lookout locations, we always prepare them. Property where you know there will be short cropfields such as beans, wheat stubble, hay, oats, and so on require lookout stands that can be entered and exited from a distance without detection by deer feeding in the fields. Sit in them just prior to the season with binoculars so you can pinpoint the exact entry location of the bucks. These stands are very important for locating a buck to target in the early season.

SCOUTING FOR OTHER HUNTERS

Scouting for other hunters is a critical ingredient to your regular success at bowhunting in pressured areas, though it is a subject that has been largely ignored in the hunting community, primarily because most writers do not have to deal with it. Only those who hunt large exclusive properties, or in areas with really low hunter density, can afford to ignore this type of scouting. Knowing where, when, and how other hunters are hunting the same property and any neighboring properties is just as important as understanding the deer's natural movement. The effect of hunting pressure on deer movement is tremendous. Extensive hunting pressure completely alters a deer population's daily pattern and, most of all, its daily timing. There are some instances in Michigan where this becomes quite obvious, such as the first couple days of bow season. Within a few days, the hunting pressure goes from zero to intense, as more than 350,000 hunters hit the woods. The bucks that were seen evening after evening feeding in cropfields just vanish, and deer sightings in general decrease dramatically. The deer that live past the first couple days become very aware that they are being hunted and react accordingly.

The simple fact is that as we attempt to pattern and hunt deer, they are attempting to pattern and avoid us. The scent and sign we leave behind and the noise we make do not go unnoticed. Deer will often discover with their noses where you were after you leave and subsequently avoid that area, at least during daylight. And contrary to popular belief, deer do notice changes in their home environment, such as missing trees or especially newly cut lanes. Mature bucks are particularly sensitive to these and other forms of human intrusion. In most heavily hunted areas, it takes only a little human scent or a subtle change for a buck to make an effort to avoid that spot or, more likely, enter a nocturnal routine. Thus understanding average hunter behavior, and how the other hunters alert deer to their presence, is vital to regular success. Ignoring the effect other hunters have on deer movement is a common mistake bowhunters make that can lead to frustration. We most often hear this expressed around mid-October, when many hunters claim that the deer just are not moving. The truth is that deer movement steadily increases throughout the fall, peaking during the rut. That movement may change from daylight to after dark, depending on pressure, but it is increasing. The truth also is that mature deer are far better at avoiding hunters than most people believe.

While you are inspecting your hunting properties, search out and follow any human sign you find. Don't limit yourself to hunter sign; just as important are other forms of human use, such as walking trails, bike trails, or forts built by local kids. On one of the properties we hunt, the landowner regularly rides his mountain bike around a system of lanes and occasionally drives his tractor down the lanes to cut wood for the winter. On another, the neighbors have a dog-walking trail along the edge of the property. The human activity in both situations has an effect on deer movement. The deer move around the human movement. In the first case, all-day hunting at that spot is not likely for us; we have only so many opportunities for all-day hunts and cannot chance one of them being ruined. In the second case, the deer are pushed onto the property we hunt relatively early in the morning. The neighbor's dog gets walked at around 9:00 A.M. It is interesting to observe how deer react to pressure that is not hunting related. After deer are accustomed to some form of nonthreatening intrusion, they usually just step aside until the disturbance is over. We have watched deer stand in cover without showing any signs of fear as people walk trails with dogs about fifty yards away. These deer simply return to their normal route as if nothing happened. Understanding the local nonhunting-related deer pressure can be of great use to your later hunting plan.

Hunter sign may include lanes, trails, flagging material, reflective tacks, and sometimes even painted trees to mark a trail. Most average hunters make the paths to their stands very obvious. Take the time to find and inspect all the stands on the property. Mark each one on your map with an O, for other hunter. Write down any information you can about each stand, such as its height, whether it is in a good spot, whether shooting lanes have been cut, whether the hunter has used bait, and how much attention he has paid to detail. Pay close attention to what you see. It is important to know how the other hunters hunt so that you can react accordingly. How stands are prepared and the surrounding sign can give you a lot of valuable information about the hunters who made them. You should be able to estimate the competence level of the other hunters by looking at their stands.

One of the first things to look for is stand height and cover. Is the stand below twenty feet, and if so, does it offer good background cover? Tree-stand hunters almost always hang their stands too low and in the open. An important detail is whether the hunter has cleared out good shooting lanes. Does he have a clear shot to the main areas he is targeting? We often encounter tree stands that are in good locations but lack good shooting lanes, making it almost impossible to get off a shot. Lack of clear shot options indicates a beginner. Is the stand in a position to take advantage of the prevailing wind? Is it on the edge of a cropfield (this is very common), along a singular travel route, or simply placed down in the middle of the woods somewhere? Is the hunter's trail to the stand well worn? The more worn the trail, the more the hunter is at that spot. Sometimes a worn trail will indicate the only stand a hunter hunts. This is not always such a bad situation. If that hunter overhunts a single spot, you at least know a spot that mature bucks will avoid during daylight.

It is important to assess all of this information to get an idea of how effective the other hunters are. The less effective, the better, as far as you are concerned. Sometimes other hunters will not be much of a hindrance at all. If all the stands are on the field edges, the hunters are actually helping you. These hunters will, in a short time, simply push the deer off the fields, and you can easily take advantage of this situation by setting up farther back in the woods in better spots. In fact, hunters along field edges will cause deer to spend more time in the woods, bettering your chances.

Your completed map and notes should provide you with some valuable information about what kinds of hunters are on the property and, more important, give you an indication of areas or routes the deer use to avoid the hunters. If you look closely at your map, you will generally notice that most stands are positioned within one hundred yards of some kind of road, two-track, trail, or field edge, particularly in areas like Michigan, where baiting is prevalent. Bait is heavy and most hunters will not carry it very far. Many hunters stay close to trails because of the difficulty associated with walking to or from stands in the dark. While hunting, either on the way in or out, you will inevitably be walking in the dark. This simple fact keeps many hunters from venturing far back into the woods. Yet another factor is general laziness. People today tend to be quite sedentary, with our cultural dependency on automobiles and computers, and the majority of hunters are no exception. If you make the effort to get beyond the normal boundaries that hunters set for themselves, you may be surprised by the positive results.

Look for zones that deer will use to avoid other hunters. Scout these zones thoroughly, and be on the lookout for alternate travel and escape routes through these areas. These alternate travel routes will usually be lightly used runways through areas that are quite thick. Do not be discouraged by the lack of use. Single mature bucks are often the primary users of such routes.

Another source of information is the landowner, who usually has an idea of how much, and when, the other hunters hunt. By knowing this, you can better hunt around them. We try to remain as invisible to the other hunters as possible. This means that if they hunt only on the weekends, we attempt to hunt during the week. Or if they only hunt evenings, we hunt mornings. Some hunters are out for recreation and do not have much time to hunt; others are serious hunters who have hunted the same way for years, regularly taking yearling bucks. These types of hunters are not that much of a threat to mature bucks in the area. They can almost be looked at as deer deflectors. The mature does will quickly pattern their hunting and react accordingly, taking the mature bucks with them when the rut phases start. So note everything you can about the other hunters in your hunting area, and keep it all in mind when planning your hunting for the coming season.

Remember, though, that every hunter has just as much right to be out there as you do. So be respectful, keep your distance, and be happy that you are dealing with hunters instead of antihunters.

TREE PREPARATION

After you have found the right spots, it is time to select and clear out your trees for the fall. This is when the real work begins. Finding the spots was the easy and fun part, easy as a walk in the woods and fun because you never know what you might find.

Clearing out trees is a topic that is taken way too lightly in most hunting literature. Most videos are filmed in managed, nonpressured areas, where mature bucks move through more open ground that does not require much work to clear shooting lanes, and most writers hunt in similar locations, or they assume that hunters already do this correctly. This assumption could not be farther from the truth. Every year in our scouting forays, we come across countless trees that have tree stands or are cleared out for hunting. Almost all of them are poorly done.

The most common mistake is a lack of shooting lanes. Other mistakes include too many branches around the stand itself that could interfere with a shot; rough bark around each step going up the tree or behind and around the stand; no clean lane through which to pull the bow up the tree; or having the stand too low, completely open, or on the wrong side of the tree. These mistakes may seem minor, but when you are hunting for mature bucks, attention to detail is of paramount importance. How many times have you heard of a hunter not being able to get off a shot at a good buck that was within range because it did not step into the open spot or approached the tree from the wrong direction? In an attempt to minimize this sort of situation, your stands have to be as perfect as possible. A big pressured buck will usually present only one opportunity per season—if you are lucky. You have to be able to respond and take advantage of that single opportunity.

Return to the spots you marked on your map and look for appropriate trees. Like most other things in hunting, the ideal tree seldom exists. Try to find a tree fifteen to twenty yards from the best available sign. This is a general rule; the stand position and distance vary from situation to situation, usually depending on how thick the ground cover is and also on the hunter's shooting capabilities. Never hunt directly over the sign you are hunting. Shot opportunities at deer that are coming straight toward you, right below you, or moving away from you are very poor shot angles for hitting vital organs, and you should never set up a tree for such shots. The tree should be large enough and have enough branches to provide decent cover at the height you prefer to hunt. When hunting from trees, we hunt exclusively from an Ambush Saddle, which means that we tend to hunt higher than most hunters, between twenty-five and thirty-five feet. This puts us up out of the deer's peripheral vision and allows us a bit more freedom of movement. The beginning procedure is the same for both tree stands and Ambush Saddles. Before screwing in any step, scrape the rough bark on either side of where the step will go, if necessary, to make climbing up and down the tree as quiet as possible. Start by attaching a screw-in step to the trunk of the tree just above knee level; because we are right-handed, we normally start on the right side. Screw in the second step at chest level, on the left. To keep your steps spaced evenly, you should use your knee on the opposite side as a sort of measuring tool. Now step up onto the first step and screw in another step at chest level on the other side. When using a tree stand, make sure you wear a safety climbing harness; if you're using an Ambush Saddle, hook up the safety strap that comes with it. No buck is worth a broken back or your life. Continue this process until you reach the desired height. You also can use climbing sticks and ladders to reach your hunting height. Once there, hang your stand. If you're using an Ambush Saddle, you screw three to six steps around the trunk at the same level, keeping them twelve to fourteen inches apart; the number of steps will depend on the diameter of the tree. These act as footrests and are used for maneuvering around the tree for potential shot opportunities. Standing on those steps, wrap the lead strap of the saddle around the tree twice, just above head level, and tie it off per the instructions. On state land, where screw-in tree steps are prohibited, we use strap-on steps in the same manner. Cranford brand strap-ons are the best of any we have used.

Once you're comfortably on the stand, it is time to take a look at what needs to be cleared out. Starting at the top, remove all branches that could possibly interfere with a shot, all the way around the tree. For this we use a small folding limb saw. You have to be open enough for clear shots yet leave as much cover as possible in areas where you will not have a shooting lane. If the tree you have chosen has rough bark, you should also scrape the bark until it is smooth enough that you do not make any noise when you rub against it. This little detail can mean the difference between success and failure at the moment of truth. If you leave rough bark on the tree, you could make noise while maneuvering for a shot.

Now, from your perch, mentally mark any branches or saplings that have to be removed to create clear shots to all of the surrounding runways within shooting range. Any runway that merges with another or several other runways should only be cleared out at the merging location. Try not to clear any more lanes than you have to, but do not leave any runway without a shot opportunity. Sometimes clearing a lane will require only a few cuts; other times it will require hours of work. Don't skimp on lane clearing. This is the point where a hunting partner can be very helpful. The easiest way to do this correctly is to remain on the stand and guide the hunter below to what needs to be cleared and what does not. If you are alone, you may need to climb up and down the tree several times to make sure that your shooting lanes are thoroughly cleared. A tool that is very helpful for lane clearing is an extendable pruning saw. These saws allow you to cut branches as high up as twenty feet, with both of your feet securely planted on the ground; they can also be helpful in cutting out-of-reach branches from your hunting location in the tree.

Clear your lanes according to how frequently you may be hunting that location. We rarely hunt from any tree more than twice per season, and we cut very wide shooting lanes. We trim wide lanes because the element of surprise allows us to get away with it. When hunting a location frequently, you allow the deer to pattern you, which makes shot opportunities more difficult. Under such circumstances, narrower lanes should be cut so that you are less likely to get spotted.

Preparing a single tree takes us, on average, about three hours, and we are relatively quick. On a good day, with a partner, we can get three trees cleared out for next fall, maximum. The important thing is to be very exact. Pay attention to detail, and take the time necessary to make your tree as perfect to hunt from as you can. Do not think that you will be able to shoot around a branch that is in the way. In low-light conditions, these branches tend to become invisible and sometimes reach out and grab arrows on the way to a good buck.

When you cut saplings out of your shooting lane, cut them as close to the ground as you can, level with the ground if possible. Cover the cut stems with leaves and dirt, and then drag the tops away into a nearby thicket or stand them up in heavy cover away from your hunting location. Try to push the cut ends into the ground and make them look as though they died naturally. Do not just put them in a big pile that is obvious to see. Cutting the stems tight to the ground and hiding the tops will help keep your tree inconspicuous to other hunters. Whenever we find cut sapling stems in the woods, we immediately begin to look for a nearby stand. Other hunters do this as well. You want your shooting lanes to be wide open but subtle. By attempting to make your shooting lanes as natural looking as possible, as if there were never a tree or bush there in the first place, you may keep other hunters from finding your trees. By fall, the new growth will help mask your spring work. Problems with other hunters hunting your trees, disturbing your hunting, or stealing your stands is a sad reality in pressured areas. By keeping a low profile, you can keep such problems to a minimum. After all of your shooting lanes are clear, climb back down your tree, removing your steps as you go. If you decide to leave the steps in the tree, at least take out the bottom six, so that the remaining steps are well above eye level and out of other hunters' sight.

The last step is to ensure that the deer actually walk past your tree. In most spots, a runway or two will be out of range. If at all possible, attempt to tighten the funnel or encourage the deer to move in your direction by blocking runways that are out of range. Usually we strategically place some cuttings in the places where we don't want the deer to go. Quite often we also use small dead trees or large branches found in the area, because what we cut is not sufficient or large enough. In this endeavor, you have to be creative. You might have to block a turn in the runway or fill in a hole in a fence. You also might open up old deer trails by your tree by cutting small saplings or removing fallen trees.

Fences can act as important deer funnels. Deer are somewhat lazy and will walk quite a distance out of their way to cross a fence at an opening, low spot, or hole. Crossing points in fences can be serious hot spots, and it is possible to help these spots along. But make sure to get permission from the property owner before altering any fencing. In an area where there is an old fence, prepare a tree nearby, and make an opening or low spot in the fence within easy shooting distance. Do this only with an obviously old, broken-down fence that is in a state of decay. Also make the crossing point more attractive by blocking any other fence crossing or simply propping up the old fence. The deer will then use your opening.

When you do all this in the spring, the deer will be used to the changes by fall and accept them as normal. Doing this kind of work in the fall, however, will alert the deer to your presence. We rarely alter state land locations, simply because alterations are easily spotted by other hunters.

After all your trees are set up and you have taken care of the detail work, look at your map and pick out the best entry and exit routes to each stand, depending on their location relative to feeding and bedding areas and when you will be hunting them, mornings or evenings. Unless you know the property like the back of your hand, by the beginning of the season, when the foliage is on, these routes will require some sort of markers to find in the dark. Wandering around in the dark looking for a specific tree is not part of the plan and should never happen. We like to use both reflective tacks and twist ties. With a flashlight, white reflective tacks can be seen from a greater distance than green ones, and they are also much easier to spot in the daytime against dark bark. In areas where we are concerned about other hunters, we use green tacks or reflective twist ties. Twist ties around small branches are very difficult to see in the daytime, and on many of the properties we hunt, there are areas of brush that we have to go through where tacks will not work. Remove all buds from any branches where you use twist ties or the leaves from those buds may hide the ties by fall. Also remove any saplings or branches from the path between your tacks, or they too will leaf out and make finding your tacks difficult later.

Now that tree is ready for hunting season. Move on to the other spots marked on your map, and clear out a tree at every spot. You might end up with more than a dozen trees from which to hunt on a single parcel of land. If so, you are on the right path. The more good trees you have prepared, the more hunting options you will have in the fall.

THE ADVANTAGES OF THE AMBUSH SADDLE

On November 2, 2004, after giving up a morning hunt during the prerut in order to vote (you must have your priorities in order), John took off for a late midday/evening hunt several hours from home. It was a cool, lightly overcast day, with no wind. At about 2:30 P.M., he was comfortably settled in his Ambush Saddle, thirty-two feet above a small, active primary scrape area. It didn't take long for the activity to start. At 2:45, a two-and-a-half-year-old eight-point came into the small zone and proceeded to check for previous doe activity. He appeared to be very nervous and soon left without marking any of the scrapes or working the licking branches over them. John had witnessed that type of behavior on many occasions and was excited about what it might mean. Younger bucks are often very cautious when entering an area that has been recently visited by a more dominant buck.

Just after 3 P.M., John heard a twig snap to his right and slowly turned his head to see a large buck passing through one of his lanes. Keeping his attention on the buck as he cleared the lane, he slowly swung 180 degrees to the opposite side of the tree in an attempt to find an opening. His hunting height made it possible to get away undetected with this move, as did the quiet mobility of the Ambush Saddle. The buck was slowly moving to a downwind position from the scrapes. Not being able to find a hole to shoot through, John swung back around to his original position, hoping that the buck would continue into the area and possibly work one of the scrapes. The big buck stopped at the edge of the cover—a mere five yards from the base of the tree—and just stood there for several minutes. Apparently satisfied that nothing of interest had recently passed through the area, he then turned and started back in the direction he came from.

John knew he was going to pass back through the shooting lane again, so he swung back around the tree for the third time. As the buck was passing through the lane at a distance of fifteen yards, John came to full draw and gave a vocal doe bleat to stop him. The shot was perfect—John watched as the huge ten-point ran about a hundred yards and expired. There is absolutely no way with a conventional, climber, or ladder stand that he would have been able to get a shot at that buck; the trunk of the tree would have been in the way from the position he was set up in. Over the past twenty years or so, while using a harness system of this style, we have had to do the same thing many times in order to get a shot. We have been hunting from an Ambush Saddle style of harness for that period of time, and wouldn't even consider changing.

John with a ten-point he bagged during midday. Without the Ambush Saddle, he wouldn't have been able to take it.

The Ambush Saddle, simply put, is a hunting system that allows for maximum mobility when hunting from trees. While John aided in bringing the Ambush Saddle to market, we both use it exclusively as an alternative to conventional tree stands. At first glance, it looks like a seat belt gone wrong. The idea is simple: You hang in the saddle from the trunk of the tree, to which you are securely fastened. You sit facing the tree with your legs straddling the trunk, and your feet rest on tree steps placed all around the tree at the same level. The steps are used for leverage while maneuvering and as footrests while sitting. To shoot, you move around the tree and into position, then straighten your legs out and lean back in the saddle away from the tree. There is no platform to stand on and nothing to encumber movement around the tree or make noise. Once properly adjusted, the saddle is very comfortable.

John in a huge angled cottonwood tree; he later took a big buck from this location. There is no way a conventional hang-on or climber could have worked on this tree.

With an Ambush Saddle you can prepare as many trees during the postseason or preseason as you consider necessary. This is because you need only one saddle to hunt from all of your trees, and it is carried with you at all times. There's no fear of going into a hunting location and discovering that your stand was stolen—which, on state lands and in pressured areas with many small parcels, is part of the hunting process, as unfortunate as it may seem. With an Ambush Saddle, you can also be sure no one will hunt your stands while you are elsewhere. And because the saddle weighs only about two and a half pounds, fits in or attaches to a backpack, and is always with you, you can react to circumstances as they occur in the field.

With the saddle, the limitations concerning the diameter and straightness of trees that will accept stands nearly disappear. At the beginning of every season John has over eighty trees cleared out and ready for the saddle. About ten or fifteen of them are new locations set up during that year while the others are old locations that get retrimmed from year to year. Only fifteen to twenty of them may get hunted during the course of the season, but if one of the spots heats up, he has a tree ready. You do not have to limit yourself to a handful of spots. Having so many trees ready for the season also allows you to rotate stands, increasing the element of surprise and reducing scent contamination of the area. Pressured mature bucks do not tolerate hunter pressure. Rotation keeps your spots fresh and productive.

John also took a buck from this leaning big oak, which he could not have done without the Ambush Saddle's 360-degree shooting mobility.

Another big advantage of the saddle is what is known as specific mobility: the saddle makes it possible to shoot a full 360 degrees around most trees. Considering that mature bucks often come from unexpected directions, this is an important advantage. Hunting pressured areas means that you have to make good on opportunities for mature bucks when they arrive, because you will rarely get a second chance. We have gone entire seasons in Michigan without even seeing a mature buck, and when an opportunity arises we want to have the absolute best advantage possible. The Ambush Saddle puts us in a position to do so.

The saddle also allows you to keep the trunk of the tree that you are sitting in between you and the deer. By the time the hunting for mature bucks gets really good, in late October and November, the foliage in most trees is gone, and your silhouette becomes visible. This is especially true in heavily hunted areas, where deer tend to look for hunters in trees. With the Ambush Saddle, as a deer approaches, you slowly ease your way around the trunk, out of sight.

The lack of noise associated with the setup is another noticeable benefit. It is very difficult to pull up and hang a stand quietly or use a climber without making noise. You'll often find that the best place to set up is close to a bedding area, and the noise made setting up a stand can have a negative effect on the outcome of a hunt. Metal stands can make noise when you shift your body weight, and snow and ice are also a problem if they collect on a stand. The saddle avoids all of these problems.

Bowhunting for mature bucks is all about being able to adapt to their ever-changing movements. Even though our plan is to have a tree ready for every potential situation, that does not always work. Bucks are very aware of hunting pressure and are always adapting their movements to it. The more expedient you are at responding to changing deer movement, the better your chances will be at tagging that big buck.

Whenever we go on trips to hunt new, unfamiliar areas we take what we call freelance fanny packs. We use them in conjunction with our Ambush Saddle. These packs each contain tree steps, reflective markers, screw-in bow holders, rope, and a hand saw. We spend the first day scouting and setting up trees, leaving the steps in each tree after it is set up. We now have trees that are ready for hunting. If we are not pleased with a location after hunting it, we simply take the steps out as we descend and either adjust our location or put them back in their respective pack. Being able to quietly adjust just twenty yards closer to a given spot can sometimes make all the difference in the world.

It is our belief that using conventional stands would cut our shot opportunities nearly in half. The Ambush Saddle and other similar styles of hunting harnesses have completely changed the way we hunt over the years, and we wouldn't even consider hunting without them. They provide unsurpassed mobility and a better chance to react to a deer's changing movements. If used properly, they can increase your chances of success dramatically.

DEVELOPING A TENTATIVE HUNTING PLAN

As you clear out your trees, you should be developing a tentative hunting plan for the upcoming season. One of the biggest mistakes of most bowhunters is that they do not hunt with a plan. By the end of April, the vast majority of your actual scouting should be done. Now it is time to sit down with your maps and notes and develop a general hunting plan for the entire season. We're not talking about planning day for day the trees you will hunt out of; that becomes a minute-by-minute decision based on the weather and immediate deer movement, current deer sightings, and hunches. But you should plan a set of locations and a number of trees for each phase of the hunting season. You also should determine what trees need to be revisited prior to the season.

We divide the season into eight phases: the early season, the October lull, the prerut, the rut, gun season, postrut, second rut, and the late season. In your notebook, list each of the eight phases as headings. Under each heading, make a list of your trees that you think are best suited to each phase. For example, a food mast location will be best for the early season, but it could be good all season if mast continues to fall. A rub line would be best during the first few days. A primary scrape or staging area would work during all phases of the rut, but it would be best during the prerut. A tree along a standing cornfield is good as long as the corn is standing. Water holes are generally best during warm weather, which is usually early in the season. Scrape lines are best during the prerut and rut. Funnels between bedding and feeding areas are best in the early season, while funnels between bedding areas are good during the prerut and rut.

We also attempt to list the individual trees in order from best to worst. There will be some overlap among phases. This is not a problem; some trees are good throughout the entire season, though there will generally be a particular time of the season to which they are best suited. This list will be a good reference for your stand rotation and which trees to hunt during each hunting period. This is far more effective than just hunting haphazardly. Gaps are a problem, because you do not want to hunt a stand at the wrong time. This could ruin its effectiveness later in the season, when the time is right, so try to have stands for each section. Now you have created a general hunting plan for the season, which you will refine as the fall approaches and over the course of the season. Although instinct plays a big role in hunting, making a plan will definitely put you in a better position than relying solely on intuition.

FITNESS AND SHOOTING

Your fitness program that you began slowly in mid-January should be reaching full swing by April and May. By this time of year, you should be doing that cardiovascular workout about four times a week. Your strength training should also be reaching a good level, about three times a week. Shooting for an hour a couple times a week will keep your muscles fit. We usually raise the poundage of our bows by about five pounds in the spring. Shooting the extra poundage throughout the summer will strengthen your muscles and make drawing your bow that much easier when you return the poundage to your normal hunting weight in the early fall.

CHAPTER 3

June, July, and August

The long, beautiful days of summer have arrived. The does are busy with this year's fawns, and the bucks are enjoying the seclusion and the full range of foods that summer provides for growing new antlers and adding body weight. There is still some preparation to be completed, even during the dog days of summer.

GENERAL PERMISSION SEEKING

Hunting permission comes and goes. In fact, there is hardly a parcel we hunt today that we hunted ten years ago. The reasons for losing permission vary considerably. In the pressured state of Michigan, bowhunting has gained tremendously in popularity in the last twenty years. In quite a few instances, we lost permission because the family allowing us to hunt took up bowhunting themselves. Many of the places where we used to hunt are now developed, in most cases eliminating all hunting. Other properties simply changed owners. When you don't own the land and are not part of a family that owns land, hunting permission depends on the whims of others and is thus in constant flux. Losing permission to hunt is just part of bowhunting. Thus your search for new hunting land never ends.

During the summer, though, your attention should turn to more general scouting. No matter what we are doing, we are always on the lookout for new hunting land. In conversation and while doing business, hunting usually comes up. Since we are proud to be hunters and do not hide the fact, most people we come in contact with talk of hunting. We always relay our search for hunting permission to anyone who might be a possible source of that permission. You never know who will be able to give you a tip on where to attain permission to good hunting property. Nonhunters are usually better sources of hunting permission than hunters, because most hunters will hunt the good properties available to them. When you discover a piece of property that looks interesting, go through the effort to land permission.

SUMMER SCOUTING

If you happen to land new permission during the summer, you must scout the property before hunting season arrives, attempting not to cause undue harm to your hunting for the season. The primary difficulties with summer scouting are the full foliage that covers up the sign from last fall and the heat. Most important, sign from the rut phases will be overgrown and not as obvious as in the spring. You will not be able to scout as thoroughly in the summer, but with some effort, you will be able to speculate on what the deer activity will be like in the fall. We use the word "speculate" because summer deer activity can be completely different from fall deer activity. The bucks, particularly, alter their movement patterns dramatically as the days shorten and turn colder. A heavily used summer runway or travel route may become completely absent of deer activity by the time the prerut arrives or as the preferred food sources change.

You should structure your scouting the same as you did in the spring, looking for all the same types of hunting locations. The later it is in the summer, the more cautious you have be about scouting in and around bedding areas. A buck spooked once or twice in late June or early July will have time to resume his undisturbed pattern by the beginning of hunting season. But in a heavily hunted area, an experienced mature buck that is spooked in late August or early September could enter a nocturnal routine prematurely and may remain in that routine until the rut phases begin. If you must scout new property late in the summer, consider scent control.

Heat is a factor that cannot be ignored while summer scouting. Ultimately, the goal while scouting in summer is to remain as undetected as possible. This means not only staying out of the bedding areas, but also scouting at times when the deer are least active. In the summer, most scouting should take place in the middle of the day, not in the mornings and evenings when it is cool and deer are more likely to be moving. At midday, most of the deer will be doing what you wish you were—lying in the shade relaxing. Running into them at this time is not good for your future hunting. As with the overall timing of your scouting, the closer it is to hunting season, the more careful you have to be about scouting during midday. Of course, scouting during the hot part of the day can be very uncomfortable. Take some precautions. Carry enough water and move slowly, and you will remain somewhat comfortable. Another answer to the heat problem is to wait for inclement weather to do your summer scouting. High winds or heavy rain will mask your movement and keep you cool.

In the summer months, big bucks like this tend to have a daytime movement pattern. Quite often, once they shed their velvet they are seen less in open areas.

All of your summer scouting and tree preparation should be completed by about the beginning of August. But summer scouting of new hunting property is a situation of last resort; any scouting that can be done in late winter and spring should be done at that time. The longer your hunting properties remain undisturbed before you hunt them, the better. Late August is when most other hunters start thinking about hunting again and doing something about it. They will begin to take an interest in the deer and start busting through the brush getting ready for the season. This sudden influx of human activity in the woods alerts the mature deer of the upcoming season. If you have played your cards right, you are way ahead of the game. Your hunting areas will remain undisturbed and possibly benefit from other hunters pushing deer into a pattern that involves your undisturbed area. It is time to do a bit of relaxing while the others are just getting started.

REFINING YOUR BODY, YOUR SHOOTING, AND YOUR EQUIPMENT

Midsummer is the time to get mentally and physically prepared for the upcoming season. Your fitness program should have reached its peak and somewhat flattened into a regular routine. You should also be shooting at least a couple times a week. The muscle aspect of shooting has to be taken care of by mid-August. About a month before your season opener, you should tune and refine your shooting and bow for the coming hunting season. For us, this means giving our hunting bows a solid tuneup for the season. After our hunting bows are tuned, we make sure that all the components are quiet, rock solid, and designed for hunting. We want our bows to stand up to the wear and tear of a long season. Anything that is not absolutely essential is removed. We each have two bows set up identically in case something happens to the first, such as a cracked limb, frayed serving, or a bow developing a creaky wheel. Unless you are a bow technician, any major problem with equipment requires time to fix. We practice regularly with both bows right up to and throughout the hunting season. A backup bow is a form of insurance that we will not miss any prime-time hunting because of an untimely equipment mishap.

This is also the time to make sure you have all the equipment you will need for the season. During midsummer, archery and sporting-goods shops will be fully stocked. By getting everything you need now, you will avoid the preseason rush. If you need anything specific that must be ordered, there is still time to do so. Hunting mature bucks requires that you be ready for any circumstance that might arise. A proper array of equipment is vital to success. Covering the multitude of situations that may arise while hunting requires a pack full of gear. The following is a list of the equipment we carry into the woods in addition to our bows and arrows, along with brief descriptions.

Backpack

A backpack is an essential piece of gear. Stuffing your pockets with a few items before heading off into the woods is not enough. We carry packs that have several exterior pockets and are quiet, made of fleece, and large enough (at least fourteen hundred cubic inches) for all of our equipment, including extra clothes. We each have at least two backpacks that we alternate regularly. Wearing Scent-Lok clothing and rubber boots is not enough to eliminate all scent; packs acquire odors as well and need to be washed periodically in scenteliminating soap.

The Badlands Super Day Pack has a capacity of 1,950 cubic inches and will hold all necessary equipment. It also comes with an unconditional lifetime warranty.

Tree Steps

We always carry at least six tree steps to replace the six we removed from the bottom of each tree when we set it up. Removing those steps helps keep people from finding our trees, stealing our steps, and hunting from our trees. If we will be hunting a tree with all the steps removed, we know how many steps we will need because we wrote it down in our records for that particular tree, and we will take that many along.

Ambush Saddle

The Ambush Saddle rolls up into a ball and weighs about two and a half pounds. Unless we are sitting in them, they are always in our packs.

Climbing Safety Harness

A climbing safety harness is essential for safety while climbing up and down trees when using conventional tree stands. The Ambush Saddle has a self-contained safety belt.

Rope

We always carry a forty-foot piece of quarter-inch nylon rope for raising and lowering our bows.

Bow Holder and Quiver Holders

While hunting, we always remove our quiver from our bow and hang both the quiver and bow from the tree. Holding on to your bow for extended periods of time is unnecessary when hunting from a saddle; hanging from a bow holder, the bow is always within inches from your hand. You do not want any added movement or possible noise at crunch time.

Hand and Body Warmers

Charcoal air-activated hand warmers and Grabber adhesive body warmers are wonders of modern technology. They increase your comfortable time on stand tremendously. After we use the warmers, we close them in small Ziploc bags. This deactivates them and allows us to use some of the twelve-hour warmers up to three times.

Extra Clothes and Raingear

If we think it might become rainy, windy, or cold, we each pack a Rivers West all-weather suit, which will take care of all three situations. We always carry extra underclothes for our upper bodies. If we sweat too much getting to our trees, we change our upper undergarments and store the damp or wet items in a gallon-size Ziploc bag and then in our pack for odor control. During cold weather, we also pack most of our underlayers and pull them on after our bodies cool down to normal temperature. We do this while on stand in our Ambush Saddle.

Folding Brush Saw

You never know when you might need to prune a branch or clear out a tree. Try to find a folding saw with sierra-style teeth; they cut much more rapidly than any other tooth design.

Rattle Bag, Grunt Calls, and Bleat-in-Heat Can

We prefer a good rattle bag to antlers. A rattle bag fits better in the pack, and when used properly, it sounds excellent. Not all rattle bags are the same; some sound good, but others don't. Try different ones in the store until you find one that sounds solid and not tinny. Grunt calls are also important pieces of equipment. We carry an inhale grunt call for up-close short-range calling and an exhale grunt call for long range. We also take along a bleat-in-heat can. This and the grunt calls should be used sparingly. Too much use of anything is likely to be detrimental to your hunting.

Rangefinder

It is easier to hit a target when you know exactly how far away it is. After climbing into our trees, we use a rangefinder to measure various distances to specific markers, such as trees. Using our markers as references, we can be certain of the distances we are shooting. Our pins are sighted in from elevated heights similar to our tree-stand placement so that the ranges we take from the trees will be from angles similar to those from which we practice.

Food and Water

Whenever we hunt, we take along water bottles and something to eat. Though we don't eat very much while hunting, a granola bar, apple, or piece of chocolate can help get us through the day. On all-day hunts, we pack more.

Other Items

Other items we take include a compass, binoculars (compact 8×32s), reflective tacks, twist ties, knife, flashlights, extra batteries, bottle to urinate into, and toilet paper.

SETTING UP FOR SCENT CONTROL

Throughout the winter and spring, scent control was unimportant. Spooking deer during that period will not affect their behavior in the fall. Now is the time to begin thinking about it again and get it ready for the fall. As the season approaches, you want to give the deer as little warning as possible. This means practicing total scent control during your final phases of preparation, in August and September.

You may be skeptical about scent control products. We were, too, until we tried them and were overwhelmingly convinced. We are so convinced that we consider the ability to remain almost totally scent-free while hunting the most important technological development in bowhunting since compound bows were introduced commercially in the early 1970s. The hunting possibilities that scent control opens up are tremendous. Remaining scent-free allows you to walk to and from your stands without leaving a noticeable scent trail on the ground. This is the first point where deer used to spook before we began using activated odor-adsorbing Scent-Lok carbon suits. It used to be commonplace for deer that crossed our trail to our stands to stop and spook. There were also certain terrain types that we simply would not hunt due to unavoidable, unpredictable, swirling winds. Wearing an activated carbon Scent-Lok suit with scent-free rubber boots has eliminated these problems. We have had mature bucks actually follow our exact footsteps to our trees without showing any signs of alarm. If that is not enough proof, we see many more foxes and coyotes since we wear Scent-Lok, and both of those animals have excellent noses. Chris even had a fox walk right up to him while he was waiting at the base of a tree one evening. The fox was so close he could have kicked it. This never would have happened without scent control technology.

We simply see more deer since we began wearing Scent-Lok clothing. The deer that used to wind us before we even knew they were there now come in unaware of our presence. And when we remain scent-free, deer can pass by downwind without spooking. Having the first deer of a hunt pass through unalarmed is like a green light to any deer following them or passing through later. If those first deer spook, however, any following deer will naturally avoid the area. On occasion we see deer test the wind and act as though they have detected some scent. These deer have always checked the wind a time or two and then have gone back to feeding and acting casual. Thus practicing scent control will, without question, increase your deer sightings. In pressured areas, where mature bucks disappear at the first hint of human scent, this is an amazing advantage. You should definitely consider the realm of possibility that remaining scent-free opens up and take advantage of it.

In our hunting, scent control has taken a position of utmost importance. But as good as Scent-Lok and other activated, carbon-lined scent control products are, they are not totally foolproof. You can never be completely scent-free. Scent control is yet another aspect of serious bowhunting where you have to be meticulous with your preparation and diligent with your follow-through. Scent control can provide you with a tremendous advantage, an advantage that was impossible just a decade ago, but all carbon-lined scent control equipment is only as good as the hunter who takes care of it. Used inappropriately or only partially, scent control clothing and other products are of little value and offer nothing more than camouflage.

Your scent control arsenal should begin with the purchase of an activated coconut carbon-lined, odor-adsorbing Scent-Lok suit. Although carbon suits can be pricey, they are worth every cent. Considering that a suit may last from five to ten years, depending on how much you hunt and whether you take proper care of it, the cost per season is minor. Carbon technology originated outside of hunting. It was first used in filtration systems in such industries as aerospace and dry cleaning and is now used regularly by the U.S. military in chemical warfare suits. Activated carbon suits are based on sound scientific principles that are impossible to deny. Activated carbon is extremely porous, with tremendous interior and exterior surface area that makes it ideal for adsorption, the adherence of organic molecules to a surface area with which they come in contact.

Proper care of your activated carbon suit is critical to its effectiveness. The suit has to be reactivated before you wear it. While hanging in a store, these suits adsorb scent and can become somewhat saturated. (The adsorption process takes place because of a molecular force known as a van der Waals bond.) To remove this scent, place the suit in a clothes dryer set on high for at least twenty minutes. This removes the scent molecules from the suit and frees the carbon to adsorb new scent molecules, thanks to a process known as Brownian molecular motion. We repeat this procedure about every five to eight hunts, depending on the weather. During warmer weather, we tend to sweat more and have to reactivate our suits most frequently. This is a little more often than called for on the label, but we like to take every scent control precaution possible. Immediately after removing your suit from the dryer, store it in a scent-free container. We place our suits in activated Scent-Lok storage bags, and then inside airtight plastic tubs. You can use plastic bags instead of Scent-Lok bags, although they puncture easily.

When hunting, don't pull on your suit until just before walking to your tree. We often witness hunters wearing their scent control clothing in restaurants or gas stations. Everywhere you wear your Scent-Lok suit, it is adsorbing odor, which diminishes its effectiveness in the woods. Wear your suit only in hunting situations.

The second piece of your scent control armor is the head cover. Wearing a head cover is vital to the overall effectiveness of an activated carbon suit. Your head and hair emit more scent than any other part of your body. It is absolutely critical to wear the head cover in conjunction with the suit. A baseball cap just won't cut it.

Activated carbon gloves are the third part of complete odor armor. We wear these gloves on the way to our trees, while screwing in the steps, and while hunting. Over the years, we have often had deer smell the bases of our trees, sometimes even inspect the steps themselves. If you screw in the bottom steps with your bare hands, you are leaving a lot of scent that could spook any deer that come close.

Rubber boots are the fourth essential part of scent control. Wearing an activated carbon suit with leather or Cordura boots will negate some benefits of the suit. These boots breathe and emit a great deal of human odor both while you are on the way to your tree and on stand. Boots that have activated carbon in them are also suspect. Activated carbon must be regularly reactivated in order to be effective. How do you activate a pair of boots? A normal clothes dryer probably would not withstand that kind of abuse, not to mention what it would do to the boots. The proper amount of heat required would also not reach the inner boot. Rubber boots are not breathable. This is both their strength and their weakness—their strength because they trap all odor inside them, their weakness because they also hold in moisture, often leading to uncomfortable and cold feet. When you wear rubber boots in conjunction with an activated carbon suit, the pant legs of your suit should be over the boots. Do not tuck them inside your boots. The reason for this is simple. Every time you take a step in rubber boots, a puff of air escapes out the top of the boot; this will leave scent on surrounding plants. If your pant legs are over your boots, the activated carbon will trap this scent. Use your rubber hunting boots for hunting and scouting only; any foreign odors in the bottom cleats of the boots, such as from oil, gas, or grease, can potentially spook deer.

An aspect of scent control that is sometimes forgotten is keeping your underclothes as scent-free as possible. Treat your underclothes in the same manner as you do your Scent-Lok suit. This means washing them in scent-free detergent, immediately drying them, and then storing them just like you do your Scent-Lok suit. We dress after we get out of our vehicle after we arrive at our hunting spots so that the clothes will carry as little scent as possible.

A scent control arsenal is not complete without scent-eliminating toiletries. Before we hunt, we shower with scent-eliminating soap and shampoo, use scent-eliminating deodorant, and brush our teeth with scent-eliminating toothpaste. Ridding the body of as much odor as possible before hunting is always our plan. This also means avoiding spicy foods during hunting season, particularly those containing garlic or onions, which cause your body to emit a strong odor. The less you stink, the better and longer your suit will function.

Scent-eliminating spray is the final element in our scent control system. We always carry a small bottle of the spray with us in our packs. When we get to our trees, or while still at our vehicle, we quickly spray down anything that might have picked up unwanted scent, such as the grips of our bows or the straps of our packs. This is just a bit of insurance. If we happened to pick up some scent somewhere, we want to make every effort possible to eliminate it. We do not spray down our Scent-Lok suits, simply because it is not necessary.

This may seem like a lot of extra work, and it is. The payoff, though, is worth the effort. Since practicing diligent scent control, we have had entire seasons go by without a single deer winding us. That never happened before Scent-Lok was available. On almost every hunt, deer are standing downwind at some point. Before scent control, these deer would spook and take any other deer in the vicinity with them, and also let deer within hearing range know that there was danger in that direction. Now these deer pass undisturbed, and the deer nearby are not alarmed. And because mature bucks are usually the last ones to come out of the cover, if you spook the first deer to pass through, the chances of a mature buck showing himself later decrease dramatically.

LAST-MINUTE STAND PREP

If everything has gone according to plan, all of your trees have been thoroughly prepared for several months now. A bit of late-summer work remains to be done before the season starts. In late August, you should do the final touch-up of your stands for the season. This means you need to tour all of your stands that you prepared in the spring and make sure they are absolutely ready for the coming season. This is a final check to make sure everything is perfect and to get any last-minute work out of the way. Over the summer, new growth sometimes fills in or blocks a shooting lane, or a few new branches may sprout on the tree itself. By late August, all important plant growth will be completed, and you may have to remove a few branches. You might also need to place steps or hang stands. Whatever needs to be done has to be completed at this time. Do not wait until a few days before the opener. This touch-up has to be done well in advance of any hunting.

When you do your last-minute touch-up, it is imperative that you remain as scent-free as possible. Before you head off to your stands, pull on your rubber boots and Scent-Lok suit, head cover, and gloves. Head to your stands during the middle of the day to help prevent detection. In late August, this means you probably will be very hot, but you want to leave the area as undisturbed as possible. If you do happen to spook the deer at this time, there are still several weeks before the season for deer activity to resume its normal pattern. If you wait too long to perform this touch-up, you will only be informing the deer of the coming season. It is also important not to make any more trips than necessary to the same hunting areas. Try to entirely fine-tune an area in one outing, no more. Most hunters contaminate their hunting areas just prior to the opener with multiple visits, thus ruining their element of surprise, and sometimes even causing the local mature bucks to prematurely alter their summer routines and revert into a more nocturnal pattern. This is one of the most common scenarios in bowhunting. Every year, this leaves hordes of hunters wondering what happened to that big buck whose routine had been like clockwork for the last half of the summer.

After doing your last-minute stand prep, get out of the woods and don't return to any of your trees until it is time to hunt them. In some situations, you will not return to a particular tree until the prerut begins, which for us is late October. Some trees may not be hunted until December. Regular checking of stands for deer activity is another common mistake hunters make. By constantly checking stands, hunters are simply alerting mature bucks and does to their presence and pushing them into a nocturnal routine. If you refrain from this sort of diligence, you can allow the deer to move undisturbed and hopefully catch them by surprise at the absolute perfect moment. Staying away from their best stands until the prerut or rut is one of the most difficult things for hunters to do, yet it is one of the most important elements to regular success on mature pressured bucks. This requires self-control, discipline, patience, and adherence to a solid hunting plan.

CHAPTER 4

September

Hunting season is fast approaching, and most hunters now are frantically scouting. But you have been getting ready for the season since January. All of your trees and stands are ready and fine-tuned, your bow is tuned and set up for hunting, and your equipment is in a state of readiness. You are ready for battle.

Just as you are going through the change from hunting preparation to actual hunting, the deer are also going through changes. With the shortening days and cooler temperatures, they begin to feed heavily in September, making them more observable from a distance. There should be noticeably more deer feeding in fields at this time of year. The bucks become more visible and are seen feeding in bachelor groups in the same fields as the does. Mature bucks and does have been going their separate ways since spring. Most mature bucks are out of velvet by the end of the first week in September, and most yearlings by the end of the third week. With the shedding of velvet, bucks feel the first surge of testosterone and begin rubbing and casually signposting. The majority of does have weaned their fawns by late September. The slight cooling of temperatures allows the deer to move more than they have been the entire summer without overheating.

September is an exciting time, a precursor of things to come. There are just a few more things you need to do before the hunting begins. In some states, the bow season starts in September, but in others, the opener is not until October, so adjust your timing to fit your local season.

LOOKOUT STANDS

In early to mid-September, your main task is to locate a mature buck to hunt during the first few days of the season. You cleared out lookout stands during the spring specifically for this purpose. These are not stands from which you will be hunting. In most instances, they are across a field or in an out-of-the-way spot. Many hunters seem to think that if they are not hunting, they do not need to sit in the woods. But preseason sits in lookout stands can be some of the most practical and useful scouting there is. It is also a great way to increase your knowledge of deer behavior. Firsthand experience watching deer is a better teacher than any book or video can ever be. Sometimes we take a camera along and get a few shots of the deer we see.

Any mature buck that you spot will generally still be following a well-established late-summer routine. The last thing you want to do is alert this buck to your presence. Even though you are not hunting and are quite some distance from the deer you will be watching, practice scent control. Your lookout stands also should have been chosen so that you can approach and depart without being detected.

We spend our free time trying to locate a mature buck to hunt the first few days of the season. We would like to claim that in this endeavor we are regularly successful, but this is simply not the case because of the makeup of most of our properties, which are small and sometimes marginal. Although some of our hunting spots are located in sections that normally contain a mature buck or two, most of the time the late-summer feeding area is not where we have permission. Sometimes, though, we manage to get the bead on a good buck. Even when we do not spot a mature buck, sitting in the woods in late summer is a great way to spend time.

In some instances, you may be able to locate a buck from a vehicle. If the property you hunt borders on a road that gives you good visibility into the property, you can spot from your car or truck early in the morning and just before dark. You can cover several properties in an evening. The problem with spotting from the road is that any mature buck that is regularly visible from an automobile will attract attention from other hunters in pressured areas. The word of such bucks generally gets around. This means that anyone who is hunting in the vicinity will go out of the way to get a crack at this buck, both on neighboring properties and on the actual property where the buck has been spotted. This makes lookout stands in areas that are protected from roads a better option. In pressured areas, it is also wise to keep the news of any sightings of mature bucks to yourself. Spreading the news of the whereabouts of a mature buck can only lead to more competition for that buck, whether through permission or trespassing

When you spot a buck, mentally mark the spot where he enters the feeding area. Note the time the buck arrives, how long he remains, when he departs, and the exact location where he exits. Bucks at this time of year usually follow a very steady routine and will do so until they are disturbed. Careful observation will give you a good idea where you must set up to intercept this particular buck. If you already have a stand at this location, you are in luck. Plan to hunt this spot on one of your first hunts. But if the buck is entering his feeding area from some other point, it is time to get to work. There is still a chance to intercept that buck when the season begins, as long as the buck and the area remain undisturbed.

During the middle of the day, while practicing extreme caution with scent control, clear out a tree at the point where you observed the buck. If there are no appropriate trees, find a spot for a natural ground blind or pop-up blind. Before using a pop-up blind for hunting, set it up in a shaded area in your yard for at least a week. This will air out most foreign odors from the fabric. Wear Scent-Lok gloves while taking it down and setting it back up in a hunting location. If possible, wait for inclement weather (high winds or rain) to set up at the new location. Because you know exactly where the early-season buck is entering its feeding area, and at what time, you should not alter the area as you would while setting up a hunting location in the spring. Clear a subtle lane to the desired shot area and get out of there. Do not linger, and do not do any more scouting, lane clearing, brush moving, or cutting than absolutely necessary. Try to keep a low profile with scent, noise, and any alterations to the environment. The buck will notice any changes.

Deer are far more aware of minor changes to their home environment than most people give them credit for, particularly mature matriarch does and mature bucks. Deer also have far better memories than most people realize. A mature doe that lives in one of our longtime hunting areas shows just how good deer memories can be. This doe has lived in the same area for several years. Five years ago, John shot a doe from a particular stand while another mature doe was standing right next to her. From that point on, every time this doe appears, she inspects that stand very thoroughly, even though it gets hunted only once or twice per season. We have watched this doe numerous times from other stands within sight distance of the original stand. We have even attempted to shoot that doe, with no success. Just as this doe has remembered where danger was, other deer notice changes in their home areas. With this in mind, it is clear that any cutting that has to be done close to opening day should be kept to an absolute minimum. After your stand preparation is completed, leave this area alone. Do not even think about setting foot in this spot until you are ready to hunt. You want the buck to continue following the same summer routine until you have a chance to hunt him. Any bit of pressure could change this pattern and ruin your first good opportunity of the season.

NEW RUB LINES AND CLUSTERS

The majority of mature bucks are out of velvet by early September. As soon as bucks begin to lose their velvet, they begin making rubs. Though we strongly recommend doing most of your scouting and tree preparation in winter and spring, and the final touches by August, new rub lines and clusters can be fantastic locations to ambush a mature buck during the first couple days of the season, and you'll find these areas only in mid to late September.

Having previously scouted your hunting areas in the winter and early spring, you should have a good idea of where any new rub lines might appear on any specific property. You have noted any old rub lines in your notebook but usually do not know whether a particular buck survived. Now is the time to find out. A word of caution, though: In heavily hunted areas, if you have already spotted a mature buck from a lookout stand and are set up for him, don't even think about walking on the property and looking for anything until you have hunted that spot at least twice.

Starting around September 20, while practicing extreme scent control, take a quick midday jaunt through each of your hunting areas, searching for new rubs. Waiting until the twentieth allows bucks time to get rub lines or clusters started; before that, there may be just a few individual rubs that are difficult to find.

With notebook in hand, check all likely locations between bedding and feeding areas. Bucks will still be feeding heavily, and early rub lines are usually located between these areas. It is best to do this during very inclement weather, preferably a hard rain or strong wind.

On properties we have hunted for years, we know the area well enough that we often do our final stand preparations—which we usually recommend doing in August—at the same time we are looking for new rubs. One visit is normally our preseason maximum, so this takes the August visit out of our scouting program. In pressured areas, there is a fine line between keeping pressure to an absolute minimum and finding early-season setups. Only knowing your hunting area intimately will allow you to make the right decision.

If you find a new rub line and it looks as though it has been made by a mature buck (see the section on hunting rub lines in the October chapter), set up a tree on that route far enough away from the bedding area that you will not spook deer with your entrance and exit. In this spot, be subtle with your trimming. Make one good lane to the runway with the rubs. If the area has thick cover, making visibility poor, clear two small lanes to the same runway. This will give you a visual lane and a shooting lane. The full foliage of the early season can dampen the noise of an approaching buck, allowing him to pass through a single lane before you can draw your bow.

Clusters of rubs are generally found along perimeter cover bordering open areas, such as along the edges of weed fields, cropfields, marshes, swamps, and openings in the woods. Treat a cluster in a small area in the same manner as a rub line, placing a stand within shooting distance and then getting out. Just as in the spring, cut saplings and brush tight to the ground, and carry the cuttings well away from your hunting area. Hide them or prop them up to make them look like a natural part of the woods. Even though some individual rubs may get revisited, we do not hunt individual rubs without other sign to go along with them.

FRESH SCRAPES

While cruising for new rub lines and clusters, keep an eye open for fresh scrapes as well. It is rare in pressured areas to find scrapes in mid to late September, but we occasionally do. They generally occur along the same runways where rub lines would be found, between bedding and feeding areas. The great thing about finding scrapes in September is that you can be almost certain that they were made by a buck with at least one breeding season behind him. Yearling bucks usually do not start scraping until the rut phases begin. If you are fortunate enough to find scrapes along a runway in September, you definitely should set up a spot to hunt. Set up as described for new rub lines.

On several occasions in September, we have found some early subtle activity at primary scrape areas. This scrape activity is the mark of a mature buck. Hunt such a location during the first day or two of the season, and then leave it totally alone until the rut phases begin.

REMOTE CAMERAS

This is the time of year when most hunters are out in the woods setting up their remote cameras or, as they are sometimes called, scouting cameras. It is very tempting to use these cameras so that you can see the bucks you are hunting, but they can be detrimental to your hunting of pressured mature bucks. Such bucks tolerate very little disturbance in their core areas before it causes them to change their habits and become nocturnal. First you have to place the cameras in the woods, creating a disturbance and leaving scent behind. Then the cameras have to be checked periodically, resulting in more disturbance and more scent.

Additionally, the cameras themselves can spook deer. We have watched as does were photographed in a pressured area with remote cameras with a flash in near-dark situations. Most of the does bolted from the flash, almost as though they had been shot. This reaction is not necessarily seen in the photos, but it definitely makes it clear that cameras can spook deer. If does react so dramatically, imagine how pressured mature bucks react. Just how severely pressured bucks react has become clear to us over the last few years. Fellow bowhunters often show us remote camera photos of bucks taken prior to the season near their hunting locations. Generally, the hunter has only one photo of a good buck, and then no more. Having been spooked, the mature buck begins to avoid the general area near the camera. This is not the case with yearling bucks, which continue to return and be photographed. These young bucks are not so wary as older bucks. They have not yet lived through a hunting season with antlers on their heads and do not sport old wounds, as do a good portion of mature bucks in pressured areas. If the photographed buck ends up getting killed later in the season, this usually happens in a different location from where the camera was positioned.

The situation is different in nonpressured areas, even for mature bucks. John has a good friend who has more than forty photos of a 190-class fourteen-point taken on his property in Iowa from a single season. That is a nonpressured buck! He also has several photos of three other really good bucks on the same property, one of which is a 180-class twelve-point. Deer that live in areas with very little hunting pressure may not react adversely to remote cameras.

We prefer to view remote cameras as something that could reduce our chances at killing a mature buck. If you decide to use a remote camera in your hunting area, you should attempt to minimize the effects it has on the deer. One possibility is to turn off the flash and set the camera for daytime use only. To keep your disturbance to a minimum, set the camera up only one time, while practicing scent control, and remove it from that spot the first time you hunt there. This eliminates repetitive intrusion into an area. The camera may allow you to confirm the daytime presence of a buck in your hunting area. The ideal remote camera would be of the infrared variety, with no flash and no noise, having a direct satellite hookup to a home computer, and never needing to be checked in the woods. Until something like this comes on the market, we do not recommend using remote cameras while hunting mature pressured bucks. Though we like photos of deer, the ones we like best are those where we are holding the antlers of the buck we have killed. A single photo like this is worth a hundred of that same buck alive in the woods.

This was the only time this buck was caught on camera. We suspect that the flash kept him from returning. In pressured areas, everything matters.

This wide eight-point was also photographed only this one time, while many subordinate bucks were caught multiple times on the same scrape.

REFINING YOUR HUNTING PLAN

In the spring, while doing your postseason scouting, you should have started developing a hunting plan for all of your hunting properties and individual trees, for the entire season. Now is the time to put everything together. You should have a notebook full of maps, marked with hunting spots, and lists of your best stands for specific parts of the hunting season. As you were scouting, you should have marked the various sign and the best times to hunt these spots. By this time of year, it should be very clear what the preferred food sources are and how the crop and food sources will be used throughout the fall. You should work out the best time to hunt each particular tree, based on your spring scouting list and on your last round of late-summer tree preparation. Daily timing is also critical; some trees are better suited for morning hunts, some for evening hunts, and some for all-day hunts during the rut phases.

CHRIS'S EARLY-SEASON SURPRISE BUCK

I wasn't planning to hunt at all. I made the long drive out to the farm to scout for two days in preparation for a planned hunt during the first or second week of November. I had not been out to this farm for a few years, so I wanted to check it out before hunting. As I neared the farm, the weather changed from partly sunny and mild to rainy and relatively cold for late September. Driving past the old farmhouse, I noticed Greg, the farmer, in one of his barns. I pulled in to announce my arrival and say hello. Friendly as usual, Greg gave me a warm welcome. Our conversation floated through many subjects, including the weather. It had been raining for about a week straight, and Greg had had a couple sightings of decent bucks, which definitely sparked my interest. At about noon, it was time for Greg to head in for lunch and time for me to get scouting. Jokingly, as we parted, I boldly commented, "With the weather like it is, I think I'll just stalk a cornfield, shoot a buck, and head home in a couple hours." We shared a laugh over my ridiculous statement and went our separate ways. Sometimes I wish I were more careful about the things I say.

I drove up the road about half a mile to the lane that led into the first part of the farm I intended to scout. The rain was still falling steady as ever, so I pulled on my raingear along with my scouting pack and headed for the woods. As I crossed the first lush, green alfalfa field, I couldn't help but notice how drenched everything was. Water was dripping from every leaf and branch, so much so that it reminded me of the Canadian coastal rain forest, where I had spent some time getting acquainted with rain. The alfalfa was bordered by a small cornfield, which butted up to a brushy fencerow, on the other side of which was a five-acre oval patch of soybeans. Instinctively, I stopped just short of the fencerow, then cautiously worked the last few steps up to the fence and peered across the little field. At the other end, only a few yards from cover, stood a doe and two fawns feeding. They were feeding contentedly, seeming hardly aware of their surroundings. I watched them and pondered my next move. After about ten minutes, those deer didn't look as if they were in a hurry to go anywhere, so I stepped slowly out into the field. In an instant, the doe took notice, stared intently in my direction, and then bounded off, taking her fawns with her. Both seemed clueless as to why they were suddenly bounding out of the lush beans. I don't like to spook deer when I scout, so I was hoping that this would be an isolated incident.

Crossing the beans, I arrived at the deep ravine that cuts through the property. This is the key terrain feature on this part of the farm, and the one I wanted to check out. The ravine is wide and brushy and splits the property in two, connecting a major bedding area to all the crops. On the backside of the ravine is an alfalfa field that is completely hidden from any road and surrounded by good bedding areas and travel routes. Setting up a few trees along these travel routes, and perhaps locating a staging area, was my intention for this afternoon. I moved slowly to the bottom of the ravine, trying not to make a sound, but just as I started up the other side, my attention was drawn to the field and several bobbing white tails flying over the small hill. Instantly I knew I had to change my game plan. It was now about 12:30 P.M., and the deer were up and moving and probably would be all day. Instead of scouting, I should probably hunt somewhere and hope for a change in the weather for scouting. Perhaps I could resume with my plan the following day.

Since there was hardly any wind, stalking a cornfield was out of the question, but I didn't have any trees ready. Glancing down the ravine, I noticed that some logging had been done, and several trees looked huntable from a distance. They were situated along the back edge of the ravine, about fifty yards from the inside corner of the back alfalfa field. And if my memory served me right, there used to be some good runways up the edge of the ravine. I decided that I would hunt from one of those trees. I turned around and walked back to my car.

At my car, I swapped scouting Scent-Lok for hunting Scent-Lok, traded my scouting pack for my hunting pack, and pulled my bow from its case. Retracing my steps, I was back at the ravine in about half an hour. Trying hard to be as silent as possible, each step deliberate and calculated, I stalked down to the patch of trees I had decided to hunt. It took only a couple seconds to make a decision. In the best location imaginable was the perfect tree. Positioned just on the inside corner of two overgrown logging paths and at the intersection of three well-used runways that led to the alfalfa, and having a good split at about thirty feet for excellent background cover, this was the tree. I got to work immediately with my tree steps and Ambush Saddle, and within ten minutes I was hanging just above the split. At the top, I only had to trim two small branches to open up clear shots to all three runways.

Inspecting the possible shot positions, I noticed a couple saplings that had to be removed on the ground. So down the tree I went. Grabbing the first sapling, I cut it out of the way and began with the second, when suddenly, in midcut, I became aware of a serious mistake. When I had reached my hunting height in the tree, I removed my Scent-Lok gloves and tossed them into my pack. I had forgotten to pull them back on before climbing down to remove the saplings. Now I had left human scent right in my shooting lane. I was angry at myself for this boneheaded mistake, but it was too late to do anything about it, so I hid the saplings off to the side in some thick brush where I was fairly certain a deer would not walk. The only thing I could do now was hope that this mistake would not come back to haunt me. Up the tree I went, brooding about my mistake. It was now about 1:30 P.M.

For the next two hours, it rained. The rain was not heavy, more like a thick mist or fog that enveloped everything, with water moving in all directions, yet without wind. At 3:30, a light breeze pushed the rain away. After sitting in the rain for two hours, I found this a welcome change. I guess the deer thought so too—it was only a few minutes later when movement caught my eye, and there, only about twenty yards away, walking down the old logging path along the edge of the ravine, appeared a single deer. Focusing my attention in that direction, I studied the button buck as he casually plucked browse from along the path. Like a happy-go-lucky teenager, he didn't appear to have a care in the world and was definitely not overly interested in his surroundings. In short order, he stepped into the shooting lane where I had cut the branches. Here he paused for a second, nose on the sapling, but showed no sign of alarm. Twitching his tail, like we would shrug our shoulders at something of little importance, he passed through, heading across the ravine toward the beans. Perhaps my mistake was not so serious after all. It wasn't five minutes later before the button buck's brother ambled along the same path. His reaction at the shooting lane was a little more pronounced. At the cut sapling, he stopped, looked around, and tested the wind, before following the tracks of his brother. How would a mature deer react?

I didn't have to wait long for the answer. About twenty minutes behind the fawns followed a very large mature doe. I surmised that this must be their mother. She didn't have a care in the world until she got to the shooting lane and her nose hit that cut sapling. She lifted her head, paused for a second, and lowered her nose to smell the sapling again. It was a double take, as though she had to take another whiff to believe her nose. Instantly she was on high alert, spending the next twenty minutes trying to find the human that had left the scent. She tested the wind, circled my tree twice, walked to the edge of the field, and peered out into the alfalfa. She walked back and stood directly downwind of me at about twenty yards, testing the wind again and again; I could hear her sucking wind through her nose. Eventually she followed the route her fawns had taken, though with extreme caution and seeming agitated. Now I had the answer to my question. If a mature buck followed the path of the other deer, I would have to try to take him before he got to the shooting lane. I scanned the lane for possibilities and found a small hole that might work in a pinch.

A couple more hours passed, in which I had to be content with watching squirrels and birds. The wind slowed to nothing, and the first gray of the coming night started to filter between the trees. Although it still looked like broad daylight out in the field, the distance I could see in the woods gradually shrank, gray mixing with the early-season green. I could see only about forty yards when a deer silently materialized at the edge of my vision, coming from the same direction as the other deer. Instantly more focused, I concentrated on the deer. Antler, good antler, and coming my way, following the same exact path the other deer had taken. A second glance was all I needed to decide that this was a shooter. The buck carried a decent rack with some unusual points, points that I didn't bother to count.

Carefully grabbing my bow, I moved into position in my saddle, anticipating a shot through the small hole before the scent-contaminated shooting lane. I was ready but the buck took his time, browsing along slowly, on pace to enter the alfalfa field just a bit after dark. Two steps before the small opening, the buck stopped, lifted his head, and scent-checked the area. He was now only about twenty yards out, and I could see him clearly. Thoughts of my mistake were racing through my head. Could the buck have smelled me already? Was he picking up on scent the mature doe had left behind? Just two more steps, I attempted to will the buck forward. Then the buck did the unexpected, as mature bucks are known to do, and turned, deciding to cut behind my tree, where there wasn't a runway, and quickened his pace. As if on autopilot, I shifted my weight and moved the saddle into shooting position. The buck was now directly behind my original position.

The buck quickened his pace, seeming now to have a set destination in mind. Searching for an opening, I spotted a small hole through which I could intercept the buck and drew. In a split second, the buck's chest filled the hole. I blatted, dropped my pin onto the buck's chest, and set my arrow free. *Whack!* The sound of arrow hitting bone and the blur of a buck bolting were all my senses could detect in the sudden flurry of movement and sound. It all happened so fast that I did not even see where my arrow hit.

As I followed the buck with my eyes, he dashed, to my astonishment, out into the alfalfa, away from the bedding area. His barreling jump into the field was where I lost track of him with my eyes. Attempting to follow him with my ears, I listened for any clue. A couple seconds later, I was met with a puzzling sound, a very loud sharp snap, almost like a shot from a .22, coming from the top of the hill in the field. Again, I was filled with uncertainty and questions. I wondered at the sound. There wasn't a branch anywhere in that field, and it was at least four hundred yards to the other side. From the feel of the shot, I didn't think the buck could have gone that far. Did he somehow circle back? With thoughts like these racing through my mind, I packed my things together, trying to do this slowly and casually. I climbed down the tree, removing my steps as I went, taking my time.

About twenty minutes later, I was on the ground and crept silently to the shot point. A quick inspection revealed nothing—no arrow, no hair, no blood, not even any scuffed leaves. I decided to take a quick look where I last saw the buck, where he bounded into the field. Moving as slowly as I could with adrenaline still pumping, I reached that point and the heavy burden of uncertainty fell from my shoulders. There on the ground was a wide spray of bright, frothy blood, clearly a lung shot.

Stepping into the field, I scanned the low hill. Just at the top, I could see the distinct curve of an antler above the alfalfa. In a sudden burst of elation, I held my bow high, gave a whoop of joy, and ran up the hill. The buck had collapsed in midstride and was lying on his side. No arrow hole was apparent. I lifted the buck's head to admire his antlers: eleven points. Then, curious about my shot, I turned him over to take a look. Under the buck lay the top quarter of my arrow. When the buck crashed, he broke the carbon arrow, which explained the loud snapping sound. Since there was no exit hole, I assumed the rest of my arrow must be lodged in his chest. After admiring the buck for a few minutes, I carried my hunting gear back to my car with the hope of getting Greg to help me with the buck.

Chris with his early-season eleven-point.

It was just before dark when I knocked on the door. Greg's wife, Vicky, answered the door and greeted me warmly. Greg was in the other room. A quick call and out he came. The first question he asked was whether I got one, playing on my comment from earlier that afternoon. My answer was that of course I shot a buck. At first he didn't believe me, which is understandable. Then, more seriously, I told him about the buck and quickly recounted the hunt. Within minutes, we were out in the field in his old Ford, picking up the deer. In another hour, I was driving home with my early-season surprise buck and making new plans for the first week of November.

As you make the last tour of your stands, keep your eyes open for any changes or obviously important factors, such as an abundance or lack of acorns or apples in a previously scouted area or a fresh rub or scrape line. Add any new information to your maps and records. A last look at your chosen stand sites should reconfirm or call into question your early-season stand decisions from spring. Some of your best stands will still be inactive at this point; for instance, primary scrape areas are generally not active until the prerut and should not be hunted until then.

When you have all the information together, develop a plan and stick to it. We usually go through our notebooks at this time and list our best stands. The list is usually ten to twenty trees long. At the top of the list are trees in primary scrape areas and staging areas. These are our overall best stands, the ones from which we have the absolute best chance at killing a mature buck. For each tree, we then write down the best time to hunt. We list our early-season trees, our October lull trees, and our late-season trees. The list helps us develop a solid rotation of hunting stands and provides a quick reminder of all stands available. Each tree should have a time or weather condition that is best. Write this information in your notebook. When that unique set of circumstances comes together, hunt accordingly. This sort of guidance can help you hunt far more effectively than simply haphazardly bouncing from stand to stand. Flexibility is important, however; your plan is not set in stone. If conditions change or deer movement is altered through some unforeseen event, adjust accordingly. The ability to adapt is just as important as your plan.

HUNTING LOGBOOK

A hunting logbook is an invaluable tool in planning your hunts when used in conjunction with your scouting notebook. Detailed information can reveal deer patterns and behavior that would otherwise remain undetected by mere casual observation. After each hunt, we log pertinent information. If you decide to do this, write down any information you feel is relevant. Include the number of deer you see, what each one of the deer was, the time the deer moved through, and any interesting behavior. It is important to note such things as what the deer were feeding on or whether a mature buck was following a doe. Besides recording any buck you see, attempt to identify the individual bucks and try to figure out what that deer was up to. Was it merely feeding, signposting, or demonstrating other dominance or rutting behavior (such as making scrapes, sparring with other bucks, or chasing does)? This information helps you figure out exactly why any individual buck passes by your stand. The biggest question that you try to answer in your logbook is why the deer are doing what they are doing. When you know why a deer has taken a particular route, you can begin to come up with a way to hunt that deer.

Weather conditions are another important part of the logbook. Note all the relevant weather conditions, such as temperature, wind, and precipitation. This combined with deer-sighting information can give clues to which stands are best in which conditions. For instance, in years when the acorn crop fails, you might consult your logbook to determine where you saw mature bucks the last time the mast failed.

Filling out logbooks might seem like a very time-consuming ritual, but it is not; in just two or three minutes after a hunt, you can easily jot down that hunt's happenings. You can return to your logbook later, during downtime in season and sometimes after the season is over, to fill in more details. A few key words can bring back a flood of memories from a particular hunt. After a couple years, these books become invaluable. We make copies of our logbooks and notebooks and keep them locked in a safe. They are that important to us.

THE IMPORTANCE OF TIMING

In order to kill a mature buck, you have to be in the right place at the right time. Occasionally this happens through sheer luck; everybody knows a beginner somewhere who walked into the woods, climbed a tree, and killed a big buck. But this sort of event is an exception. To kill mature bucks with any regularity requires careful planning. We cannot emphasize enough how important proper timing is to the outcome of your hunting. Besides seasonal timing, which involves developing a plan for the entire season and saving your best trees until they are ready to hunt, there are other forms of timing that you must consider in order to be regularly successful at hunting mature bucks. One is your own daily timing, and another is the timing of other hunters. Understanding when other hunters hunt is critical to using them to your advantage.

Daily timing means the times you arrive at and depart from your stands. By nature, mature bucks are more nocturnal than the other deer in the herd. This is a simple truth that most hunters are unable or unwilling to consider. Most hunters disregard this fact and arrive at their morning stands a few minutes before first light or, even worse, a few minutes after first light. Hunters on this time frame are unwittingly pushing any mature bucks in the area ahead of them into the bedding area. If a buck has been spooked, you won't be able to shoot it, and your chances at it during the remainder of the season will diminish as well.

The solution to this problem is simple, but it requires strong will and endurance: You have to get to your stand first, before a mature buck starts his predawn morning return. This means arriving and being set up in your stand a minimum of one hour before first light. By first light and daylight, we mean the first hint of light, not actual meteorological sunrise, which is at least half an hour after first light. In some cases, you need to arrive up to two hours before daylight, depending on the distance between bedding and feeding areas and the habits of the mature buck you are after. Your early arrival means finding a route to your stand that does not spook the deer you will be hunting later in the morning. Sometimes this includes walking a long way, usually through the woods or swamps. Walking through open fields in the morning will just spook the deer you are after. Climbing out of bed this early in the morning is often very difficult, especially because you will be sitting in the dark for up to a couple hours. This may seem like a long time to sit in the dark, and it is, but it will be well worth it if you see that buck you thought was totally nocturnal sliding undisturbed toward his bedding area right at the crack of dawn or getting up out of his bed and moving back by you at midday.

When you are in your stand so early, you will on occasion have deer pass through before daylight. It may seem counterproductive to sit in your tree and have deer pass by that you cannot shoot. Allowing these deer to pass undisturbed is extremely important. Mature bucks that pass through in the dark and bed down might return later in the morning. This will happen only in a spot that is undisturbed. During the rut phases, mature bucks have a midday movement pattern and quite often use the same route to exit their bedding area as they did to enter it.

It is also important not to leave your stand too early during your morning hunts. This is absolutely critical during the rut phases, when bucks come out of their nocturnal routine. Bucks have a natural pattern of movement during the rut phases that has them on their feet at midday, sometime between 10:00 A.M. and 2:00 P.M. On morning hunts, it is important to stay on stand until 2:00 P.M., if possible.

You need to arrive at your stand early for evening hunts as well—the earlier, the better. Again, you want to be set up in your stand before the deer are up and moving. Deer tend to be even more cautious in the evening than they are in the morning. If you spook deer back into the bedding area on your way to your stand, the chances that a mature buck will pass through the area are virtually nil. The longer you are in your tree before the deer move through, the better your chances of seeing a mature buck.

Yet another timing aspect that most hunters overlook is their evening retreat from stands. Most hunters simply climb down out of their trees the minute shooting light is gone, whether there are deer nearby or not. It is important to time your getaway. If you spook deer on your way out of your tree in the evening, deer are likely to remember the disturbance and possibly avoid that spot in the future, particularly mature deer. You have to take every precaution available not to spook deer near your stand on the way out. This may call for endurance. If deer are around your tree when it gets dark, you should wait until they are gone before climbing down. Sometimes this means waiting in your tree for an hour or more after dark before you can attempt a getaway. The longer it is dark, the more comfortable deer become, and the less likely they are to associate your late departure with future danger in a single spot. Like your entry route, your exit route should be such that you can leave the area with as little disturbance as possible. In some areas with very high deer populations, it is nearly impossible not to spook deer from time to time during your entries and exits, but keeping it to an absolute minimum is always the goal. Don't walk out through a field or food source where the deer are feeding. Find a way out of the woods where you are least likely to disturb deer, even if this means a long walk. It is better to walk an extra half mile and preserve your chance at a mature buck than to walk a hundred yards and potentially ruin that chance for the season.

Using other hunters' timing to your advantage is important if you hunt in pressured areas. Most hunters are far more predictable than deer. They hunt the same time frame day in and day out, quite often their entire lives. Most hunters arrive at their stands just before daylight. With this time frame in mind, hunt accordingly. Other hunters commonly push deer ahead of them with their arrival. If you know when and where they are hunting, and where the nearest bedding area is, you possibly can benefit from this situation by being set up in your stand much earlier, a minimum of an hour before daylight. The deer that a hunter on a normal time frame pushes ahead of him will be conditioned to the hunter's arrival time; this is because most hunters who hunt this time frame usually overhunt their stands. The deer will not go far before resuming a normal pace. Your early setup could help you intercept these deer before they enter their bedding area.

The other side of normal hunter timing in the morning is the time of departure. Most hunters are out of the woods by 10:00 A.M. Mature deer get used to this situation and simply wait to move until after the hunters depart. By remaining on stand longer, until noon or, even better, 2:00, you can take advantage of this situation. Deer move more during the middle of the day than most hunters are aware of. Although this movement increases dramatically during the prerut and rut, it is not exclusive to that time of year. The deer remain in areas with perimeter cover, and therefore you rarely see them as you go about your daily business. Stands for midday hunting have to be in cover where deer feel comfortable moving during daylight. They must also be far enough from the bedding that you can approach a stand and sneak back out without being detected. These stands can be hunted in two ways. Either you can simply remain on stand longer than the other hunters, perhaps hunting all day, or you can hunt the second shift, from 9:00 or 10:00 A.M. throughout midday. Usually we continue to hunt until our normal evening departure. Do not burn yourself out with frequent midday hunting prior to the rut phases. Save most of your long-term midday attention for that period of the season.

For evening hunting, the situation is the reverse of that in the morning. Many times we have been sitting in a tree and had hunters pass by just a few minutes before prime time. These hunters usually sit for an hour or two, and then pass back through prior to or right at dark. The deer get used to this sort of evening hunting time frame and often move around the hunters. Get into the woods as early as possible, and you will often be rewarded with deer sightings in the middle of the afternoon, before most hunters are in the woods. In pressured areas, this type of dedication and persistence is required for consistent success.

The key is to establish a time plan that puts you in the right place at the right time. The more time you spend in the woods, the better your chances will be, but mere hours on stand are not enough. You must clearly plan your time to intercept both normal deer movement and movement caused by other hunters. In your general hunting plan, you should establish a daily time plan for each tree, each area, and each phase of the season. Developing a plan will, without question, make you a better hunter and separate you from the other hunters in the area.

FINAL EQUIPMENT CHECK

Inspect your equipment one final time to make sure everything is in perfect condition. It is important to check your bow for any sound on the draw. This might include a tick of the cams or the sound of your arrow sliding across the rest. It is critical that your bow be absolutely silent on the draw, in all weather conditions. If it makes any sound, fix the problem immediately. Although it is also important that your bow be relatively quiet during the shot, we feel that too much attention is given to this and not enough to the sound of the draw. After you shoot, the damage is done, but if a deer hears you draw, it is more likely to spook both before and during the shot. String jumping, or actually string ducking, occurs when the noise a bow makes during the shot causes the deer to duck your arrow before being hit. It is almost impossible with modern compounds at shot distances of less than twenty yards. A deer that is already tense and on alert before a shot is far more likely to react to the noise of the actual shot. Inspect all of your other equipment for anything that could be a problem, and take care of anything that could cause trouble.

At this time, we also put our hunting equipment through a couple of dry runs. We set up in a tree with our Ambush Saddles at the edge of a yard while wearing all of our hunting gear, exactly as if we were hunting. We then shoot a few arrows to check our shooting in a simulated hunting situation. This means shooting at targets placed at different sides of the tree and at different angles to emulate hunting shots. To make this as realistic as possible, we sometimes shoot only one arrow at each target. While doing this, be aware of how your hunting clothes affect your shooting. Perhaps you will notice your bowstring slapping the arm of your jacket when you shoot to the right or behind you. This problem can and must be alleviated with a few strategically placed safety pins. You might also have to adjust your sights slightly. If you take the time to run through this procedure, the effort could save you an unpleasant surprise after the opener.

KEEPING FIT

We recommend that you end your fitness program in September. The long walks and long hours on stand should be enough to keep you in form throughout the season. In fact, during a normal hunting season, each of us loses about ten pounds. This is a lot, considering our light, 150-pound frames. The only exercise we recommend during the season is continued shooting. Too often hunters stop shooting their bows once they begin hunting. In 2004, John talked to a fellow hunter from Iowa who missed a 180-inch fourteen-point late in the season because he had not shot his bow in three weeks. When he eventually shot it, it was shooting six inches low. It is important to practice at least three times a week from the height at which you plan to hunt. This will keep your shooting muscles in shape, allow you the opportunity to detect any changes to your bow, and keep you confident for when that shot at a mature buck opens up.

After the season starts, the most important aspects of fitness are a healthy diet and sleep. During the season, both of these areas tend to get neglected, and hunting is conducive to neither one. To keep up your energy level during the season, it is important to try to eat a balanced diet. While hunting all day, this is hard to do. To combat this problem, we always eat as well as we can while not hunting and supplement what we eat with vitamins.

CHAPTER 5

October

October is a month of tremendous change in the whitetail's world. The days become shorter, and the weather changes dramatically, from summerlike during the early part of the month to cold and barren of foliage during the later part of the month. The change in whitetail behavior is as dramatic as the change in weather, as they rapidly alter their docile late-summer routines with the approaching rut and the onslaught of hunters.

Bowhunting in October in most northern states is essentially divided into three phases. The first phase is the early season. The second is what most hunters refer to as the October lull. And the third, if conditions are right, is the beginning of the prerut. Being able to anticipate the dramatic changes of October and react quickly to these changes are of primary importance for regular success on mature pressured bucks. For each of the three phases, you have to develop a hunting plan.

THE EARLY SEASON

In our home state of Michigan, the season opens on October 1. The first three to five days of the season can provide a tremendous opportunity to kill a mature buck, if you have prepared and hunt with care. At this time of year, the mature bucks that were unmolested during preseason are still following a late-summer routine, which includes feeding in day-light. These bucks will continue to follow this routine until they are disturbed.

Deer do not differentiate between hunting pressure and scouting pressure.

With their last-minute scouting, a lot of hunters alert the mature deer to the upcoming season. There are many stories of mature bucks that spend the entire summer feeding evening after evening in the same field, only to seemingly vanish into thin air a minute before hunting season begins. This disappearing act is largely due to untimely and intrusive field-edge scouting and setup too close to the opener.

The major problem with hunting field edges is the approach and departure. If you decide to hunt a field edge in the morning, you will most likely spook deer out of the field while on the way to your stand. On the other hand, if you decide to hunt a field edge in the evening, you will most certainly spook deer with your exit. Once deer are spooked off a field in the evening, the mature bucks normally will no longer enter that field to feed until after dark. Therefore, if the mature buck you are after does not pass by the first (or possibly the second) time you hunt the edge of that field, you will probably be out of luck in that spot. The trick becomes finding a way to cut off the buck before he enters the field or his bedding area in the morning, while keeping a low profile so as not to alert him and other mature deer of your presence. If you alert this buck to your presence, your next opportunity might not be until the prerut, if at all. If, however, you have scouted from a distance during preseason and are sure that a mature buck will enter a field at a particular spot before dark, go for it. Hunt this spot a time or two; if you are unsuccessful, back off. Having a big buck's movements patterned this tightly is an unusual circumstance that you should take advantage of.

Back in September, you should have attempted to pattern the movements of a mature buck and perhaps set up an early-season stand for that particular buck. During the first few days of the season, hunt that spot. If you were fortunate enough to find a good rub line during preseason or postseason scouting, these locations also are good bets during the first few days of the season. Mature bucks will follow their normal travel routes, including rub lines, until they are disturbed.

Feeding staging areas are also points of special interest at this time. These areas offer cover within close proximity, generally thirty to fifty yards, of the eventual feeding area. Mature bucks sometimes linger here before entering the feeding area after dark. A feeding staging area is usually a convergence point of several runways, often with numerous rubs, and always in a travel corridor. There must be enough cover for a mature buck to feel comfortable during daylight. The cover will also allow you to enter and depart from your stand undetected on evening hunts. If one of these spots exists on your property, include it in your early-season stand rotation.

The window of opportunity to intercept early-season mature bucks in pressured areas is short. The weather is usually nice and warm at the beginning of October, and just about everybody will be out bowhunting. The deer catch on to the onslaught of hunters fast. Try to buck the trend. Do not overdo it. Hunt your early-season stands an evening or two, and then, if you are not successful, back off. Begin hunting secondary stand locations, which include all those in funnels or travel routes between bedding and feeding areas. These are the spots where anything can happen. Stay away from your rut-phase stands.

Food-Source Hunting

During early to mid-October, deer continue to put on fat for the winter. This coincides with the acorn drop throughout the North. The deer ravenously feed on acorns wherever they are available. When there is an abundant crop, acorns are the deer's preferred food source, though other browse and crops make up at least a portion of their diet. You should take advantage of this situation.

Because oak trees are so important to our hunting, we have made an effort to understand some of their basic biology. We are mainly concerned about the frequency of acorn mast in the oak tree species found in our hunting areas. In the areas we hunt, the main types of oaks are northern white oaks, northern red oaks, bur oaks, and northern pin oaks. White oaks are one-year species, flowering in the spring and producing acorns that fall. This means they are capable of producing acorns every year. Red oaks are a two-year species. They flower in the spring but do not produce acorns until the following fall. The time between good mast years is usually longer. One-year species produce a good acorn crop about once every two to three years, and two-year species once every four to six years. Yearly crop failure as a result of late frost or insect parasites is common among oaks. To make acorn mast even more unpredictable, individual trees in a stand of oaks are not necessarily synchronous. Two red oaks standing next to each other might produce acorns in opposite years. And some trees simply produce more acorns than others. (For more detailed information on oaks, consult *Oak*

Forest Ecosystems, by W. J. McShea and W. M. Healy.)

This knowledge can be helpful in planning your hunting. If you make note of the oaks in your hunting areas and identify them according to species, this gives you a general idea of how often particular trees can produce acorns. Then, while doing your August or September final stand prep, check the oaks for acorns. This can be done easily with a set of low-power binoculars. Put oaks with a good crop into your hunting plans.

Deer prefer white oak acorns over red oak. White oak acorns contain a lower level of tannins, which give acorns a bitter taste. If you are confronted with the choice to hunt white or red oaks when both types of acorns are available, it is better to hunt the white oaks. Location, though, is often more important than the type of oak, as deer will feed on any type of acorns. The best oaks for hunting early-season mature bucks are those that are well back in the woods, surrounded by cover, and close to bedding areas. Most deer stop there in the evening before moving on to more open terrain and in the morning before entering the bedding area. When the acorn crop is small, deer will compete for the acorns that are available. Finding an oak full of acorns in an area with an otherwise poor acorn crop can be a shortcut to a nice buck. If you allow several deer to pass undisturbed, a mature buck may arrive to feed under this tree during daylight.

Always be on the lookout for oaks with good acorn mast. Acorns are a main food source even in the best agricultural areas.

Another food source that should not be overlooked during your early-season hunting is apple trees. Deer simply love apples. Isolated trees bearing apples will attract deer as well as, if not better than, an oak dropping acorns. If there are apple trees on your hunting property, try to figure out whether they are late or early apple droppers. Some trees will be full of apples only for the first week or two of hunting season; most yellow or green apple varieties, for instance, tend to fall early. Other trees will have apples throughout the entire fall. Hunt the trees when they are dropping apples. The deer will definitely be tuned in to this food source.

Depending on the amount of oaks and apple trees on your hunting property, you will usually have a relatively short window of opportunity to hunt them as food sources, normally a few weeks. Some years, however, both the acorn and apple drops last the entire season. Judge the situation and hunt accordingly.

Standing corn is yet another important food source to hunt. A cornfield acts as a feeding area, bedding area, and travel corridor for all deer, including mature bucks. Because standing corn offers almost total security, deer move in and out of it as though it were a bedding area. This creates a movement pattern completely opposite of that found in other cropfields. Mature bucks commonly leave cornfields in the evening and return to them in the morning to bed down. Hunting in standing corn and around the perimeter of the field can lead to success. While hunting the perimeter of a cornfield, look for areas of good cover bordering the corn. The transition from cover to cover allows a big buck to feel secure about crossing that point during daylight.

Another place to hunt at this time is travel routes leading to alfalfa fields or beanfields. After the first few days of the season, hunting pressure will stabilize, and so will deer movement, which will definitely shift to more nocturnal activity, as far as the mature bucks are concerned. This is the time to hunt those secondary spots where anything can happen. Do not hunt your rut-phase stands at this time. This means staying away from primary scrape areas and rut staging areas. The only exception would be if you found some preseason scrape activity in a primary scrape area while scouting. This is a rare situation in pressured areas, and a hunt or two is warranted.

Rattling

One early-season tactic that has been successful for us is rattling. Early-season rattling is different from rattling during the rut and prerut. The bucks at this time of year are not yet aggressive toward one another. Any sparring that takes place is casual, though the local bucks might be seriously establishing or reaffirming their rank for the upcoming rut. On several occasions, we have witnessed yearling bucks sparring with older individuals. This was obviously no challenge to the larger buck. Most sparring is preceded and followed by nonchalant browsing, as if nothing happened. Any sparring that takes place attracts the curiosity of any other bucks in the vicinity, which never rush in aggressively but sometimes stop to watch the sparring and even, on occasion, walk over and join in. We have witnessed up to four different bucks sparring on and off. This lighthearted attitude at this time of the season means that aggressive antler clashing will likely cause a buck to hightail it into the thickest cover available, and perhaps even make it impossible to rattle him in later in the season. Light antler tickling, however, might spark that same buck's curiosity and entice him to walk in and see what the boys are up to. If you decide to do early-season rattling, stay nonchalant and low-key. John has taken three big bucks during the first days of the season that responded to light sparring sequences.

We have had our best success with early-season rattling in the mornings. A buck with a full belly and a contented demeanor returning to his safe zone is simply more likely to investigate a sound out of curiosity than is a buck moving in the afternoon. And curiosity is the main reason deer respond to rattling in the early season. In the evening, deer, particularly mature bucks, move slower and pay much more attention to their surroundings as they rise and approach feeding areas. Open feeding areas always have the potential to harbor danger, and bucks are very aware of this. There is also more general human activity in the evening than in the early morning. Our most successful rattling has taken place after we have heard other bucks sparring nearby, visually spotted a buck in the distance, or heard deer moving nearby that we knew would not come close without a little coaxing.

When you hear two bucks sparring in the early season, you know that they are in the mood for a little riff. When they quit sparring, try to imitate exactly the sounds the bucks were making with your rattling bag or antlers. Do a short and subtle sparring sequence, perhaps twenty seconds long, and then wait. If you hear them coming in your direction, do not rattle again. If you rattle for twenty to thirty seconds, a buck can lock in on your exact location, and no more rattling is required. Rattling again could potentially spook that buck. If a buck does not respond, attempt one more short sequence, and then hang up your rattling bag for the remainder of the hunt. It is common for hunters to rattle too much. It is particularly important not to overdo it in the early season. If you rattle too much or too aggressively now, the bucks can become conditioned to it and may not respond during the prerut or rut. The superaggressive rattling often shown in numerous hunting videos is extremely unrealistic to normal hunting conditions in pressured areas and should never be emulated.

In early October 1999, John was on a morning hunt in a big-woods area in northern Michigan. It was very foggy that morning. At about 8:00, he heard a couple deer moving through the woods about a hundred yards away, heading toward a large, marshy bedding area nearby. On a whim, John decided to give rattling a try. He rolled the sticks in his rattle bag together lightly for about thirty seconds. After he finished, he could hear that the deer had turned and were now casually moving in his direction. As the deer got closer, he could hear them munching on acorns. Eventually he could see two sets of legs under an oak about forty yards away, but he could not tell what kind of deer they were. The way they acted so casually, John thought they were a doe and fawn. After feeding for a few minutes under that tree, the deer turned and started walking straight back in the direction from which they had come. John pulled out his grunt call and gave one short grunt. The deer turned and walked straight back toward him. John was pleasantly surprised when a mature eight-point followed a mature ten-point out of the fog. These bucks were moving so casually that it appeared they did not have a care in the world. Both bucks were obviously three-and-a-half-year-olds. When the ten-point was at twelve yards, John released his arrow. The buck bolted fifty yards and collapsed into the tall, green ferns. These bucks obviously had responded to John's rattling out of pure curiosity. Aggressive rattling would have sent them into cover.

Hot-Weather Hunting

Hot weather is a condition hunters often encounter during the early season. This is most often the case in states where the opener is in September, but high temperatures commonly occur well into October. Extreme hot spells or long Indian summers keep many hunters out of the woods. High temperatures late in the season also curtail deer movement dramatically. The hotter it gets, the less the deer move. Sitting in the woods when the mercury rises above 80 degrees F can be downright torturous, but if you have a hot-weather option planned, a heat wave can be a blessing in disguise. As soon as the thermometer rises a couple days in a row over the 70-degree mark, it is time to think about water.

Deer, like all other animals, need water, and the hotter it is, the more water they require. The best place to hunt during hot spells are water holes in areas nearly devoid of water. Deer will key on these spots and travel long distances to get a drink or bed near them if they offer perimeter cover. The smaller the water hole, the better. A small water hole will concentrate deer in an area where you will be able to get off a shot. One of the areas we hunt has a swale with a spring that always contains water. The only other nearby water source is a small stream almost a mile away. Though the swale always sees some use, deer activity in this spot increases tremendously during hot spells. When the temperature rises for a few days, we always make it a point to hunt near that swale. In areas with a lot of water, such as rivers or swamps, the deer still need to drink, but a drought or hot spell has less effect on their behavior simply because water is more plentiful and easily available, which makes pinpointing exact locations nearly impossible.

So when it gets hot, head to the overall driest areas and find out where the deer are drinking. Hunt these spots immediately. They are exceptionally good only as long as it remains hot and dry, although if a water hole is an isolated drinking source, it will be used year-round. Even when a mature buck is in a mainly nocturnal time frame, if the temperature is hot enough, he has to have water at some point during the day.

Both morning and evening hunts next to water can be equally productive. Deer often stop to get a drink before heading off to the bedding area for the day. If you are in position at least an hour before daylight, you could very well get a chance at a good buck before he enters the bedding area. After being bedded all day in hot weather, deer also go directly to water for a drink soon after getting up for their evening movement.

Another option for hunting water holes is to head to your stand just before the hottest part of the day, usually between 11:00 A.M. and noon, and then tough it out until dark. If the water hole is surrounded by good cover and fairly close to a bedding area, deer will pay it a visit throughout the afternoon, particularly just after the hottest part of the day, after 2:00 P.M. To get through such a hunt requires mental toughness and attention to scent control. The hotter it is, the more you sweat and stink. Take a lot of water to drink so that you do not overheat. Despite the suffering, we have arrowed a few nice early-season bucks this way.

Hunting Rub Lines

Hunting along rub lines can be particularly promising during the early season and can be generally good spots throughout the entire season, sometimes even during the October lull. Recently a lot of attention has been given to hunting rub lines. Indeed, rub lines can provide excellent hunting, but we do not consider them the overall best spots to hunt. For one thing, at the exact time mature bucks begin moving more during the day, the prerut, they also alter their movement patterns away from their normal bedding-to-feeding-and-back routine. This means that quite often, bucks abandon their rub lines when the chances are best to see them during the day. And although we have had success with rub lines, the makeup of our properties makes hunting them quite difficult. Most of our hunting properties are small and usually contain only a tiny fragment of a rub line. In this situation, it is sometimes impossible to get into the optimal hunting position—a spot where we have a chance to see a buck during daylight. Often we are left guessing at the fence line where the rub line goes and are too far from the bedding area to be sure of a daytime encounter. We counter this problem by using topographical maps and photos, but sometimes we just cannot pinpoint where the buck is going. This makes timing an encounter with a particular buck far more difficult than if you have the entire rub line to work with. We take what we can get and hunt the portions of the rub lines the best we can, which sometimes even means ignoring them.

Even a small water hole in a relatively dry area can receive a lot of traffic.

The best things about a rub line are that you know a buck made it, you can get an idea of that buck's general size, and you know you are hunting a preferred travel route of that particular buck. If a buck is left undisturbed throughout the early season, he will still follow his rub line, possibly even during daylight.

It is important to understand the basics about rub lines before hunting them. When you find a rub line, try to follow it until you know where it leads in each direction. Early-season rub lines are found on travel routes between a buck's bedding and feeding areas. You can differentiate the general time of day a rub line is being used by noting what side of the trees the rubs are on. If they are on the side away from the bedding area, they were made as the buck was on his way to bed down. This usually means the buck is using the rub line in the morning. If the rubbed side is facing the bedding area, the buck is using that travel route to reach a feeding destination, most likely in the evening.

When hunting rub lines during the early season, whether on a morning or evening hunt, the closer you sit to the bedding area, the better your chances are of seeing a mature buck during daylight. Mature bucks tend to be the last deer to leave a bedding area in the evening and the first to arrive in the morning. This means they are the last to arrive at a feeding area and the first to leave. These feeding area arrivals and departures usually take place under the security of darkness. But take care to arrive at your stand undetected by the bedded deer on evening hunts. If the deer become aware of your arrival in the evening, they will either remain bedded until you leave or take another route to the feeding area.

Judging the size of a buck by his rub line can be difficult. You can never be absolutely sure of the size of a buck making rubs until you actually see him. There are, however, some characteristics that will give you a good indication of the size of the buck making the rubs you are looking at. The initial thing to look for is rub size. Generally, bigger bucks rub on bigger trees. This is normally a good indicator of a buck's size, but not always. Every buck has a unique antler configuration, sometimes making it nearly impossible for a big buck to rub on big trees. Chris hunted a buck like this for a couple seasons. The tall-tined ten-point had a very narrow inside spread, not more than twelve inches, and extremely long main beams, which were less than an inch apart at the tips. This buck always rubbed tiny saplings, usually breaking them off at about waist height. We also hunted a large, mature eight-point that rubbed trees less than three inches in diameter. Conversely, John witnessed a small four-point rubbing his antlers on a tree that was at least eight inches in diameter. This, too, can be misleading, because more than a single buck can and will use a rub.

After you look at the size of the rub, consider the rub height. Mature bucks are taller than immature bucks and tend to rub higher on trees. Also inspect any small trees or branched trunks surrounding a rub for tine marks. Tine marks on trees that are more than eight inches behind or next to the main rub indicate a good-size buck. Along the same line, look for tine marks above or below the actual rub. These marks are signs of tall tines or a wide spread. The rub itself also holds a few clues. If the peeled bark of the rub is severely frayed, this indicates a buck with pearling at the base of his rack or several small points. These are characteristics found almost exclusively on big bucks. Rubs made by small bucks tend not to have fraying of the bark; they look almost as if someone rubbed the side of the tree with a piece of metal pipe. Yet another indicator that a mature buck made a rub is broken branches. It takes long, solid tines to have enough leverage to break branches. Rubs made on large, horizontal limbs are almost always made by mature bucks. Another sign that a big buck is in the area is rubbed or shredded bushes. Only mature bucks will tackle entire bushes, sometimes reducing them to a bunch of broken stems. Mature bucks sometimes have a particular type of tree they prefer to rub. One big mature buck we hunted unsuccessfully for several years went out of his way to rub small cedars. This buck's rubs were severely frayed and obvious from a distance. When you look at rubs, check for any unique characteristics. This detail can help you identify a particular buck's rub line.

During the season, if you notice a new rub line on your property while entering or exiting your hunting locations, follow it and decide on a stand location. For rub lines used in the morning, position your stand as close to the bedding area as possible, yet still far enough from it that you will not spook the deer that are bedded within it as you leave for the morning. The reason for hunting as close to the bedding area as possible is so that you might catch the buck during daylight. The farther you are from the feeding area, the better your chances are of doing this. On pressured property, hunting rub lines found during the October lull will likely be unproductive, but as long as you stay away from your rut-phase locations, they do offer a possible opportunity. While hunting rub lines is written about extensively and shown on videos and TV, keep in mind that the vast majority of all these hunters are hunting extremely managed, nonpressured property. In such areas, mature bucks will follow a set daytime routine of following a rub line during the entire season.

If you find a fresh rub line during your last-minute preseason stand prep, plan a hunt for that spot within the first few days of the season. Bucks, if left undisturbed, follow a steady routine during the initial part of the season and, with luck, are not yet nocturnal. After a disturbance, the buck will probably continue using the rub line, but only after dark, until the hormonal surge of the rut reduces the buck's interest in feeding. At this point, a buck may abandon his normal travel routes completely to concentrate his attention on does and the travel routes they are using, which are usually not the same routes mature bucks use. The reason for this is simple. Outside of the rut, does avoid mature bucks and their normal travel routes. When the surge of testosterone forces mature bucks to their feet during daylight, they must change their routine to intercept does. Bucks change not only their travel routes, but sometimes their bedding areas as well. This means that you can be pretty sure a buck will use his rub line during the early season and October lull, but not so sure after the rut phases begin. Once a mature buck changes his routine during the rut stages, new rub lines will appear.

CHRIS'S 2004 TWELVE-POINT

During the 2003 October lull, I discovered a perfect staging area—a point of tall goldenrod and low brush jutting into a mix of alfalfa, corn, and beans. It was adjacent to a huge, deep draw that served as the local bedding area. Between the point and the draw was a short strip of open woods. This was one of those rare spots that served as a feeding staging area, a rut staging area, and, as I would later find out, a primary scrape area. Immediately I cleared out a tree in what I thought to be the best spot.

Three weeks later I returned to this new spot on a morning hunt. I didn't have to wait long for the action. Only a few minutes after daylight, I glanced toward the draw and there, standing less than forty yards away, was a great, tall-tined ten-point. The big-bodied deer fed contentedly for a few minutes, as I slowly swung around the tree in my Ambush Saddle to get in position for where I anticipated the shot would be. The buck, however, had other ideas. He turned and walked quickly through the strip of woods across the side of the draw. He was moving fast and angling slightly away from me, so I immediately spun back around the tree in an attempt to find an opening for a shot. Within seconds, the buck was in the only opening available, standing slightly uphill from me.

I guessed the distance at just under thirty yards and let my arrow fly, only to watch it drop under the buck's chest. He took two bounds, looked back, and slowly vanished into the thick draw. Upon retrieving my arrow, I noticed a couple of things. First, the buck had been almost ten yards farther away than I had estimated. And second, he had been walking down a tiny runway that was littered with rubs on tiny saplings, most of which were broken off just above knee level. I hadn't noticed these before. They were obviously rubs made by the ten-point, and this was one of his main travel routes. The runway was slight and may have been used by this buck alone. I quickly cleared out a tree that would give me a better shot at his runway.

I hunted that spot three more times that year. Twice I spooked a bedded mature buck at my tree in the dark, despite arriving almost two hours before daylight, proving that that big buck had my number. On those hunts, a couple of yearlings passed through, but I knew my chances at the big boy were slim. The third hunt gave me an opportunity to watch one of the yearling bucks for almost two hours, from 12:30 to 2:30 P.M., as he worked a couple of scrapes and then bedded down less than twenty yards from my tree. With all of these encounters in mind, I could hardly wait for the 2004 bow season to begin.

A quick late-summer scouting foray to this spot revealed that the little runway was again being used. It was once more littered with rubs. For my first hunt at this spot, and only my fourth hunt of the season, I chose a clear, unseasonably cold morning. The temperature was just above freezing as I settled into my saddle two hours before daylight. Slowly, the stars faded away and the sun rose above the trees, bringing with it a drastic rise in temperature. By 9:00 A.M. it had risen more than 30 degrees, to a little over 60 degrees, and I still hadn't seen a deer. Now sweating, I removed my outer layers and settled back in, determined to hunt until at least noon. About fifteen minutes later, movement caught my attention along that little runway. Peering in that direction, I could see a deer's leg. The deer moved a little closer and the next thing I noticed was antler in the shadows. It took a few more steps and I could make out a good rack with at least two tall points on each side and good mass, indicating what I thought was an eight-point.

Deciding instantly that this was a shooter, I paid no more attention to the rack. With my bow already in hand, I readied myself for the shot. As if someone had scripted everything for me, the buck casually walked right up the runway. He was behind a small tree only a step or two from my shooting lane as I drew my bow. Unaware of anything out of the ordinary, the buck stepped into the shooting lane at a distance of sixteen yards, stopped, and, as if on cue, looked in the other direction. Instantly my arrow was on its way, disappearing in the buck's chest. In a flash, he vanished into the goldenrod. Within seconds, there was a light crash, followed by silence.

After I slowly collected my gear, it took me half an hour to get down to my arrow, which was covered in light, frothy blood. An ample sixty-yard blood trail revealed, to my pleasant surprise, a perfectly typical, heavy-antlered twelve-point. The buck dressed out at over 200 pounds.

Chris took this twelve-point from a spot that served as a feeding staging area, rut staging area, and primary scrape area.

THE OCTOBER LULL

Those dreaded middle weeks of October are here. The deer activity in general has dropped off from the early season, and the bucks, especially the mature ones, have all but vanished. The rut is not yet in gear, and there is little action in the woods. It is important to understand why this happens mid-October. By understanding what the deer are doing, you will be able to react successfully to the situation. Do the deer stop moving during the October lull? Absolutely not. In fact, their movement steadily increases throughout the month. But the time of peak deer movement, especially that of mature bucks, now tends to be after dark, particularly in areas with heavy hunting pressure. The October lull is a natural phenomenon in deer behavior, but it is reinforced by hunting pressure.

Around mid-October, trees and underbrush begin to lose their foliage. The days get shorter and the weather grows colder. As the lush green of summer gives way to the barren woods of fall, the deer become naturally uncomfortable with their environment. In places where they enjoyed a long summer of excellent cover, they can now be seen from long distances. This sudden opening of the woods causes deer to become somewhat more nocturnal; mature bucks are naturally the most nocturnal animals in any deer population, so it becomes clear when most bucks are moving during the October lull. The bucks remain in this nocturnal routine until the hormonal surge of the rut pushes them back into more diurnal movement. The interesting thing is that this is a completely natural process. It happens even in areas with little or no hunting pressure.

Intense hunting pressure compounds and intensifies this situation. If you overhunt your best stands during this time, you will be alerting the deer to your presence, which will cause the deer, notably the mature does and bucks, to avoid this spot, at least during daylight. Every time you hunt a tree, you make noise and leave traces of scent. The deer that naturally pass through after dark will note your presence. Any time you spook a deer, doe or buck, or leave traces of your presence, you reduce your chances at taking a good buck in that location for the rest of the season.

So how do you hunt the October lull? This is the time to practice extreme caution and, most of all, *patience*. Your stand rotation should be similar to that in the early season, with a concentration on hunting travel routes and funnels between bedding and feeding areas. This is also the time to be hunting your secondary stands, those in out-of-the-way places such as a single oak in a standing cornfield or that odd tree in a big woods. Hunt trees that are on less frequently used travel routes in good cover and with a primary food source nearby. Most of your secondary stands should offer some potential for taking a good buck. Others, such as an oak in a standing cornfield, could offer a relatively good chance. In pressured areas, the majority of bucks three and a half years old and older are very nocturnal during the lull, and there is nothing you can do about it. Just hunt out-of-the-way locations that offer excellent cover and hope for the best.

Even during the lull, you are most likely to have success if you regularly rotate your stands. If you hunt the same tree or trees night after night, the deer will become wise to your hunting and react accordingly, avoiding that location. Your best trees, however, should be saved for the moments when they are absolutely ready to be hunted and your chances for taking a mature buck are greatest. The prerut and rut are to bowhunting what the play-offs are to most major sports, the time when things get really intense. All this may seem obvious, but judging from the number of hunters who hunt from the same handful of trees outing after outing, sometimes year after year, and complain that all the deer have disappeared, not everyone has caught on.

THE PRERUT

The prerut is the phase just prior to the main rut, when the bucks are ready to breed but the does are not quite in estrus. The surge of hormones associated with the shortening days and colder weather rouses the mature bucks into a much more active routine, as they start moving during the day in their core areas in search of estrous does. Because the does are not quite ready, however, the bucks are busy signposting and scent-checking but do not yet abandon their core areas, as they often do while chasing during the peak of the rut, when their ranges expand. This pattern of confined daytime movement is a very short-lived phenomenon that provides the most important window of hunting opportunity in the entire year. You simply must take advantage of this situation. In our area, the prerut usually begins around Halloween and lasts between one and two weeks. This varies slightly from year to year, depending on the weather. If you are serious about hunting mature bucks, this is the best time to be out in the woods.

We have suggested a somewhat similar hunting routine throughout the early season and the October lull, but now it is time to change gears. This is the start of the "play-offs," and it is time to put in long hours. It is important to react to the alterations in deer movement patterns. Your emphasis should now change from hunting travel corridors between feeding and bedding areas, early rub lines, and secondary stands to hunting your best spots— primary scrape areas, rut staging areas, and funnels between bedding areas.

Primary Scrape Areas

In recent years in the popular hunting literature, scrapes have gone from being considered paramount hunting spots to mere secondary locations. This mild dismissal of scrapes and primary scrape areas as prime hunting locations is the result of studies that conclude both that the majority of scrape activity happens after dark and that scrapes are often visited by more than one buck. These studies solidly refute the old adage that a scrape is a particular buck's calling card. This dismissal of scrape hunting is also backed by a lot of frustrated hunters who have put in time watching scrapes with minimal success. We, however, hold firmly to the belief that primary scrape areas are focal points of buck and doe activity during all phases of the rut, and thus are of absolute importance. Rather than being an indicator of how much or how little bucks use these areas, scrape-hunting failure can usually be attributed to faulty recognition, flawed setup, and improper hunting.

Recognizing a primary scrape area should be easy. What could be more obvious than a bunch of scrapes confined in a small area? It's not quite that simple, however; scrapes alone do not make a primary scrape area. Other ingredients have to be present as well. Primary scrape areas are found in corridors or zones with concentrated deer movement. The scrapes are normally in areas that are relatively open yet surrounded by perimeter cover, such as a small, brush-littered clearing with some small trees interspersed in it. The opening, though, generally is relatively close to a bedding or feeding area or in a funnel. The open area has to be such that there are enough low-hanging licking branches for several scrapes. Licking branches are the most important part of scrapes. They are a main source of communication between all mature deer, which mark them with scent from several glands, including their forehead, preorbital, and nasal glands, as well as with saliva. The size of primary scrape areas can vary considerably. Some are as small as twenty yards across, while we have seen others up to eighty yards long. This variance and the fact that hunting pressure alters both when and how deer use primary scrape areas, and can even influence where they are found, are the main reasons hunters have difficulty with them. However, pinpointing such a spot with all of these ingredients is a huge step to regular hunting success.

It is also important to understand how bucks and does use primary scrape areas. They are always found in areas where the deer feel secure and move through on a regular basis. Most of them are perennial, meaning that unless there is some drastic change in terrain or movement patterns, such as a housing development, acorn mast, or change in crop rotation, deer will use them year after year. There is usually some activity in these areas year-round; at a very minimum, the licking branches will be used by the bucks and does the entire year. This scent marking increases dramatically during the rut phases. Licking branches are a center of communication. As the rut approaches, bucks increase the actual scraping activity, which is called signposting, just as with rubs. The ground-pawing part of scrapes is the most noticeable for us hunters and has been given the most emphasis in hunting literature. But we consider licking branches the more important part of the scrape combination for hunters to pay attention to. The more licking branches a scrape has, the more it is being used. We have seen scrapes with as many as twenty well-used licking branches over them. These multiple licking branches indicate that the scrape is being used frequently by both bucks and does. The more a scrape is frequented, the better your chances at successfully hunting it.

The dominant buck in the area uses the primary scraping area and is responsible for opening most of the ground scrapes, usually the larger ones. This is a sign of dominance, though other mature and younger bucks use these scrapes as well. Because these scrape areas are in high-traffic corridors, does pass regularly by the scrapes, sometimes inspect them, and on occasion mark the licking branches. The does, through scent checking and general familiarity with the local deer population, know which bucks are using the scrapes. This is important later when the does start coming into estrus. As a doe enters her breeding cycle, she gravitates toward primary scrape areas. The rut is a two-way street. Mature does tend to show a preference for particular bucks and know where to find them. We have witnessed this type of doe behavior. Usually a single doe shows up at a primary scrape and just loiters, perhaps urinating in a scrape or marking a licking branch, but mostly just casually browsing, looking, and waiting. If you witness this sort of behavior, pay close attention to your surroundings; a mature buck could step out of cover any moment.

Matriarch does usually attempt to seek out the dominant buck in the area. It is sheer speculation, but we believe this increases the likelihood of being bred by the dominant buck and having superior offspring. Bucks are well aware of this and check their primary scrape areas for estrous does. The bucks begin checking during the prerut, well in advance of any does coming into estrus. Bucks may stop and work their scrapes when they scent-check, or they may scent-check their scrapes from downwind.

Deer rut behavior is often presented by other hunters as though the bucks chase the does, which want nothing to do with them. This is not the case. The does want, and need, to be bred during their short estrous cycle and focus on primary scrape areas when they have the opportunity to search for a mature buck. Therefore, it is extremely important not to spook does by overhunting your primary scrape areas before they are ready. During the prerut, the surge of hormones the bucks experience causes them to be up on their feet and moving, far more during the day than earlier in the season. Mature bucks usually return to their bedding areas in the morning on a time frame similar to that during their pressured October lull routine, usually one to two hours before daylight in pressured areas. The bucks bed down and then get back up, usually between 10:00 A.M. and 2:00 P.M., to scent-check their primary scrape areas and the perimeters of bedding areas. They may also bed before daylight in or near a primary scrape area. Bucks use the most direct routes possible— as long as they have adequate cover—to reach the destinations they have in mind. This means that the exact moment mature bucks begin to move more during shooting hours, they also abandon their normal travel routes between bedding and feeding areas. Hunting these destination points is the best way to be regularly successful on mature bucks.

About the time the prerut should be starting, check your primary scrape stands for activity. On an evening hunt, about an hour earlier than normal, practicing extreme scent control, sneak to your primary scrape stand that you set up during your postseason scouting. Check the scrapes for activity. If the scrapes are not yet active, turn around and leave the area. Because you arrived earlier than normal, you should have enough time to get to another stand, a secondary stand, or even another hunting area. You do not want to spook the buck you are after with an untimely hunt in his primary scrape area, before he comes out of his nocturnal routine. Hunting pressure can cause a buck to abandon a primary scrape area in favor of another or to only scent-check it under the cover of darkness, and you want to make certain that this does not happen. Repeat this procedure about every four days, until the primary scrape area becomes active. When you find that the scrapes are active, hunt the tree that evening and again the next morning. Be sure to arrive and be set up at least an hour and a half before daylight.

Now is the time to change your hunting plan. Up until this point, you should have hunted a stand rotation that included hunting a particular tree no more than once a week. Now, during the short prerut, it is perfectly acceptable to hunt a tree several times, perhaps even several days, in a row. Several hunts, and long hours on stand, will provide you with maximum opportunity to intercept that mature buck you are after. Hunting all day is also a good tactic for the prerut. The bucks are becoming restless and often move during midday, signposting and scent-checking for the first estrous female. Primary scrape areas are often visited between 10:00 A.M. and 2:00 P.M. Make every effort to spend as much time hunting near your primary scrape stands during the prerut as possible; the buck you are pursuing could show up at any time. Be very careful not to spook does. Does under your tree at this time of year are like buck magnets; the more doe activity, the better.

If the activity at the stand ceases, move to another location. Hunt a stand a couple days, and then rotate to the next. Don't put too much hunting pressure on a mature buck, which can push him back into a nocturnal routine. If the pressure is overwhelming, an experienced buck might remain totally nocturnal throughout the entire rut. Two bucks John took during the 2004 Michigan season were taken over primary scrape areas, during the prerut, and during midday.

Rut Staging Areas

Recognizing rut staging areas can be difficult because of their lack of concrete recognizable parts. Rub lines or scrape lines are easy to identify, as they both consist of certain distinct sign. Even primary scrape areas have constant identifiable elements in the form of scrapes and licking branches, making them easier to identify. Rut staging areas can contain rubs and scrapes, or none at all, and vary with changes in hunting pressure, the local buck-to-doe ratio, and the preferred food source at the moment. The general structure of staging areas also varies considerably between big-woods and agricultural areas. This ever-changing, somewhat slippery character of staging areas makes them difficult both to recognize and to describe. We sometimes have problems locating them and occasionally discover them while hunting high-traffic areas with good cover during the rut phases. After you learn how to recognize staging areas and how to hunt them, you will describe them only with superlatives.

It is important to understand why bucks use rut staging areas. A mature buck with a breeding season under its belt knows that moving during daylight is dangerous. Instead of wasting energy chasing every doe across the countryside and making themselves vulnerable to predators, as young bucks do, mature bucks try to conserve as much energy as possible. A key aspect to saving energy and reducing vulnerability is staging areas. Bucks use staging areas to intercept estrous does, while remaining in areas with cover that are fairly secure from predators, mainly hunters. Even during the prerut and rut, most mature buck movement is nocturnal, particularly in pressured areas. A buck usually returns to cover before daylight, but instead of entering his regular bedding area, as he did during the early season, he will stage and wait for an estrous doe that might pass through. This is a lot more productive than running all over the place checking for does like young bucks do. From a single high-traffic staging area, a mature buck can check many does for receptivity without wasting energy. The more hunting pressure there is in an area, the more likely a buck is to demonstrate such behavior.

If a buck is undisturbed and a doe passes through, he will get up or stay downwind and check her for receptivity; if she is in or close to estrus, he will follow her or push her into an area of good cover. If the doe is not in estrus, he may bed back down or wander off through the best available cover. This practice provides mature bucks far more security than pursuing does in open areas. Actual breeding out in the open by mature bucks is extremely seldom. If it were common, more hunters would witness it. If nothing passes through to a buck's liking, he will get up later in the morning, usually between 10:00 A.M. and 2:00 P.M., and scent-check his core area. While scent-checking, the buck usually passes through other staging areas, primary scrape areas, funnels between bedding areas, and funnels between bedding and feeding areas. A buck's scent-checking tour takes him through high-traffic areas that offer good cover. If a buck does not find a doe in the midday period, he will probably bed down and stage for the remainder of the day in or near a high-traffic area to catch the evening doe traffic in the opposite direction.

Staging areas vary greatly, but there are some general characteristics to look for. In agricultural areas, staging areas are most often found between the preferred feeding areas and the bedding areas. If the preferred feeding area changes, so does the staging area. An agricultural staging area will have cover between itself and the feeding area. This cover might be as simple as an overgrown fencerow, or it might consist of a buffer of woods or thick brush. One of the staging areas we hunt is bordered on the crop side by a nearly impenetrable patch of briers. The staging area itself, where the does pass through, is usually relatively open. This allows a buck to hear, smell, and, by simply standing up, see deer passing through. The size of the open area is not standard. We have hunted staging areas as small as thirty yards across and as large as one hundred yards long. The open area is usually bordered on the side away from the feeding area with thick cover that provides a quick escape. Staging areas always have several runways passing through them and often contain some fresh rubs and one or more scrapes. A primary scrape area is sometimes also used as a staging area. Bucks choose these areas because of heavy deer traffic. When a buck stages, he beds just inside the cover. From this point, he can depart quickly if a predator happens through. These agricultural staging areas are more defined and easily recognized than those in big-woods areas.

Staging areas in big woods are far more seldom. This is due to the lack of constant concentrated food sources, which makes the everyday movement of does far more erratic and less predictable. These staging areas have basically the same structure as agricultural staging areas but are less defined. The buck will search out an area with cover in which to stage, a spot that gives him a good position from which to detect any approaching does or predators. It will have a good escape route and possibly rubs and scrapes. Any point where deer movement is somewhat concentrated is a good place to look for staging areas. Big-woods staging areas will be found near or bordering feeding areas, primarily oaks in the North. Other places to look for them are at sudden breaks in terrain (such as bases of oak ridges, saddles, fresh cuttings, funnels, or edges of swamps) and known bedding areas.

The area's deer concentration, buck-to-doe ratio, hunting pressure, and baiting have a lot to do with whether you will find staging areas and how much the bucks use them. In areas with a very high deer population, mature bucks will stage during prerut but rarely during the main rut, because during the main rut they are almost always with estrous does. In areas with many does and few bucks, a mature buck will stage during prerut but will not have to during the main rut. On the other hand, in areas with very low deer concentrations, particularly in big-woods areas, the bucks cannot afford to stage. They could wait days until a doe shows up. Bucks in such areas are forced to seek more to find an estrous doe, and their range during the rut phases may expand up to several times. These bucks move a great deal during daylight. Excessive hunting pressure in or near staging areas will have a dramatic impact on the amount of use they receive. A buck will use a staging area only if he feels safe there. If the security of this area is breached, the buck will move elsewhere to intercept does, which will also change their pattern. Constant pressure in such areas will force the bucks to use other staging areas or pursue does only in the security of darkness.

Baiting also disrupts the use of staging areas. Baiting generally alters a deer herd's basic movement patterns dramatically. This has a detrimental effect on staging areas. A baited area often becomes a staging area and offers an extremely small destination point for many does. The main problem is that mature bucks associate bait with danger, so they usually stage at bait strictly after dark or from a distance downwind.

JON'S BICYCLE BUCK

John's son Jon worked a little faster the entire day to get off work about an hour early. It was late October, the prerut was beginning, and it was a crystal-clear day, one of those days where anything can happen in the deer woods. He was full of anticipation and in a bit of a hurry. He had waited for weeks to hunt his favorite tree; today was the day. After a quick double-check of his hunting equipment, he loaded it into his truck. Finally, he lifted his light aluminum-framed mountain bike into the bed of his truck and set off.

The drive was quick to his parking spot on state land. With steady, practiced hands, he pulled on his Scent-Lok suit and pack. Jumping onto the bike, he began his ride. This state land gets pounded around the edges, but back in about half a mile, there is not much hunter action—none, really, until gun season—and motor vehicles are not allowed. This leaves a gap in hunter activity that the deer seem to be well aware of. Jon covered the mile ride in a matter of minutes and pulled off into a thicket to hide his bike. He attached his bike to a middle-size poplar with a long cable lock to prevent theft. Then he walked the last couple hundred yards to his tree as silently as he could.

Jon unloading his mountain bike for the long journey deep into state land.

The red oak was an unlikely, yet perennial, hot spot. On the edge of a very large, marshy bedding area with a long, grassy island through its middle, the tree was off the end of a long point of poplars that extended to larger woods farther to the southwest. The tree was both a food source and part of an open funnel, with nothing but grass on two sides. Bucks bedding in the marsh tended to move just inside the edge until they got to this tree. At this point, they crossed into the poplars, even though they had to cross fifty yards of short grass to do it. The only tree between the woods and the bedding area was this oak. The bucks took this path because it had more cover than any other, even though more cover meant only a single tree and a few bushes.

Jon slid into his Ambush Saddle and settled in about twenty-five feet above the ground. It took a few moments for his mind to slow down from the rhythm of a hard day at work and get into the hunting mode, but soon he was taking his time soaking in the golden clear October afternoon. He was watching the birds about half an hour later, honestly not expecting any activity so suddenly, when the sound of a deer approaching in the bedding area drew his attention to the point. Straining his senses in the direction of the bedding area, he saw the brown of a deer suddenly materialize just inside the edge. In a few steps, a yearling four-point ambled out into the open. The little buck checked the open areas for any signs of danger and then made a straight line to Jon's oak. The acorns were thick on that tree and, more important, on the ground under it, and the little buck obviously had acquired a taste for them. For at least half an hour, the buck fed intently under the oak, seldom lifting his head to scan for predators. The buck's ears kept swiveling back toward the bedding area, and when he lifted his head and stared into the thick stuff, Jon knew more deer were approaching.

Within minutes, another buck walked steadily out of the cover. This buck's little rack carried three points, instead of four. Both were typical yearling bucks for the area, which produced very few mature bucks and where a big buck was any that scored more than a hundred inches. The instant the three-point spotted the four-point, it took an aggressive posture, laying its ears back against its neck, tilting its head slightly to one side, and angling at the four-point from the side. Not wanting any part of a fight, the four-point bounded a few strides out into the open brown grass and proceeded to feed, or at least pretended to browse on whatever edibles may have been out there. The three-point, obviously feeling pretty good about himself, decided to demonstrate his dominance by working a scrape for a few minutes. He went through the whole procedure, working the licking branch, pawing the ground, and then urinating down his legs into the bare patch on the ground. After he was finished playing the part of the boss, the three-point took the four-point's position under the tree and began feeding on acorns. The two bucks were feeding in peace, and obviously avoiding one another, when yet another buck appeared on the scene.

This time a spike stepped out of the bedding. Although this buck had only two points, it was a yearling equal in stature to the other two bucks. The spike walked directly toward the oak. Seeing this, the three-point again took an aggressive posture. With ears laid back, head tilted and lowered, he stepped toward the approaching buck. This time, though, his intimidation did not work. The spike took the same posture and stepped up to spar. For several minutes, the two little bucks pushed each other around in what looked like a very even match. When their mock battling took them a few yards from the tree, the four-point would slide in for a couple acorns. When the fighting stopped, the four-point would abandon his spot under the oak for the other two, which would feed side by side for a while, but then seemingly without warning resume their sparring. This went on for more than an hour.

Jon was enjoying the constant activity. He was satisfied with his hunt, and not really expecting anything more, when the sound of another deer approaching caught his attention. The two battling bucks did not stop or seem to pay any attention to the approaching deer. The lack of the deer's attention led Jon to believe that the incoming deer must be another young buck. You can imagine his surprise when a heavy-tined eight-point stepped out of the brush a mere thirty yards away. For the area, a buck of this caliber, a three-and-a-half-year-old, was extremely rare. The buck stood at the edge of the brush for several minutes, looking over the situation and observing the little bucks. Upon the appearance of the older buck, the pair stopped sparring and began quietly feeding. It was almost as if the buck were saying to himself, "I came out here for this." With three bucks all feeding within fifty yards, the mature buck slowly made his way to the oak. He, too, seemed to know of the abundance of acorns.

Totally unaware of Jon up in the tree, the big buck fed to within range. Instead of being content merely to watch, Jon had picked up his bow and was preparing for a shot. Casually the buck approached, but as big bucks usually do, he seemed to keep something between himself and a clear shot, to the point of frustration for Jon. The deer had closed the gap to within fifteen yards but was still standing behind the one overhanging branch that prevented a clear shot. "One more step, just one more step," thought Jon, but the buck stopped once again to survey his surroundings. With all his senses focused on the deer, the wait was torture and seemed like an eternity. The buck took his time, looked all around, scent-checked the wind, and then looked all around a second time, his ears swiveling in all directions. It was almost as though he sensed something but could not pinpoint exactly what. Finally dropping his head to feed, as if he once again did not have a care in the world, the buck took two steps forward. Now he was broadside. Almost instantly, Jon drew his bow, placed his pin just behind the buck's shoulder, took a deep breath, and let the arrow loose. The arrow buried into the buck's side, about an inch behind his shoulder, exactly where Jon had aimed.

The buck was knocked to the ground, as though he had been shot by a gun, and kicked his legs in a running motion. Now instantly nervous about his shot, thinking that somehow he must have spine-shot the buck, Jon reached for a second arrow. Just as he had it nocked, the buck leapt to its feet and bolted straight east along the edge of the bedding area. Now somewhat dejected, and completely unsure of a shot that had looked so good, Jon followed the buck with his eyes until the animal vanished from sight. Listening intently for another couple seconds, he followed the deer with his ears until he heard the sound of breaking brush, then silence. If not for the unusual behavior of the buck after the shot, Jon would have sworn that he had heard the buck crash. Uncertainty is the only way to describe Jon's emotions. The shot appeared to be perfect, but the actions of the buck after the shot were unlike any that he had ever witnessed. He hoped that what he had heard was indeed the sound of the buck expiring in a heap, but he was not quite sure. Jon waited in his stand for at least another hour, until dark. He did not want to make any noise that might spook the buck, so he decided to play it safe. After what seemed like an eternity, he climbed down his tree to inspect the point of the shot. A quick look was all that was needed to boost his spirits considerably. The ground and the arrow were covered with frothy red blood, the sure sign of a good double-lung hit. Flashlight in hand, Jon quickly walked back to his bike and began the ride back to his truck. He drove home to get some help finding his buck and getting it out of the woods.

Returning to the scene about two hours later, Jon was accompanied by his longtime friend and hunting companion, Jeff, and a dark green plastic ice-fishing sled for dragging. The tracking proved easy. For more than a hundred yards, the two of them followed the blood trail. Jon was just mentioning that with so much blood loss, this deer could not have made it much farther, when Jeff spotted the buck. His next comment was an expletive about the buck's body size.

With the life gone out of him, the buck had toppled headlong into a thicket of briers and saplings with such force that its antlers were hung up in the small trees. The entire front half of the deer was suspended in the air, and only its hind legs were touching the ground. Its antlers were so completely covered in brush that it was impossible at first even to count points. It took some effort to pull the buck free from the tangle.

After a bit of pulling, it was clear that the buck had an exceptional set of antlers for the area and was indeed one big-bodied deer. It carried eight points, with long main beams that almost touched in the front, and had good mass. Later that night, after a long drag back out of the woods, Jon and Jeff had the buck weighed. It topped the scales at just over 180 pounds dressed. Any buck that dresses over 150 pounds in central Michigan is an exceptional animal.

The journey was worth it, and Jon took home this eightpoint.

Staging areas are of interest to bucks only as long as does are using the nearby food source. When a food source dries up and the does move to other food sources, the bucks alter their movements to intercept these does. A good staging area might suddenly become devoid of deer activity when the crops are picked or the acorns are done falling.

Hunting rut staging areas is similar to hunting primary scrape areas. Wait until the prerut to hunt these spots. We have had our best success hunting these locations in the morning. Because mature bucks bed in these areas before first light, an extra-early arrival time is essential for such hunts. If you want to have a chance at a buck that is using a staging area, you have to be there first. When does pass by later in the morning, there is a good chance that the buck will show himself. Rut staging areas are also an essential part of a buck's scent-checking routine during late morning and midafternoon. A staging area located near a constant food source can provide action throughout the entire rut.

Funnels Between Bedding Areas

Funnels between bedding areas, thick cover that allows bucks security of movement during daylight, are super spots to hunt during the prerut. Mature bucks almost always take the route with the most cover in the daytime. These travel routes are used extensively in a buck's scent-checking routine, often during the middle of the day. Your setup should be in a position in the funnel from which you can shoot the funnel's entire width. If this is not possible, choose a spot that provides the most shot opportunities to the best sign. Bucks passing through such funnels have a destination in mind and usually are moving quite expediently. If the funnel is too wide to cover, tighten it by stacking brush, which deer will rarely walk through. We do not recommend doing this in season; by doing this the previous spring, deer movement will be confined to around your tree by the time hunting season arrives. When your primary scrape and rut staging areas begin to heat up, it is time to include funnels between bedding areas in your hunting rotation. These funnels are also great all-day spots.

New Rub Lines and Clusters

Once the prerut begins, we abandon all early-season and October lull rub lines. However, any time we move through our hunting area, we look for new fresh sign, such as rub lines or clusters of rubs. New rub lines found during the rut phases mark a buck's new travel route, and new clusters of rubs mark a destination point. The thicker the cover is around the rub lines, the more likely they are being traversed during daylight, possibly midday. Fresh rub lines and rub clusters definitely warrant a hunt or two.

Tarsal Glands

Scent is a key element in the world of white-tailed deer. Using scent for bowhunting is so popular that it seems as if everyone is using some scent or another. In pressured areas, this has had some negative consequences. Mature does and bucks in many areas have come to associate scents with hunters. That this happens is just a matter of time, if you use a particular scent every time you hunt. The key to scent use is timing and moderation. If a hunter squirts doe-in-heat scent on the ground every time he walks in the woods, the effectiveness of this scent will diminish after just a few uses, particularly if it is the early season. Using sex scents too early in the season is a very common mistake hunters make. If you use a sex scent, wait for the prerut. Scent overdoses are just as detrimental. Deer will definitely be on alert if it suddenly smells as if a hundred foxes ran through the woods peeing all over everything or a herd of coons is somewhere just up ahead. Any scent use has to be well considered. Scents work, it is an undeniable fact, but if you don't know how and when to use them properly, it is better to go scent-free.

The scent technique that we most often employ is using real tarsal glands. Every year, we collect the tarsal glands from any bucks and some from the does that we shoot. We then vacuum-pack, label, and freeze them until next season. Each label states whether the tarsal gland is from a buck or doe, the date it was shot, and the quality, rated as to muskiness for the bucks and closeness to the rut for the does. This gives us a steady supply of scent for the upcoming season. When the time comes to use a tarsal gland, we just pull one out of the freezer and thaw it out. If one of us kills a buck with particularly strong-smelling tarsal glands during the season, we store them in airtight plastic bags in the refrigerator and use those the same season. The fresher, the better. The most important reason to use tarsal glands is that you can be absolutely sure that you are getting real scent that is not overly concentrated or stale. With tarsal glands, it is almost impossible to create a scent overdose. Second, tarsal glands are free. If you are not able to cut them off deer that you or your friends have shot, you can usually get them for nothing at deer-processing operations. If you are pursuing mature bucks, try to find the strongest, muskiest-smelling tarsal glands you can that are not rotten.

The best time to use tarsal glands is during the prerut. Use them at your best spots: primary scrape areas, rut staging areas, and funnels between bedding areas. While on the way to your stand, stop about one hundred yards or so from your tree. With a safety pin, attach a tarsal gland to a six-foot-long piece of string. We almost always use tarsal glands from mature bucks. The scent of a mature buck in another mature buck's core territory can definitely arouse his curiosity. To make the situation even more enticing, we sometimes use two tarsal glands, one from a buck and one from a doe. You can imagine how interesting the scent combination of an unfamiliar buck and doe is to the dominant buck in the area. Drag the tarsal glands behind you, crossing as many alternate runways as possible. Then hang them on a branch about fifteen yards from your stand at about deer-nose level, from which the wind will blow the scent through the woods. Hang them in a spot where you can get a good shot at any deer that comes close. When a buck crosses the scent trail, chances are good that he will follow it. We have had excellent success with this scent technique, especially during midday.

As with any other tactic, use tarsal glands in moderation. If you attempt a tarsal gland drag at a primary scrape area and it doesn't work, don't attempt it again at that spot. Spreading out your scent use is vital to success. Try using the tarsal gland drag at several different locations, but never regularly in a single spot. Each time you repeat a scent procedure, the chances of having a mature buck respond decrease. Thus it is also vital to use a scent drag only during daylight hours in the prerut and rut, when bucks are most likely to respond.

Before you begin using rut tarsal glands, there are a few more things to consider. We always hunt our best spots during prerut clean on the first hunt. This means no tarsal gland drags the first time out. If a big buck is already using a specific location, there is no reason to attempt to lure him in. There is a good chance that he will come in on his own in a leisurely manner, and a gland drag may alter his routine and make him more aware of his surroundings. Also, tarsal glands from mature bucks will often spook subordinate and young bucks. They also spook does not yet in estrus, which want nothing to do with mature bucks. If you are not hunting for big bucks, do not use mature buck tarsal glands.

Rattling

You can make your tarsal glands even more effective by using them in conjunction with rattling. The combination of an olfactory attractor and an acoustic challenge can work magic during the prerut. This is the best time of the entire season to rattle. The bucks are signposting and seeking that first estrous doe. They are ready for the rut. They are also still true to their core areas, which will change when the chase stage of the main rut begins. This means that if you are in the core area of a particular buck and rattle, the chances are good that he will hear your call. The sound of two bucks fighting or, more likely, sparring can bring that buck to his feet.

Most bucks, especially in heavily hunted areas, respond to rattling extremely cautiously. This means that if the buck responds, he will probably circle downwind of the rattling at quite some distance. In pressured areas, even the most dominant bucks exhibit this behavior, largely because of the vast amount of faulty calling the deer have experienced throughout their lives. Calling is a fun hunting technique that hunters tend to overuse, and many attempt it throughout the entire season, often at the wrong times. Any buck that hears rattling week after week all season is unlikely to respond, and if he does respond, his approach will be with utmost caution. After the buck has circled downwind, he will scent-check for the source of the sound. This is where the use of the tarsal gland becomes important. If the approaching buck smells another buck or, better yet, a buck and doe, he is likely to put his nose to the ground and follow the scent trail. Sometimes bucks become so intent on following the scent that they almost throw caution to the wind. This can be the case if the dominant buck in the area responds.

When you rattle, it is imperative that you keep this buck behavior in mind. Unlike what you often see in television shows and videos, aggressive antler smashing seldom works in typical hunting areas. Most fighting or sparring that takes place in average deer populations is very short, with most conflicts being avoided by intimidation and body language. Keep your rattling sequences short; twenty to thirty seconds is long enough. During this time frame, start a sequence with about five seconds of aggressive rattling to get a distant buck's attention, and follow it up with grinding and light sparring sounds. Heavy horn beating often causes bucks to hightail it in the other direction or not respond to the rattling at all. Complete two or three rattle sequences at five- to ten-minute intervals during a hunt, and then put away your antlers or rattle bag. Rattling more than once or twice a week in a particular hunting area is too much in most cases. Less is better when it comes to rattling, if you want to use the technique effectively.

The best time to rattle is right at first light. Mature bucks may still be on their feet at this time, moving toward bedding, and are far less cautious after a night of moving undisturbed than in the evening. Bucks also are less likely to respond after they have bedded down. The best places to rattle are those where bucks feel comfortable moving during daylight, such as primary scrape areas, staging areas, funnels between bedding areas, and along the edges of standing cornfields. A cornfield is a special circumstance for rattling, and one of the few cases where we recommend hunting a field edge. Mature bucks feel comfortable in standing corn, and quite often the dominant buck in an area will take up residence in a cornfield. At the break of daylight, that buck is usually on his feet in the corn, and by rattling at first light, you may be able to persuade the buck to step out of the corn, or come close to the edge, for a few minutes.

This does not mean that rattling is not effective in the evening; it is. The problem with evening rattling is that bucks often wait to respond until last light or, worse, just after dark. This means that after you rattle, you will often encounter a buck in the dark as you descend from your stand or are walking out. This only reinforces that buck's hesitation to respond to rattling and other calling in the future. It also increases the likelihood that a buck will remain in a nocturnal routine throughout the prerut, a common situation in areas with heavy hunting pressure.

CHAPTER 6

November

Bowhunting in November for mature pressured bucks across most of the midwestern and northern states is dominated by three events: the continuation of the prerut, the rut, and gun season. The continuation of the prerut allows several more days to hunt a mature buck while he is still following some semblance of a pattern before the full-blown main rut. During the main rut, mature bucks frequently toss caution to the wind as testosterone takes over. Big bucks are much more vulnerable than at any other time of the season. They rarely have patterns during this period; anything can happen at any time of the day. In many states, including Michigan, gun season opens right in the middle of the rut. This sudden onslaught dampens deer movement dramatically, and in pressured areas, it eliminates the vast majority of bucks, thus changing the face of the rut.

The best thing about November is that this is when mature bucks are most vulnerable, and your chances for killing a reclusive monarch are better than at any other time. In record books, November always dominates with nearly 60 percent of the archery entries, even in states where gun season takes up a good portion of the month.

CONTINUATION OF THE PRERUT

During the first week of November, your hunting situation is very similar to that of late October. The timing of the prerut and rut varies from year to year, depending somewhat on the weather. If your best stands—primary scrape areas and rut staging areas—did not become active in late October, continue checking them. If they are going to have any activity at all, it should happen by the first week of November, at the very latest. If activity starts, begin hunting as described in the October chapter. It is now time to heavily hunt a rotation of your best stands. Stick to that rotation as long as there is continued sign of mature buck activity. That means concentrating on primary scrape areas, staging areas, funnels between bedding areas, and fresh rub lines or scrape lines. When the prerut is rolling, it is acceptable, and even advisable, to hunt your primary scrape areas a couple days in a row, if you practice strict scent control and can enter and exit without detection. With the main rut fast approaching, this is the time to pull out all the stops, which means putting in as much time on stand as possible and using some other hunting tactics.

Decoys

Decoys can work like magic during the prerut and rut, if used properly and in moderation, pulling bucks into shooting range that otherwise would have passed by out of range. Although a decoy can work at any time of the season, simply because deer are curious animals, we normally don't use them until the prerut, when the bucks' testosterone levels are peaking. In open areas in the early season, the first deer likely to move are the does. Does that enter an open area and spot a decoy will likely approach and inspect the fake deer. The inspection almost always ends with the doe stomping the ground, playing peekaboo with the decoy, snorting for several minutes, and then bounding off spooked, taking any other deer in the area with her. So if you set up a decoy too early in the season, you will be severely diminishing its effectiveness later in the season, during the prerut and rut, when the bucks are most active in daylight. As with any other tactic, you want to wait until the perfect moment to employ it. When bucks are searching for estrous does, they are most likely to be attracted to a decoy.

THE LUCKY ELEVEN: JOHN'S 1982 ELEVEN-POINT

t was already early November, and I had yet to hunt one of my best spots.

I The large poplar was positioned at the end of a draw that cut into a mature woodlot to the north. The small forest consisted mostly of very mature poplars and was interspersed with large oaks, beeches, and maples. There were also a few small cuts where the mature poplars had been removed, which provided another attraction and a source of browse for the deer. The deer used the draw as a main travel route to the main bedding area, about a ten-acre patch of very thick red willow. The bedding area was located across an overgrown pasture straight to the north. There were well-worn runways along both sides of the draw that followed the edge of the thick underbrush filling the low spot. The runway on the west side of the draw had several rubs along it and the occasional scrape. There was a banner crop of acorns that year, and I knew the deer would be using that draw in the mornings on their return to the bedding area. I had already seen two good bucks nearby from another tree, and I really wanted to hunt there. The catch was that the tree near the draw required an east wind, which is rare to begin with, particularly in northern Michigan in the fall.

Finally, at the end of the first week of November, I got my chance. That morning I woke up and walked outside to check the weather. The wind was blowing lightly from the southeast, and the mercury had risen to about 40 degrees F. Though it was not raining, it was misty and damp. Excited at finally having the chance to hunt one of the trees I considered among my best, I was dressed and out the door in a matter of minutes. The walk to the tree was more than half a mile, which I covered as quickly as I could. The long walk and climbing up the tree an hour before first light had caused me to sweat and overheat. It was not even daylight before I was shaking from chills caused by having damp, sweaty undergarments. Back then, I did not layer properly or dress down for long walks, or carry a backpack with extra clothing. Learning to dress properly and carry extra clothes in a pack came about after many years of suffering on stands.

Through my shivering, I attempted to concentrate on hunting. The deer traveled predominantly north in the morning and south in the evening, but with the rut starting, they could come from any direction. Sitting on two two-by-fours nailed about twenty-five feet up in the poplar, I reviewed the situation at first light. The best shot was about ten yards to the west runway, and my second shooting lane allowed a thirty-yard shot to the east runway, along the far edge of the draw. The early morning passed without much action, except for my shivering. The biggest event was the sun rising over the horizon, bringing with it that long-wished-for warmth. I think every bowhunter knows how much relief those first rays of sunshine can provide on a cold morning. By about 9:00, the sun was up and I was warm and comfortable again.

Just as I was beginning to enjoy hunting again, two does and a single fawn meandered past, following the far runway along the east side of the draw. The deer moved out of the woods into the overgrown pasture toward the bedding area. A few minutes behind them followed a yearling four-point. The young buck had his nose to the ground and was obviously intent on catching up to the does that had just passed. At the time, I was just a couple years into the transition from shooting any buck to strictly pursuing those two and a half years old or older, so I let this one pass. Like most hunters in their youth, it was still difficult for me to let shootable bucks pass. However, I knew there were two nice two-and-a-half-year-old bucks in the area, and I wanted to get an opportunity on one of them before the fast-approaching gun season. The area I was in was absolutely pounded by gun hunters, who shot any legal buck. The odds that one of the bucks would live beyond two and a half were virtually zero.

It was just about 11:00, and now warm and sunny, when I caught a bit of motion out of the corner of my eye. A quick glance was all I needed to confirm that one of the big bucks was steadily making his way down the draw. His nose was glued to the ground, following the track of the deer that had passed earlier. Like the four-point, this buck, too, was obviously following the nearly two-hour-old scent of the does. One of those does must have been in estrus or close to it. As focused as the buck was on the lingering scent, everything seemed to be unfolding perfectly, except for one problem: If the buck continued to follow the does, he would eventually present a broadside thirty-yard shot, but my comfortable shooting range was, and still is, twenty-five yards or less. I hesitate to take shots any farther than this, no matter how open. Even though I had been shooting in a league for several years and was very proficient with my equipment, a thirty-yard shot at a whitetail was a tough situation. Shooting at targets while standing in perfect position, and never having to worry about what the target is going to do, is quite different from shooting at live, moving animals from awkward positions and angles, not to mention having to deal with the additional excitement.

With gun season only a week away, I knew this would most likely be my only chance at one of the two nice bucks, so I decided to attempt the shot. The buck was about two steps from the opening when I drew my bow. Those last two steps came quickly. With my thirty-yard pin already on the buck's chest, I blatted to stop him. He halted immediately and stared in my direction, though he appeared to be looking under me. Careful not to rush the shot, I settled my pin behind the buck's shoulder, exhaled slowly, and let the arrow fly. Still concentrating on my shot placement, I watched the arrow disappear into the buck, though a little farther back than where I had aimed. The deer sprinted south, into the overgrown pasture, and out of sight. After the shot, I was filled with that rush of emotion that every hunter has while shooting deer. I was positive that I had just made a fatal shot, though a little worried about recovering the buck. It looked as if I had just made a liver shot, or perhaps even a gut shot. I had tracked deer shot like this many times before and was aware that things could get difficult.

Not wanting to spook the buck if it was bedded nearby, I waited another hour before unleashing my safety belt and climbing down the tree. Trying to be as quiet as possible, I collected my things and sneaked to the point of the shot. There was good blood right at the point of impact. I also inspected my arrow, which was lying on the ground a couple yards behind where the buck had been standing. It was covered in dark blood and had a little brown grit on it. More than likely I had hit the buck in the liver and paunch, which meant he already may have expired or he may not die for several hours, depending on which arteries were cut in the liver.

Since I had to walk through the overgrown pasture in order to get out of the woods, I decided to carefully follow the blood trail to the pasture before making a decision on how to proceed. While I was tracking, I was careful to scan the woods up ahead for a bedded buck. Deer with this sort of wound will often bed down only a short distance from where they were shot. Barely in the weed field, I found five spots were the buck briefly bedded, moved a few yards, and bedded again. It was clear that the buck was not bedded in the old pasture and had made it to the thick and wet bedding area. The decision was easy. I broke off the tracking to give the buck time to expire.

After going home, shooting my bow, and doing some odds and ends around the house for a few hours, I returned to the blood trail wearing my hip boots. I picked up the trail and followed it into the thick red willow. It was tough going, and I found no more blood after another hundred yards. I attempted to search the bedding area by doing circles, walking runways, crawling through thickets, and trying to think like a deer. It was all to no avail. It was almost dark as I dejectedly left the bedding area, with the feeling that I had covered every inch of it. I would have to return in the morning to resume and widen my search. I felt that I must have pushed him out of the area.

I don't think I slept a wink that night and was up at daylight. I called in to take a day off from work, and as soon as it was light enough to see, I headed back to the woods. On the northwest side of the bedding area was a small, L-shaped open woodlot. To the north, the woodlot was bordered by a small hayfield. Since I had covered the bedding area fairly thoroughly, I decided the first place I wanted to search for the buck was in those woods. The hayfield had a tractor lane along its edge, which ended at the woodlot. Taking advantage of that tractor lane, I drove to the edge of the woods and parked. Stepping out of my car, I glanced across the field and noticed something white lying in the alfalfa, not fifty yards away. A closer look was all it took to find my buck. I must have pushed him out of the bedding area the evening before, and he just couldn't go any farther. The fact that the buck expired in the open and that I had parked my vehicle that close was simply a stroke of luck. Occasionally, luck plays a big role in bowhunting.

The two-and-a-half-year-old eleven-point was a very respectable buck for the area. My arrow had passed through the front of his stomach and the back of his liver. Though I waited before tracking this buck, I did not wait long enough. If I had waited a few hours longer, I may have been able to follow a blood trail to a dead deer, which is far better than circling for a dead deer—most of the time, this is like looking for a needle in a haystack. This buck helped confirm that patience is required on any questionable hit. The more patient a hunter is after a questionable hit, the better the chances will be for recovery. I was fortunate that this buck was shot in an agricultural area, where bedding areas and places for deer to hide in general are usually small in size, compared with those in big-timber areas with big swamps. In a different area, that buck may very well have never been recovered, because I pushed him that evening instead of waiting overnight.

Use decoys only in areas where deer beyond your shooting distance can see them; in areas of heavy cover, they are not needed. If a buck is using a travel corridor that is unhuntable because of a lack of trees or suitable ground cover for a ground blind, or if he is out of your range, such as on a neighboring property, these are perfect situations for decoy use. Clear out a stand in the best tree you can find with visibility to the travel corridor the buck is using. Place the decoy in a position where it is visible from the buck's travel corridor. If the buck passes through and does not notice the decoy, grunt or bleat to get his attention. If he stops and looks, the visual attraction of the decoy should lure him into range. If the buck notices the decoy on his own, let him move in without any coaxing; remain silent and get ready for a shot. Attempt calling only if the buck loses interest for some reason.

Whether to use a buck or doe decoy depends on the time of season. From early season through the prerut, we use a doe. Mature bucks are seeking those first estrous does during the prerut, and they are likely traveling alone, which is the perfect scenario for using a doe decoy. These bucks will almost always come in to check out the fake doe. During the rut, when most mature bucks are with estrous does, it is rare that they will respond to a doe decoy. A buck decoy, on the other hand, will test their territorial dominance. Young bucks may be intimidated by a buck decoy, however, and spook if the decoy has antlers that are superior to his. A decoy that spooks deer before a mature buck shows himself can possibly keep the target buck from approaching. Therefore, if you are in a good location, before you set up a decoy, always hunt the stand clean. This gives you an opportunity to intercept any buck that is passing through naturally. A buck passing through an area that is completely natural is more comfortable and not necessarily on high alert. The minute anything is out of the ordinary, the awareness level of both bucks and does increases.

To set up a doe decoy, place it at a comfortable shooting distance, quartering slightly away. If a buck approaches, it will likely approach from the rear. To use a buck decoy, set it up broadside. Bucks almost always approach other bucks head-on, though occasionally they will just charge in and ram the decoy from the side. Always place a decoy upwind in a spot where it can be seen from a distance. It should also be set up far enough away from your location that if the buck circles downwind of it (about five yards at the most), he will not be right below your tree. When setting up a decoy, take every precaution not to leave any human scent on it. Spraying it with scent killer once set up is a good idea.

We have tried just about every manufacturer's decoy and have settled on two: the Montana and the Carrylite. Both have advantages and disadvantages. The Montana is an actual print of a doe on fabric that folds up similarly to a pop-up blind and fits in a backpack, making it extremely portable. Although it looks very real from a distance, it is two-dimensional and cannot be seen from straight on or behind. The Carrylite is a hard plastic decoy with more detail than other hard-bodied decoys. It is three-dimensional, which is definitely an advantage, but it is cumbersome to carry and can be noisy to set up. Trimming off some of the plastic, however, makes it much quieter to set up. If we had to pick just one, it would be the Carrylite.

When using a decoy, you can combine it with other tactics, thereby providing attractions for all three of the deer's main senses: a decoy for their sense of sight, a scent drag for their sense of smell, and rattling or calling for their sense of hearing. This involves using a real tarsal gland or fresh estrous urine as a scent drag to the spot where the decoy will be set up. Best of all is to use two tarsal glands, one from a mature buck and another from a doe. Make sure that your scent drag crosses as many runways or travel corridors as possible. After your decoy is in place, attach the tarsal glands to the decoy; under the tail is best. On morning hunts, do a rattling sequence at first light. If your rattling attracts the attention of a nearby buck, the scent trail and decoy will usually get that buck to come in close enough for a shot. If your first rattling sequence is not effective, try again in ten minutes. When hunting pressured areas, do not rattle beyond the second sequence. In nonpressured areas, you can perform a rattle sequence once per hour and let the decoy and scent do their work the rest of the time. If you are going to hunt through midday, try a rattle sequence or two between 11:00 A.M. and 2:00 P.M.

This Montana decoy will fool any interested buck. Its downside is that it is not three-dimensional, so it cannot be seen from the front or rear.

In-Season Scouting

By early November, it will be clear whether your spring scouting has produced the desired results in the form of active primary scrape areas, staging areas, and funnels between bedding areas. If these areas do not show the buck sign you expected, you have no alternative but to do some in-season scouting now. Most of the time, a change in, or lack of, expected deer movement is caused by an unforeseen disruption. In pressured areas, this is usually due to other hunters, but it also might be a result of crop rotation, property development, or even your own mistakes, such as overhunting an area.

If your plan is not working, it is time to adjust. Flexibility and a willingness to change are necessary attitudes at this point in order to have a successful season. The key now is to adjust while having as little impact on deer movement as possible. This means scouting only while practicing total scent control, wearing a complete Scent-Lok suit, headgear, gloves, and rubber boots. It also means scouting during the middle of the day, when the majority of deer are least active. There is always a risk at this time that the mature buck you are pursuing will be up and moving, but unfortunately, this risk is unavoidable. If at all possible, scout during heavy rain or high wind. Heavy rain covers the noise you make while scouting and dilutes the scent that you inevitably leave behind after preparing a hunting location. High wind is the weather condition in which deer are least likely to move, because it makes it very difficult for them to detect danger. The moving branches and the sound of wind passing through the trees make both seeing and hearing difficult for deer, and the deer's nose is also at a disadvantage, as scent disperses very quickly. Therefore, most deer bed down and wait until after the winds subside to move.

When you begin in-season scouting, the first step is to find the cause of the disturbance, if possible. After you find the source of the problem, attempt to discover how the deer have reacted. Study after study has shown that deer do not abandon their home ranges; they are just good at moving their centers of activity and avoiding us. You might find that the hot primary scrape area has been moved just a couple hundred yards away. Immediately set up and hunt any such spot you find, or one with a heavy concentration of does. When scouting during the prerut, find the best fresh sign available, and either hunt it that evening or immediately leave the area and return to hunt later. If you continue to walk around your hunting property, you diminish your chances at taking a mature buck. The window of opportunity during the prerut is short, and you have to take advantage of it.

Scouting in bedding areas can be detrimental or awesome, depending on the situation. Don't scout small bedding areas in a locale where the deer have many other options of places to bed. If spooked, the deer likely will leave the small bedding area and bed somewhere else. Some bedding areas are very large, allowing the mature bucks to pursue does during daylight hours without ever leaving the bedding area. Here, any spooked deer will just move to a different portion of the same bedding area. Under such circumstances, include the bedding area in your in-season scouting. Always use extreme caution regarding scent, noise, and alterations in size of shooting lanes. Keep tree trimming to an absolute minimum, leaving lanes a little narrower than normal. One nice thing about hunting in a bedding area is that you can hear a deer coming before it gets into a shooting lane, giving you ample time to get ready.

The ideal location for a stand in a bedding area is wherever several runways merge or intersect. In large, thick bedding areas, it is not uncommon for there to be some all-day activity from all the deer during the rut phases, not just the mature bucks. With this in mind, you want to be where the most sign or runways are within shooting distance.

When hunting bedding areas, be in your location well before first light—in pressured areas, an hour and a half at an absolute minimum. Make as little noise as possible whenever entering or exiting a bedding area. The prerut is a time when you must be aggressive yet careful; if you stay outside a large bedding area and wait for the action to come to you, after a week or two you will probably be planning your next season's strategy, hoping the buck you were pursuing makes it through gun season.

Another bedding area situation is in thick stands of small pines, spruces, or cedars with the lower branches reaching the ground. Here the deer are likely to move among the branches in the daytime. It is worth taking the chance of spooking deer out of that type of bedding area by setting up a subtle hunting location. These areas of thick conifers are so attractive to deer that they will return within the next day or so, even in pressured areas.

Mock Scrapes

If you have checked a previously well-used primary scrape area a couple times without finding any sign of buck activity, yet there is other deer activity, and you cannot locate another primary scrape area nearby, it is time to do some encouraging in the form of mock scrapes. The opening of scrapes may entice a local mature buck into action, or at least to include your spot in his routine. Since it is best to hunt with as little disturbance as possible in pressured areas, you should use this tactic only as a last resort. Unlike in nonpressured areas, where hunting tactics work with great frequency, responses to artifical noises, sign posting, and visuals are less common in pressured areas and can be counterproductive. During midday, wearing scent-free clothing and rubber boots, use a stick to remove all the leaves and grass from two or three of the old scrapes. Then, with a bottle of buck urine, doctor the scrapes liberally. Break a couple small branches over each scrape at about eye level, and put a few drops of forehead gland scent on them to create mock licking branches. When finished, drag a buck tarsal gland back out of the woods and hunt another location. The tarsal gland scent may attract a mature buck in the area to your scrapes. The scent of an unfamiliar buck is a direct challenge to other mature bucks and may be enough to encourage a buck to make that scrape area part of his rut routine.

Check the scrapes a couple days later, following the same procedure. If the scrapes have been worked, hunt there immediately. (You should already have a stand location set up and ready to hunt at this location.) If the scrapes are still inactive, douse them again with scent and come back in a couple more days. Usually, once is enough to spur a buck into action during the prerut.

You also can make mock scrapes near an active scrape area that does not offer a good tree to hunt from or on parcels that have spots well suited for primary scrape areas—with good doe traffic and perimeter cover—but where there are none. Many hunters attempt to create primary scrape areas by making a couple mock scrapes in or close to high-traffic areas early in the season and doctoring them up frequently. In pressured areas, the extra human visits to high-traffic areas during the October lull, while the mature bucks are still nocturnal, can alter deer traffic and awareness and be detrimental in the long run. We try to keep things as natural as possible until we are certain our plans are not working out. Unmolested and natural conditions nearly always yield the best results in pressured areas.

Freelance Hunting

Many people make hunting trips to new places in November to take advantage of the prerut and rut. When visiting a new place for a short-term hunt, being able to judge and react to deer movement patterns immediately is essential. The ability to adjust to ever-changing deer movement is critical to growth as a hunter and being consistently successful. You do not have time to wait for things to happen, and you have not had a chance to prepare during the previous postseason or preseason. We refer to this sort of hunting as freelance hunting. It could be considered aggressive hunting—it's a time to pull out all the stops and go for it.

Whenever you plan to hunt a new area, obtain aerial photos and topographical maps before you go; these are available on the Internet. With these photos, even though they may be a couple years old, you can pinpoint areas in which you would like to concentrate your scouting efforts. Most major terrain features, such as funnels, valleys and draws, inside corners, marshes and swamps, and bedding areas, will be fairly obvious. Knowing where these areas are, rather than just blindly walking onto a property, saves you time, and time is limited while freelance hunting.

If we are going out of state for a week, we take several freelance hunting packs. We spend the first day of our hunt preparing hunting locations, so on that day we also carry an extension cutter and saw. When we arrive at the property, we immediately head to the best spots that we have already pinpointed on our photos, while practicing extreme scent control. Look for the best spots you can find, including primary scrape areas, staging areas, funnels between bedding areas, inside corners, and well-used travel routes between bedding and feeding areas. There is not enough time on such hunts to explore every aspect of the property in detail.

While freelancing, if there are options, we try to pick trees that require the least amount of trimming, so that we leave the least amount of scent in the area as possible. This also allows us to set up multiple trees in a short period of time. When we discover a good tree, we clear it out immediately, and then move on to the next area of interest. In a single day, we are able to get three to five trees ready to hunt with our Ambush Saddles. If a tree is in a good location, however, we will take the time to set it up even if it requires several hours to do so. On one out-of-state hunt, John had to cut down fourteen trees that were six inches in diameter or larger in order to get a shot from a huge cottonwood with a twenty-degree lean to it. This four-foot-diameter cottonwood was located in the middle of an active primary scrape area and was the only available tree large enough to hunt from. On John's second morning hunt from that tree, he rattled in and took a very nice buck.

Hunt the best spot the next day, and if you are satisfied with your location, hunt there again. If not, adjust your location or rotate to another prepared tree. While freelance hunting, you do not have to be quite as concerned with overhunting a stand. The key is to optimize your hunting time to intercept a mature buck. If you hunt a stand that does not meet your expectations, pull your steps on the way down and put them back in the freelance pack. Using such a system in conjunction with an Ambush Saddle, it is easy to move to a tree a hundred yards away. You can have a new tree set up in a matter of minutes, and silently.

Besides an Ambush Saddle or tree stand, your arsenal for freelance hunting should include a pop-up blind, decoy, rattle bag or antlers, calls (grunt and doe bleat), and several scents: doe in estrus, buck urine, real tarsals, and forehead gland. Because your time is limited, it is perfectly acceptable to attempt all the tactics you have in your repertoire. (Short-term hunts in areas with less hunting pressure are discussed in chapter 13.)

THE RUT

After the more predictable patterns of the prerut end in early November, the main stage of the rut begins in our area. This is the time when anything can happen. The mature bucks begin chasing and tending does, which is both positive and negative for hunters. On the positive side, the mature bucks are much more likely to move during daylight hours. On the negative side, they abandon their previous patterns and follow hot does on very unpredictable routes and often out of their core areas. This aids in leveling the playing field for all hunters; even someone who is doing everything wrong has a chance at a mature buck during this period. However, if you've done your homework, you can put yourself in a better position to take advantage of the rut.

It is important to realize that bucks do not completely throw caution to the wind during the rut. In pressured areas, you will seldom witness a mature buck following a doe out in the open during daylight. In fact, mature bucks in highly pressured areas might remain almost completely nocturnal throughout the rut. For a long time, it has been accepted as common knowledge that a buck will chase an estrous doe wherever she may take him. To some extent this is indeed true, especially with young bucks. Mature bucks are different, however. Their breeding is far more ritualized. Not only do these bucks go after does, but the mature does with several breeding cycles behind them also pursue the mature bucks as they approach estrus. This assures that the dominant bucks do most of the breeding. These bucks also chase differently. If a doe happens into the open during daylight hours, mature bucks usually attempt to push the doe back into some cover.

Chris witnessed exactly this type of buck behavior during the second week of November 2003 on a tract of state land in Michigan. Just before noon, a doe trotted from a thick ridge covered with underbrush and pines into a small opening that bordered on open hardwoods. She stood in the opening as a big buck slowly walked to the edge of the thick stuff. After the buck was in sight, the doe proceeded farther into the hardwoods. The buck then turned and went back into the thick stuff. The doe actually turned and ran at him, sort of like a dog that wants to be chased. The buck just looked at the doe for a second and continued back over the ridge. The doe lingered in the opening for about another minute, then followed the exact tracks of the buck over the ridge. That mature buck refused to expose himself in those open hardwoods. We have witnessed this sort of behavior on many occasions in pressured areas, but on out-of-state hunts in less pressured areas, we have seen no evidence of it.

When a mature buck encounters a near estrous doe, he follows and stays with her. A doe is in estrus for twenty-six to twenty-eight hours. During that time, the buck remains with the doe. After the initial breeding, he will breed the doe, on average, about every four hours. In between breeding, the buck and doe will often bed down near one another. The buck will also attempt to keep all other bucks away from the doe. After the doe is finished with her estrous cycle, the buck will immediately search for another estrous doe, resuming his prerut routine of scent-checking primary scrape areas and using staging areas to intercept does. While buck traffic through these areas continues, signposting, such as working scrapes and rubs, generally decreases. Bucks are usually too busy with does to spend time signposting. In their search for estrous does, bucks also visit other areas with high doe traffic.

JOHN'S MUZZLELOADER TEN-POINT

I have been chasing mature bucks for a very long time, well before it was commonplace. In the early years, there was very little information out there about hunting mature bucks. Knowledge about deer hunting was hard earned and available only through hands-on experience. Though I made every mistake there is to make, some hunts stand out as being pivotal to the development of my future hunting style. Those hunts were the ones on which unique circumstances brought about a huge gain in knowledge of deer behavior and how to hunt, almost like someone clicking on a light. One of my most memorable and important hunts took place about a quarter century ago.

It was 1981, and for the previous two years I had been pursuing a big state-land buck that I had yet to see. In 1980, another hunter had seen the buck in early October. That hunter described the buck as a magnificent ten-point, with a wide and very tall, basket-shaped rack. Though I had never seen him, I wanted this buck badly. It was the first time I attempted to pursue an individual buck.

The buck seemed to be bedding in a large marshy area consisting mostly of cattails and nearly crotch-deep water, with a small island of high ground in the center. About two hundred yards from the northwest corner of this cattail marsh was another large swamp, which was a mix of cattails, red willow, and swamp grass, with some small dry areas covered with tamaracks and cedars. Both of these bedding areas were located in an oversize section dominated by mature hardwoods, mostly oaks and maples, but with small pockets of poplars and beeches. In that area, there were no crops for several miles. This meant that the deer foraged somewhat randomly throughout the woods, feeding mostly on acorns, beechnuts, and other natural browse. This kind of area is tough to hunt for an individual animal. Without a defined preferred food source, it is very difficult to pinpoint constant travel routes, because the deer wander a great deal. The marsh had the typical network of runways radiating from it, spaced about twenty yards apart, which looked like deer highways. I had already learned, though, that runways like these can lead to false conclusions. It doesn't take a lot of deer traffic to trample weeds and cattails and churn up soft dirt, making it look as though every deer in the county is passing through a particular spot. Soft dirt makes tracks look fresh for a long time.

During the previous two bow seasons, I hunted rub lines and individual scrapes whenever I could. Rub lines with occasional scrapes led into bedding areas in several locations. The routes this buck was using were easy to identify. The tracks he left behind were huge, and the trees and bushes he rubbed on were totally demolished. Though I saw several bucks while hunting in these locations, I never saw the big guy. I didn't yet understand how mature bucks reacted to heavy hunting pressure, particularly that rub lines generally are not the most productive stands while hunting in pressured situations. And the area this buck called home got slammed with hunting pressure.

Now, with about twenty-five more hunting seasons of experience, I understand why rub lines are not that productive for pressured bucks prior to the rut phases, though they are very effective in nonpressured situations. The reason is simple. In areas with extreme hunting pressure, most two-and-a-half-year-old bucks are already almost completely nocturnal during the early part of bow season, not to mention how nocturnal a really mature five-and-a-half-year-old buck that lived on state land would be. This means that through most of the season, rub lines—buck travel routes—will be used only after dark. And waiting to hunt these rub line spots until the rut phases is not really effective. Generally speaking, if there are mature bucks in an area, they will do most of the breeding. Before the does start coming into estrus, they usually do not want anything to do with the mature bucks, so they attempt to avoid the travel routes that the mature bucks are using. This is why hunters seldom see mature bucks and does together before the rut phases begin. You may see younger, subordinate bucks attempting to chase does around and feeding together with does, but this is only because young bucks are like teenagers who don't know what to do with the sudden surge of testosterone flowing through their bodies.

Once the rut phases start, the mature bucks begin moving during daylight, pursuing estrous does. Since the does had been avoiding the bucks' regular travel routes, the bucks have to change their routes to intercept them. This means that as soon as a nocturnal pressured buck begins to move more during daylight, he changes his movement pattern, sometimes even changing his bedding area. Fresh rub lines and scrapes that suddenly appear during the rut phases are therefore definitely worth hunting, because there is a possibility of a daytime sighting. It is also very likely that new rut-phase rub lines and scrapes will show up in areas with heavy doe traffic.

Bow season that year passed without any luck. On opening day of gun season, I hunted at home in Clare County, with no success. Though I knew that the area where the big buck lived was probably crawling with gun hunters, I just had to give that buck one more shot. On November 16, I headed back to southern Michigan. Arriving at midday, I decided to pull on waders and head out to that island in the cattails. At that time, I ordinarily would not go into a bedding area to pursue a buck, always fearing that I would spook any buck I was after. And on that afternoon, I probably did just that. Stepping onto the dry ground, I was shocked at the amount of buck sign. There were rubs everywhere and many scrapes. A few yards onto the island, I found something that to that point I had seen only a couple of times. Positioned almost centrally on the island stood an oak tree with low-hanging branches. Under nearly every branch was a large scrape, and over each scrape were numerous licking branches. There were at least ten scrapes. I was looking at a very hot primary scrape area. Within a few minutes, I found a natural ground blind in a deadfall downwind of the scrapes and settled in for the afternoon. That evening, several does and two small bucks crossed the high ground, checked the scrapes, and disappeared back into the cattails. I was definitely in the right spot.

I had a feeling that the big buck would pass through that island at some point, so I decided to hunt the entire next day. The next morning, I was in my ground blind a couple hours before first light. I just did not want to spook that big buck. At about 8:00, the first deer of the morning stepped onto the island, and my jaw nearly dropped to the ground. This was the buck I had been hunting for the previous two years. Both his rack and body were huge. In fact, this was the biggest buck I had ever seen while hunting up to that point. Unfortunately, he was out of range. The big buck skirted the other end of the high ground at a distance of about 150 yards, which was simply too far for my side-lock .54-caliber muzzleloader, which had iron sights and shot round balls. The accuracy of that old muzzleloader was a far cry from that of modern, scoped, in-line muzzleloaders shooting sabots. I watched as the buck vanished back into the cattails and hoped he would return later in the day.

During the course of the day, a few does, a couple small bucks, and a decent eight-point crossed the island about sixty yards from me. The eight-point was a good buck by Michigan standards, and in any other situation I would have shot him. But I wanted a shot at the big guy (in fact, he was all I could even think about), so I held out. Although there was heavy hunting pressure all around this spot, it was obviously an isolated area where the deer felt comfortable moving during the day.

About half an hour before dark, the big buck stepped back onto the high ground. Once again, he was at the other end of the island. This time, though, he walked straight at me, toward the scrapes under the oak. At a distance of about sixty yards, he abruptly stopped. I was downwind of the scrapes, and he was forty yards on the upwind side. He stood stone still, peering in the direction of the scrapes and toward my hiding spot. I could sense that something made him uncomfortable. The buck was facing me head-on. Now I was in a dilemma. It did not look as though the buck would stick around for very long, but a straight-on shot was definitely not the greatest. I was fully aware that with my muzzleloader, I could shoot only about a five-inch group at a hundred yards, from a bench. Having already shouldered my muzzleloader, using a shooting stick as a rest, I had to decide quickly whether to shoot and, if so, whether to aim for the neck or chest. There were a couple small branches in front of the buck's chest. Big bucks in pressured areas rarely give you a second opportunity, and this was the second time I had seen this buck in one day. *Bang!* Decision made.

A cloud of white smoke filled the air, blocking my view. Immediately I jumped out of my blind and scrambled about ten yards to the side, to see around the thick smoke. The buck was lying on the ground, attempting to move. I reloaded as quickly as I could, struggling with clumsy adrenaline-charged fingers. Shouldering my muzzleloader, I cautiously moved in for a second shot. At a distance of about ten yards, I put an insurance round into the buck's chest. After the adrenaline wore off, I could hardly believe what I was looking at. The buck had a huge body—later he weighed in at 287 pounds dressed—and he had antlers to match, an almost perfectly typical ten-point. For five years, this buck was the Michigan state record with a muzzleloader.

Though I shot this buck with a muzzleloader, the circumstances surrounding this deer changed my bowhunting dramatically. I began to go out of my way searching for scrape areas like the one I found under that oak, which I eventually began calling primary scrape areas. Eventually I started to figure out how to hunt them. I also began to better understand how pressured bucks use their travel routes both before and during the rut. This buck was nocturnal until the rut, and even then he moved during daylight only in a remote area inaccessible without waders.

John's 1981 ten-point. Even in pressured areas, the occasional buck grows to maturity.

Although mature bucks do most of the breeding, subordinate bucks often are able to get in on the action. In pressured areas with low mature-buck-to-doe ratios, this is a common occurrence. The rut, particularly in the North, is quite synchronous, with most does coming into estrus at approximately the same time, and there is simply not enough time for the mature bucks to do all the breeding within the normal two-week span. Subordinate bucks will also check, and use, the primary scrape areas and staging areas in an attempt to locate an estrous doe; we have witnessed it on many occasions.

Taking advantage of this behavior is the key to hunting the rut properly. This means continuing to hunt the same locations as during the prerut, as well as travel routes with heavy doe traffic. Your best spots will be active during the rut, but the dominant buck you are pursuing will be far less regular in his movement than during the prerut. The good thing is that the other mature bucks in the vicinity are also expanding their ranges and moving more. This causes overlaps, with bucks scent-checking the primary scrape areas of other bucks and following does into the other males' core areas. The extensive roaming the bucks do at this time during daylight hours gives all hunters an excellent chance. It is not uncommon to see several bucks on a single hunt during the rut, even in pressured areas.

Stick to your best spots if the activity warrants it, and spend as much time on stand as you can. All-day hunting is advised whenever possible. During the rut phases, the more time you spend in the woods, the better your chances will be, as long as you avoid spooking the deer and practice diligent scent control. During the rut, a mature buck's natural routine, when not with an estrous doe, likely has him scent-checking during midday, between 10:00 A.M. and 2:00 P.M. If you cannot hunt all day, a possibility during the rut is what we call second-shift hunting, heading to your stand at about 9:00 A.M. Hunting this time frame allows you to get extra sleep and still puts you in position to take advantage of that midday mature buck activity. Remain on stand until dark whenever possible.

Another way to hunt the rut is to concentrate on does, which are the central point of the bucks' lives at this time. Vital to this endeavor is that the does continue in their normal routine, unspooked. Spooking does during the rut, just like any other part of the season, is extremely damaging to your chances of killing a mature buck in that location. Does will change their routine when spooked, and the bucks will alter their movements accordingly.

Moon Phases

In recent hunting literature, there has been a great deal of information on the effects of the moon phase on the timing of the rut. Though we do not deny that the moon phase may have some effect, a host of other factors are far more important to both the timing and intensity of the rut and have stronger implications on hunting pressured mature bucks. Most moon phase studies have been done by studying enclosed deer that do not get hunted or extremely nonpressured deer on large tracts of very exclusive property. It would be similar to studying the nighttime walking movements of humans in a secure rural town and assuming they would be the same as in a crime-laden inner-city setting; you simply cannot compare the two. In reality, throwing hunting seasons and pressure into the mix totally changes the equation.

Despite numerous claims that the intensity of the rut depends on moon phases, they have only minimal effect on the rut behavior during daylight hours in pressured areas. The absolute most important factor determining daytime rut activity by mature bucks is hunting pressure, period. Nothing pushes rut activity under cover of darkness more than heavy hunting pressure. The next factor is the immediate weather conditions, including wind, cloud cover, temperature, and precipitation. Nothing sets the rut in motion better than a solid late-October cold front. And nothing slows it down more than a heat wave. The mature-buck-to-doe ratio also has a major effect on rut activity and intensity. The more mature bucks there are, the heavier the competition and the more rut activity. In Michigan, the main rut phase generally falls at the same time every year, starting the second week of November and reaching its peak by about the middle of the month. The time for the rut in the North is limited, and the length of daylight plays the most important role.

In our experience bowhunting pressured bucks, we have noticed that the moon's greatest effect is on deer's immediate movement reaction to the moon phase, regardless of rut phase. Mature buck movement during the various moon phases differs from that of the rest of the deer. Mature bucks move less on evenings when the moon is coming up full and the sky is clear. They continue to move less after dark and throughout the night when the moon is near its full stage and unprotected by cloud cover. With cloud cover or light rain during the full moon phase, the activity level increases dramatically. The reduction in evening and night movement when the moon is in or near its full stage is compensated by more midday movement. On the other hand, if there is a new moon, the deer move more in the evening and morning and less during midday. The implication this has on your hunting is obvious: When the moon is full and the sky is clear, you should work some midday hunting into your routine during the rut phases.

GUN SEASON

In pressured areas, gun season has a huge impact on deer movement and on the herd itself. In states such as Michigan, Pennsylvania, and New York, to name a few, with well over half a million gun hunters, the gun opener changes the hunting dramatically. In a single day, in some areas of pressured states, up to 80 percent of the annual gun buck harvest is taken. Most parts of these pressured states have more than twenty hunters per square mile. In some areas of Michigan's northern Lower Peninsula, hunter densities reach up to eighty per square mile; this means the hunter density is higher than the deer density in some cases. To top it off, gun season takes place during the middle of the rut. With most of the bucks gone, the few survivors have more does to breed, some of which will not be bred during their first estrous cycle, contributing to a more intense second rut than in nonpressured areas. Daytime rutting activity seemingly disappears, with almost all chasing taking place well after dark. If there is one single event that causes most deer to become nocturnal, it is opening day of gun season. Bowhunting after this point can be very frustrating, but with planning, there are ways you can react successfully.

If you decide to bowhunt during the gun season opener, look for escape routes, the tighter the better. In pressured areas, on opening morning, normal deer movement can be forgotten; the deer are just looking to get out of harm's way. A thick funnel leading to the thickest bedding area available should be your stand site of choice. Remaining on stand the entire day is recommended; a high percentage of mature bucks are taken in midday during gun season.

John took this ten-point buck with a muzzle-loader on state land in 1983.

Hunting the Postrut (Tail End of the Main Rut)

In the North, the rut is synchronous, meaning that most does come into estrus at about the same time. This is considered the main rut and generally occurs over a two-week period, from about November 5 until 20. (These dates are approximate and vary a few days in either direction from year to year.) A few does may come into estrus early or after this period. The late phase of the rut has an effect on buck behavior that hunters should understand and take advantage of.

When the main rut subsides, the mature bucks will have become more comfortable moving during daylight hours, but with the majority of does having been bred, these bucks will now move back to their core areas, if they left them. Since the bucks' testosterone levels are still high, they spend more time searching for and pursuing the few late-estrous does. The tail end of the main rut creates much more competition for the few estrous does that remain. The mature bucks' previous irregular main rut movements with estrous does are now over, and they will go back to their more regular prerut patterns.

The date and intensity of the gun season opener, along with how much property you have available to hunt, will determine whether you are able to experience a natural late-rut to postrut phase. A gun season opener in mid-November in a pressured area will push most late-rut buck activity under the cover of darkness. Also in pressured areas, most bucks are killed during gun season, almost negating the positive aspects of the late rut. This is the case in Michigan in the areas we hunt. In states with a late gun season opener, the last week of November or early December, the postrut should present opportunities for mature bucks even better than the prerut. If there is no gun season during the main rut, the mature bucks move much more regularly during daylight hours, pursuing estrous does. Once the main rut subsides by late November, the mature bucks are accustomed to and more comfortable moving in the daytime than they were prior to it. In areas with light overall hunting pressure, even a mid-November gun season has little effect on natural deer behavior. The same holds true for exclusive areas such as hunt clubs, large leases, large tracts of private land, and even some small tracts that border large areas of property that do not get hunted. These types of areas exist in even the most pressured states. In areas like this, the postrut should happen as we described.

In nonpressured areas, hunting the postrut is exactly like hunting the prerut. The mature bucks are on a daytime routine, with a great deal of movement (just as in the prerut and rut) taking place at midday, between 10:00 A.M. and 2:00 P.M., when bucks are scent-checking their core areas. In nonpressured areas, both mornings and evenings are also good, because the mature bucks have not come to associate danger with those periods. Stick to your stands in primary scrape areas, staging areas, and funnels between bedding areas as long as they show signs of activity.

Unfortunately, because of a mid-November gun season, we have rarely witnessed pronounced late-rut buck behavior in our home state. The gun season in Michigan is simply too intense in the areas we hunt. We have had a great deal of experience and success with this rut phase in less pressured states, however, such as Iowa, Kansas, and Illinois.

CHAPTER 7

December

By December, the main rut is over, although there may be an active second rut. In most states, gun season is over and has taken its toll, and the woods are practically empty of bowhunters, except for the few committed souls willing to brave the elements. Bowhunting now is a test of will, dedication, and endurance, but it is a beautiful time to be in the woods. It is an exhilarating challenge to be able to hunt during extremely cold weather for long periods of time.

KEEPING WARM WHILE COLD-WEATHER HUNTING

The first step to successful hunting in winter is staying warm. With the right clothing and accessories, winter hunting can be an enjoyable experience. When you are warm and comfortable, you can stay on stand longer, increasing your chances of success.

Foremost, because of your proximity to the animals you are hunting, any clothing you wear must be absolutely silent. This factor becomes more critical the colder it gets. To make matters worse, sound travels farther in the winter; with the foliage gone, little exists in the woods to absorb or damper sound. Before we wear any clothing, we test it by hanging it outside in below-freezing temperatures or placing it in a freezer overnight, then rubbing the material together. If the clothing produces any sound, we will not wear it hunting. Most fabrics containing nylon and most waterproof clothing, because of the polyurethane or Teflon membranes, fail this test, though not all do. If the clothing has a deep napped fleece or other quiet fabric on the exterior, it may be deep enough to mask the noise; most microfleece fabrics, however, do not. Many shot opportunities are lost because of noisy clothing at crunch time, and the colder it is, the stiffer the nylon or synthetic membranes become, making them even noisier when you move.

Dressing properly for cold weather will help you tough it out, in comfort, when the mercury drops. Layering your clothes is essential, as it provides you with the flexibility to adjust to both changing weather conditions and your body temperature during the hunt. The clothing required to remain comfortable while sitting on stand for several hours is totally different than that necessary while walking. Layering allows you to adjust your clothing to the conditions, keeping you comfortable in all situations. A single thick, insulated suit just does not cut it. We used to wear all of our clothes when walking to our stands, and though we abandoned that practice years ago, we still see many hunters doing it. Unless it is an extremely short walk to get to your hunting location, your inner layers will become damp with sweat by the time you arrive at your stand. Moisture conducts heat and cold at a much faster rate than air, which means that when you are wet from sweat, you get colder much faster than when you are dry.

Our solution to this problem is simple: We wear as little as possible on the way to our stands, in order to keep our bodies cool, and carry the rest of our clothes in our packs. After we arrive at our stands and are set up, we then change our clothing. Initially, we undress somewhat and allow our upper bodies to cool down from the walk in, and then we replace the upper-body bottom layer, which for walking in was just a long-sleeved T-shirt, with wicking long underwear. We layer over that the rest of our packed-in clothing and place all clothes that we took off in airtight plastic bags to prevent any odors from escaping. Another possibility is changing a couple hundred yards from your stand, and then slowly stalking to the stand to avoid working up a sweat. Whatever you do, it is critical to remain as dry as possible during cold weather. This will increase the time you can remain on stand comfortably. Make sure you get to your stand early enough to allow for the extra time this cooling down and changing process will take. Also, running late to your stand creates more stress and can cause added perspiration.

Let's consider winter clothing from the inside out, the logical order when getting dressed. Start with a layer of moisture-wicking long underwear, top and bottom, and a pair of thin moisture-wicking socks. The next layer should be a light wool sweater or insulated top, a pair of sweatpants or insulated bottoms, and a pair of thick socks. Despite advances in synthetics, wool remains one of the only materials that will keep you warm after becoming damp or wet. During extreme weather, one of these initial top layers should have a turtleneck to keep the wind from going down your neck. The next upper layer is an insulated vest, which provides warmth to the body's core while avoiding bulk that would restrict arm movement. If it is windy, raining, or snowing, we each wear a Scent-Lok liner topped by a Rivers West suit as the exterior layer, along with a Scent-Lok head cover. During extreme weather, the wind will rapidly penetrate any layers, insulated or not, outside the windproof layer and render them ineffective for warmth. Handle any clothing you wear over your Scent-Lok suit just as you would the Scent-Lok suit itself, keeping it odor-free, storing it in a scent-free bag, and wearing it only while actually hunting.

To keep our hands warm, we usually wear noninsulated Scent-Lok gloves. While sitting, the hands can be tucked away in a scent-free, soft, quiet muff. The muff is strapped around the waist once on stand and is totally out of the way during shot opportunities.

Our heads are covered with Spando-Flage face masks followed by Scent-Lok head covers. During extreme weather, we wear over this some sort of insulated caps, usually radar caps with earflaps that can be used if needed, or stocking caps. Since these hats are worn as outside layers, over the Scent-Lok head cover, they must also be kept scent-free.

Very helpful to keeping warm during winter hunting are Grabber air-activated body warmers. These body heat pads have an adhesive backing that you attach to the outside of your innermost layer of clothing. Do not attach them directly to the skin; they produce enough heat to cause minor irritation or even burns. They stay warm (not hot like hand, toe, and other warmers) for twelve hours. When on stand in cold weather, we attach a couple body warmers in various places: on the lower back, in the kidney area, and on the chest. If it gets really cold, a body warmer on each upper leg works wonders. We do not put these on until we are on stand and our bodies have cooled down somewhat. These body warmers are simply amazing and will increase your comfortable sitting time dramatically. Toe warmers for boots, hand warmers for gloves, and foot warmers are also available. Your toes are usually the first thing that gets cold while hunting. A heat source directly over the toes keeps them warm longer in rubber boots and makes hunting far more comfortable.

You can use these adhesive warmers more than once. Because they are air-activated, you can shut them off by pulling them off your clothing, sticking them together, and placing them in an airtight Ziploc bag. To use them again, just pull them out of the bag and reattach them to your clothing. If you follow this procedure, a single warmer can last two or three hunts. Using body warmers can reduce the amount of clothes you have to wear, making hunting more comfortable and increasing both your total time on stand and the time you can spend sitting still.

Rubber boots are a must when hunting scent-free, so your winter clothing arsenal should include a pair with removable pressed wool liners, such as the Glacier Bay model by Ranger. The biggest problem with rubber boots is that they do not allow moisture to escape, causing your socks to become damp from sweat and your feet to get cold. This is yet another compromise to stay scent-free. We minimize the discomfort by making sure that both the boots and liners are dry before we begin hunting; this is done with an electric boot dryer. When we hunt stands that require long walks, we wear plastic bags between our socks and boots. Once on stand, we replace those socks with dry ones that we packed in, putting the damp socks into the plastic bags before placing them in our packs. Our liners and socks are dry, giving us much more time before our feet get cold. When purchasing boots, it is important to know that their temperature ratings are for walking, not sitting.

REMAINING UNDETECTED IN WINTER

Though paying attention to detail is critical at all times of the season, it is most critical while winter hunting. After sitting in freezing temperatures for a few hours, bows tend to make noises that were nonexistent during warmer weather. To find out if your bow has any potential noise problems, leave it outside overnight, and then draw it. Another problem area in cold weather is the arrow rest. Nothing seems to be amplified more in the cold than the sound of an arrow sliding over a rest, and the commonly used plastic covering simply does not suffice with pressured whitetails. We use stick-on fuzzy moleskin padding on our arrow rests. This is the only product we have discovered that allows us to remain silent while drawing our arrows in the extreme cold. Make sure you adjust your sights after adding moleskin, as it may cause you to shoot a few inches higher.

Quiet stands are an absolute must in extremely cold temperatures. Commercial tree stands often creak, and those noises seem to be amplified in cold weather because of the expansion of the metal. Another problem is that the foot platforms hold snow and ice, making it nearly impossible to change your foot placement without making some noise that any deer nearby can hear. Ambush Saddles allow us to hunt without the risk of a noisy stand or crusty snow or ice giving our positions away.

Tree selection is another area of concern while winter hunting. With the lack of foliage at this time of year, many of your early or midseason trees are now less than optimal, for the simple reason that the cover in the woods is gone. When looking for trees to clear out for winter hunting, it is very important to find ones with some background cover. This kind of cover can take the form of other trees behind you or branches on the tree you're in, just as long as you don't have open sky behind you, which will leave your silhouette easy to pick out. Good sources of background cover include large crotches, conifers, and oaks that have held on to their leaves. It will be necessary to hunt somewhat higher, in other types of trees, than earlier in the season. The added height will minimize your chances of getting detected as a result of motion as a deer approaches.

THE SECOND RUT

Several factors contribute to an active second rut. Frequently in areas with a skewed buck-to-doe ratio in favor of the does, as in most pressured areas, a few adult does are not bred during their first estrous cycle. The timing of gun season can affect the intensity of the second rut. The gun season in Michigan opens on November 15, which in most years coincides closely with the peak of the rut. Because the majority of bucks are killed during the first few days and the remaining bucks take on severe nocturnal habits, some does are not bred during their first cycle. Approximately twenty-eight days after a doe's first cycle, she again enters estrus, placing the second rut during mid-December. The biggest factor causing the second rut, however, is doe fawns that have reached puberty. These fawns often enter their first estrous cycle in December. Doe fawns in agricultural areas are more likely to come into estrus during their first season than are those from big-woods areas.

The second rut is far more subtle than the first. With the majority of crops picked and most foliage becoming less palatable, the center of doe activity shifts to the best food sources available, and the bucks follow. This creates more precise destination points and deer that are easier to pattern, but in pressured areas, most movement takes place after dark. The deer, naturally, begin to conserve energy, so there is far less chasing. There also is far less scrape and rub activity, and nearly all of it is done at night. What little signposting bucks engage in usually takes place in travel corridors between bedding and feeding areas.

The second rut is difficult to hunt, particularly if you are pursuing mature bucks in pressured areas. Intense gun-hunting pressure will have pushed any mature bucks that are still alive into a much more nocturnal routine, and even yearlings will move mostly at night. If the pressure subsides a great deal toward the end of gun season and during the first week or so afterward, which is normally the case, bucks will cautiously resume some movement during the day. This shift coincides with a natural shift to daytime movement by all deer during the cold winter periods. Any area you hunt after gun season should offer good ground cover through which a buck will feel comfortable moving during daylight hours.

This twelve-point was taken by John during the second rut, on December 17, 1997.

As with the first rut, hunting the second rut means finding the does. This entails finding travel routes to the best available and most used food sources in the area, as well as pinpointing the route the mature buck is taking. Mature bucks usually use a different route from the one the does take. For instance, John shot a big twelve-point during the second rut in December that followed his own runway, which offered more cover, through the middle of a woodlot instead of taking the well-used travel routes along the edge of the woods like the other deer. Check the main and secondary travel routes to the main food sources for fresh scrapes, rubs, and large tracks. Buck sign, scrapes, rubs, and large tracks in areas without cover were likely made or left during the security of darkness.

If you scouted during the previous postseason and were in the woods in January, you should have a few spots in mind for this time of season. Check these spots for signs of a good buck. Your stand should be positioned at a point where you can get in and out without being detected. This late in the season, spooking deer will be even more detrimental to your hunting than it was before gun season. And again, scent control is absolutely critical.

Although second-rut activity is concentrated on travel routes to and from feeding areas, bucks still demonstrate some normal rut behavior and movement patterns, though far less pronounced than during the main rut. Bucks will still return to staging areas and bedding areas before daylight, and later in the morning get up and scent-check the edges of bedding areas, and travel routes where they intersect bedding areas, for estrous does. As in the prerut and main rut, this movement often takes place between 10:00 A.M. and 2:00 P.M. The best stands for hunting this movement pattern are usually the same ones that were best during the prerut and rut, as long as the main food source has not changed.

POSTRUT WINTER HUNTING

As the rut periods come to a close, all whitetails start feeding heavily again. The deer now move less, yard up in hard winters, and are generally less active until spring.

When postrut winter hunting, food is the key to everything. Find the preferred food and you will find the deer. Travel routes between feeding areas and bedding areas are your best bet. In northern regions, dense cedar swamps are primary feeding and bedding zones in which the deer will stay until spring. You will likely spook deer with your entry, but if the swamp is large enough, other deer may pass by as the day progresses. In agricultural areas, the primary preferred food sources in the winter are picked cornfields, beanfields, hayfields, and winter wheat fields. Large areas of oaks with good acorn mast that was not consumed during the fall will also be key places to find feeding whitetails. Be opportunistic and hunt wherever the deer are currently moving.

PART II

SPECIAL SITUATIONS

CHAPTER 8

Hunting in the Rain

You listen to the local evening weather report in preparation for tomorrow morning's hunt; a cold, steady rain is the forecast. Hoping that the weatherman is wrong, you set the alarm anyway. The alarm goes off, and you get up and look out the window to see a steady rain. The outside thermometer reads 40 degrees. The weatherman was right. The dominant side of your brain tells you that you are not hunting this morning, but the "I'm a dedicated bowhunter" side temporarily overrides it, forcing your body to go through the motions of pacing for several minutes while debating whether to hunt or not to hunt, before you crawl back into your warm bed. Does this sound familiar?

Any dedicated bowhunter knows what it is like spending hours on stand in the rain. First there is a smattering of drops, followed by a steady fall, until eventually water is running down the tree trunk in streams and dripping off branches from above, directly onto your head in exactly the same spot, drop after drop. The mere mention of rain causes most bowhunters to shudder and think about staying home for the day. Depending on the volume of rain, temperature, and wind conditions, hunting in the rain can be one of the most miserable experiences there is, so when it rains, most bowhunters stay out of the woods, sipping coffee in a warm kitchen, knowing deep inside that they should be out there hunting.

But this is unfortunate, because they are missing some of the best hunting to be had. This is a time when a bowhunter's true dedication is tested. Depending on how hard it is raining, your chances of seeing a mature buck can be very good. Mature bucks feel comfortable moving during the daylight in the rain, regardless of the time of season. From the first few days through the October lull and all phases of the rut, the odds of your seeing a mature buck moving in daylight are much higher when it is raining. Through years of observation, we have been astonished at the regularity with which we see bucks in the rain—even in areas with heavy hunting pressure. John hunted one fourteen-point buck for four years and finally shot it in 1997. During that period, he saw it only three times. The first was during a downpour while he was doing some midday in-season scouting; the second was while on stand all day in a steady rain; and the third, the day he arrowed that old buck at straight-up noon, was marked by a sudden snow squall that dropped a couple inches on the ground within an hour. That buck lived in an area that got hunted extremely heavily, and he seemed comfortable moving in the daytime only during periods of precipitation.

Whether buck movement during rain is a natural phenomenon or is caused by the lack of hunters in the woods in pressured areas on rainy days, we are not quite sure. It is likely a combination of both. Bucks tend to move during rainy weather naturally, and because they rarely encounter hunters on these days, they learn to associate rain with safety. When there are no consequences for actions, those actions are likely to become more regular. While this is obviously speculation on our part, our past hunting logs back up these movement patterns and big-buck sightings on rainy days.

That the ability to move in silence over the wet ground also makes mature deer feel more at ease, becomes very obvious when you notice the drastic difference in how they move. On dry, calm days, they take a few steps and then stop to listen and look for any possible predator's reaction to their movement. On days with light drizzle or light rain, mature bucks move with a regular pace and are not concerned about the noise they are making (or not making). There has also been some proof that fresh scent is easier to detect in damp environments. Bloodhounds work best in mildly wet conditions, and as any rabbit hunter can tell you, beagles have a much easier time trailing in damp conditions. Thus during a light rain or drizzle, a whitetail's sense of smell likely becomes more acute.

Rain comes in different intensities. We have found a light drizzle to moderate steady rain to be the best for buck movement. Heavy rain accompanied by heavy wind or thunderstorms will cause deer to lie low. However, they do move just before and after any heavy rainfall. During the

2003 season, Chris had a big mature buck come in under just such circumstances. He was in the woods clearing out a tree on a cold and very windy day. At 11:30 A.M., he was about halfway through clearing out his shooting lanes when the gale suddenly stopped and it began to rain. Chris finished his tree preparation as fast as he could, walked back to his car, and changed into his hunting gear. By 12:30, he was settled into his Ambush Saddle. A steady and relatively heavy rain fell for five hours, during which time he did not see any deer. Then the rain stopped as quickly as it started, and the sun dropped between the clouds and the horizon. It was not five minutes before a doe and two fawns walked right beneath his tree. A few minutes later, two bucks materialized in the tall grass of an overgrown pasture. Both bucks carried eight points, the first a good-size yearling, and the second a heavy-beamed mature animal with at least a twenty-inch inside spread. The yearling passed easily within range, but the big boy moved through just out of range. Both bucks passed unscathed. Both of us have had other, similar experiences.

According to the logs we have kept over the years, more than 30 percent of our sightings of mature bucks (three and a half years and older) in our extremely pressured home state of Michigan have been during rain or snow. This is an extraordinary number, considering that only a small percent of our hunting takes place on such days. For this reason, we go out of our way to hunt on most rainy days—exactly the opposite of what most hunters do. Hunters that have the privilege of hunting nonpressured areas for whitetails rarely hunt in the rain, because they do not have to do so to take big bucks. But if you hunt pressured areas, rather than dread the rain, keep in mind just how well bucks move in such weather.

There was a time when hunting in the rain required suffering. For years, there just was not any raingear that was quiet enough for bowhunting; everything contained PVC, which is noisy and stiff. For durability in all hunting applications, manufacturers used nylon exteriors over the PVC, adding to the noise factor. The best we could do in those days was to wear wool, which retains some insulating qualities when wet. This meant we would get wet, but as long as it was not too cold, we would remain on stand as long as we could hold out. Modern waterproof membranes and exterior fabric technology have changed this situation dramatically.

Raingear for bowhunting has to fulfill several criteria. First, it has to keep you dry. Second, it has to be quiet. Third, it has to allow freedom of movement. Fourth, it should not cause you to sweat, making you soaked from the inside out. And fifth, it must be durable. These are the biggest problems that raingear manufacturers have had to overcome.

Well over 90 percent of all modern hunting rainwear offers two types of waterproof membranes: polyurethane and Teflon. The rest is PVC-lined or made from a Tyvek-type material that is best known as a house wrap. Unlike PVC, polyurethane and Teflon membranes offer freedom of movement. Both of these materials are also noisy, but they are attached to the inside of quiet fabrics, such as polyester fleece or microfabric (brushed polyester). The key to making a suit quiet is to have enough depth or loft to the exterior fabric to mask the noise of the membrane underneath.

"Waterproof" and "breathable" are two words that should never be used in the same sentence, let alone next to each other. The tests used to label a waterproof suit as being "breathable" are rather meaningless. They are no more than simple vapor transfer tests that practically any materials other than rubber and cellophane could pass. There are no waterproof suits that you can blow air through. They are either waterproof or breathable (permeable); they cannot be both. Any waterproof suit can be used as a windproof suit during cold, windy days for exactly that reason: It does not allow airflow through it. To test this concept, we took a brand-name noninsulated, "waterproof, breathable" jacket and draped it over a big three-speed fan. We turned the fan on high and lit a match on the other side. The flame never flickered. We then turned the jacket over to test airflow from the other direction, and the results were the same. Even though the fan was so powerful that it made the jacket look like half of a balloon, not enough air passed through it to alter the flame of the burning match. Breathability of any waterproof suit has to come through venting, consisting of visible openings that allow airflow.

JOHN'S RAINY-DAY ELEVEN-POINT

B ack in 1975, there was no quiet waterproof clothing for bowhunting up close. The only rainwear available at that time was extremely noisy and uncomfortable. I worked at a local sporting-goods store at the time and tried to keep up on all the latest technology in hunting gear. Because of the lack of adequate waterproof apparel, however, when I went bowhunting in the rain, I wore quiet cotton work coveralls over whatever layers were needed underneath to try to keep warm. During heavy rainfalls, I got drenched, and if it was cold out, I would usually get sick and then spend the remainder of the season hunting with a severe cold or flu. I loved bowhunting and the mystique of the white-tailed deer that much and still do.

It was raining hard that cold November Saturday morning. When the alarm went off and I looked out the window, I started to shiver just thinking about what I was going to do. But it was my day off, and I was going hunting no matter what. The positive experiences I had had hunting in the rain up to that point were few, but I was still hungry to learn as much about hunting under adverse conditions as possible.

Because of the heavy rain, I had to choose a location where a deer would be relatively easy to find without a blood trail—a place without thick undergrowth for quite a distance. By the time I got to the base of the big oak I was going to hunt from, I was soaked from the waist down from walking about half a mile through tall, wet weeds and ferns.

This hunting location was unique. The large oak served as a single-tree funnel between a thirty-five-year-old mature white pine plantation that was totally open underneath the canopy and a mature hardwood forest consisting mostly of small pin oaks, with short ferns that the deer bedded in. The big oak stood alone about twenty yards from the pines and fifteen yards from the corner of the woods. On the other two sides were old hayfields that had not been cut in years and were now weed fields. The normal deer pattern was to feed in the weed fields at night and go into the pines at daybreak, mill around there, and exit into the woods later in the morning.

By 8:30, I was soaked to the bone and starting to get cold chills. A couple does and a spike had come out the back side of the pines and crossed the smaller weed field at about 8:20, but other than that moment of excitement, it had been a miserable morning. At 9:10, a six-point exited the pines and crossed the small weed field. I decided to stick it out until 9:30, which was about an hour and a half earlier than I normally would leave, but I did not think I could tolerate the cold any longer than that.

At 9:20, a very respectable buck stepped out of the pines, following a runway that went within five yards of the base of my tree. I was not very high up in the oak, maybe eighteen feet, and it had lost most of its leaves. When walking in the rain, deer tend to keep their heads lower to keep the rain out of their eyes, making a hunter in an open tree with no background less likely to get spotted. As the buck slowly walked toward me through the twenty-yard gap, he kept his head down as expected. As he passed by at five yards, I took the shot. The hit looked good. The arrow should have passed through the top of the buck's right lung and the center of his left lung.

The buck turned and ran across the smaller weed field, which was about one hundred yards across, and disappeared into the woods on the other side. Any time a lung-shot deer goes more than one hundred yards, I question whether both lungs were hit. My adrenaline was pumping, and I was not feeling very cold anymore, but I knew I had to give that buck some time in case only one lung was hit.

After thirty minutes, I could not wait any longer. I was cold again and had to start looking. I climbed down, pulled the arrow out of the ground, and inspected it. The rain had not yet washed all the frothy blood from the arrow. I had watched where the buck entered the woods, and now I went right to that spot to start looking for blood and farther ahead for a carcass. Within fifty yards, I saw the buck lying in the ferns with his head up. He was looking at me and trying to get up. At a distance of twenty yards, I nocked an arrow and shot the buck again through the chest. His head went down, and after several minutes, he expired. Upon inspecting the fine eleven-point, I found that my first arrow had passed through the top of the buck's right lung and the center of the left lung. It was without a doubt a good wet hunt, with a fine eleven-point as a reward.

John's 1975 eleven-point, which he took without wearing any raingear.

Over the years, we have had many rainwear products tear or get punctured very easily. It can happen while walking to and from stands in the dark, crossing fences, going through briers, or climbing trees. A couple years ago, Chris even poked a quarter-size hole in his neoprene waders while crossing an icy river in late November. Needless to say, the rest of his day hunting was a great deal more uncomfortable than usual.

For years, we have worn our nonwaterproof Scent-Lok suits as our outer layer and carried a packable, lightweight, semiquiet waterproof suit in our packs if rain was in the forecast. We put these on only if it started to rain. We have kept away from the all-in-one waterproof carbon-lined suits for several reasons. The main reason is that it rains only occasionally, and it would not make sense to wear nonbreathable raingear when it is perfectly dry most of the time. A second reason is that they are only semiquiet. Another huge problem is that the heat needed to reactivate the carbon liner will eventually delaminate the taped seams of the waterproof membrane, ruining the suit's waterproof capabilities.

Scent-Lok and Scent Blocker both make three-in-one rain suits with zip-out camouflaged carbon liners that can be worn as exterior garments when it is not raining. This allows the use of the outer rain shell only when it is necessary, and the inner suit can be reactivated as needed without ruining the waterproofing of the outer.

Rivers West's H2P all-weather hunting apparel is a product that, for us, has revolutionized hunting not only in the rain but also in the cold and wind. Developed in the rain-rich Northwest, it has several qualities that make it perfect for bowhunters. Most important, it is completely waterproof, and its stitch design eliminates the need for taping seams. The H2P fabric is also extremely quiet and very puncture-resistant. It has awesome tensile strength and four-way stretch similar to Lycra. It is naturally windproof as well, so we often wear it as an outer layer in wind or other cold weather. The deep fleece on the inside of the membrane makes the suit very warm, actually too warm for wearing in temperatures much over 50 degrees. This clothing also allows some airflow through venting so that perspiration can evaporate. A problem we had with other raingear was getting it dry after wearing it; not so with Rivers West's apparel. We can put this clothing in the dryer without fear of delaminating any taped seams, because there are none. It is also machine washable. Rivers West's waterproof systems are superior to any other raingear we have ever used.

In early November 2004, John decided to go bowhunting in Missouri. After purchasing a couple plat books for the area he wanted to hunt, he made some phone calls and received permission to hunt an eighty-acre parcel. During the first day, while scouting the property and preparing some trees to hunt from, he spooked a wide ten-point with a doe out of a small bedding area and watched them run across a large picked cornfield. That was the buck he would pursue. Sign from this and other bucks was very prevalent on the parcel, but there were no primary scrape areas or funnels of heavy traffic to focus on. After setting up three trees to hunt from, John was ready to start hunting the next morning. The weather forecast predicted rain for the next few days, and when he woke up before dawn, it was indeed raining.

Whenever John leaves his home state of Michigan to hunt in one of the known big-buck states, it would take a tornado to keep him out of his tree. After settling into his Ambush Saddle an hour and a half before first light, he hunkered down for the beginning of what was to be four days of gut-wrenching sitting from before daylight until dark.

The first morning, he sat in what he thought was the best of the trees he had prepared. By noon, he had seen just one doe and two fawns—time to move. He moved to another tree and was settled in by 1:00 P.M. That afternoon, several small bucks passed within fifteen yards. The second day was a carbon copy of the first, as far as the weather was concerned. It rained on and off all day. But having moved to a different tree away from the core bedding area dramatically changed what John saw. A big half-rack walked right under his tree just after first light, and at about 9:00 A.M., he saw what he thought was the big ten-point with a doe about 120 yards away in some tall weeds. They were not coming in John's direction, so he decided to try to rattle him in. The buck immediately responded to the rattle bag and came within 25 yards before stopping and offering John a perfect shot opportunity. It was a beautiful nine-point, which John reluctantly passed on. At midday, he moved back to the tree he was in the previous evening and saw the same few smaller bucks.

The third morning, John returned to the tree from the previous evening and stayed there all day. It was still raining on and off the entire day, with the temperature hanging around 40 degrees. He saw seven bucks that day: six smaller ones and, late in the morning, the big ten-point chasing a doe in the area of the tree John had been in the previous morning. It did not take him long the next morning to figure out what tree he was going to hunt from. Every buck he had seen near the one tree was a big one, and every buck he had seen near the other was a small one, and the smaller bucks never even wandered in the direction of the other tree.

The fourth morning, John again woke up to see rain out the window of the motel room. He was getting pretty worn out from the all-day sits in the rain, but he wanted that big buck. Perched in his saddle before daylight, he could hear a buck chasing a doe in the nearby standing corn. The buck would chase her for thirty seconds or so, and then John would not hear anything for the next five or ten minutes. This went on until daylight, and the noise kept getting closer to his hunting location just twenty-five yards from the corner of the field. By daylight, they were within one hundred yards of John's tree. At 7:30, the doe busted out of the corn and stopped about forty yards away in some tall weeds. John was pleasantly surprised when the big ten-point ran out of the corn right in front of him in an attempt to circle around the doe and push her back into the standing corn. At a distance of twenty yards and broadside, while at full draw, John blatted to stop the buck. The shot was good, and after running about one hundred yards, the buck expired. He had ten very symmetrical points and a twenty-two-inch inside spread. John had worn his Rivers West Ambush Jacket and Trail Pants all four days in the cold and rain and stayed dry and warm the entire time. It was nice to be able to wash and dry the suit each night. Having to get back into clothing with a wet exterior is not very comfortable.

Rain presents you with a golden opportunity that you should take advantage of, regardless of the time of season, especially if you are hunting pressured property. Watch the weather forecast, and when it calls for a light rain all day, make plans to get out hunting. Even during the early part of the season, when mature bucks tend to be more nocturnal, there is a good chance that they will be moving. Before the rut phases, hunt feeding areas that offer perimeter cover. During the rut phases, protected feeding areas and rut-hunting locations can be productive in the rain. Despite the rain, you still have to practice extreme caution with scent control, or you can contaminate a good spot and cause mature bucks and does to avoid it later.

Proof that hunting in the rain is productive: John took this ten-point after several days of sitting in the rain, from daylight until dark.

One distinct disadvantage when hunting in the rain is that the water will eventually wash away a blood trail. Depending on the volume of rain coming down and the terrain, blood-trailing deer in the rain can be difficult to nearly impossible. Close shots with a good double-lung hit are a must. Even under the worst conditions, a double-lung-hit deer should be easy to recover if you know the area you are hunting.

In the early season, hidden food sources, such as a stand of oaks or an apple tree near a bedding area, are particularly good rainy-day spots. One evening during a steady daylong light rain, Chris shot a mature eleven-point on a travel route to a protected food source. Any spot in the core area of a mature buck that you have somewhat patterned is a good bet. During a light rain, deer movement in the morning will likely be a little later than normal and will usually continue throughout the entire day in an area that offers cover. This means that all-day hunting is a good bet when it rains. If you cannot hunt all day, try to remain on stand until at least 2:00 P.M. If you cannot get out early, hunt in midday, from 9:00 A.M. to 3:00 P.M. If you can hunt only in the evening, get on stand as early as possible, as deer generally move earlier than normal on rainy evenings. During the prerut and rut, get to your best stands—those in primary scrape areas and staging areas—and plan on spending the whole day. The mature bucks will be moving and, with luck, may come by your location. The bottom line is, big bucks move under certain rainy conditions, and you should be out there.

CHAPTER 9

All-Day Hunting

Whenever our time constraints allow and the seasonal timing and conditions are right, we hunt all day. We definitely consider all-day hunting to be one of the most important tactics in the pursuit of mature pressured bucks. Although this is one of the most talked-about methods to hunt whitetails, it is the most seldom practiced. The vast majority of bowhunters just will not sit all day, and some just can't. And we admit fully that it is extremely difficult to remain on stand from dark to dark. Sitting in one spot for up to sixteen hours requires willpower, special preparation, and planning. Hunting all day can vary from being full of action to being quite boring. It is, however, always a test of your desire to give every last effort to tag the mature buck that you know is in the area.

The first step to hunting all day is to understand why you should attempt such an endurance marathon in the first place. All deer have a pattern that involves midday movement throughout the entire year. Midday movement is particularly important during the rut phases. It goes largely unnoticed by hunters, however, because much of this movement takes place in areas of good cover or very close to bedding areas. As a prey species, deer are naturally shy animals that feel most comfortable around some sort of cover. When they live in heavily hunted areas and relate humans to danger, their need to be in or very near cover increases during daylight hours. The amount of daytime deer movement and, particularly, the distance deer travel at this time relate directly to the amount of hunting pressure in a given area.

During midday, deer usually feed or move, but they are not usually visible in the open, where they could be seen from cars or by hunters in open areas. As the season progresses, this midday movement continues, though the amount of movement, particularly that of mature bucks, fluctuates widely. The October lull sees a general reduction in midday movement, caused by both hunting pressure and the dramatic opening of the woods when the trees and underbrush lose their foliage, making once secure areas clearly visible to predators. The drop in daytime activity continues until the rut begins to kick in. During the prerut and rut, the deer's daytime movement pattern increases dramatically, reaching its pinnacle during the main rut. Mature bucks are often on their feet at midday, either traveling with does in estrus or scent-checking and searching for them. This will generally be the case in both pressured and nonpressured areas.

In pressured areas, a mature buck's movement pattern during the rut stages is usually as follows: The buck returns to a staging area or bedding area half an hour to an hour and a half before daylight. He beds down, or stages, for a passing estrous doe. If a doe passes that is in or close to her estrous cycle, the buck rises and pursues that doe. If a doe that arouses his interest does not pass through, that buck gets up, usually sometime between 10:00 A.M. and 2:00 P.M., and scent-checks the perimeters of the bedding areas in his core area, or the bedding areas themselves, for any possible estrous does that may have passed by earlier that morning. In doing so, he follows the route with the most cover from bedding area to bedding area. Interestingly, when mature bucks move during midday, they always seem to have an agenda, or certain destination points and routes, in mind. They move very steadily through the woods, seeming almost oblivious to their surroundings. The steady pace and determination are a great departure from a mature buck's usual attitude of extreme caution. In the afternoon, the buck beds down again until dark, at which time he resumes his search for estrous does.

THE FREELANCE BUCK: JOHN'S 2001 EIGHT-POINT

In mid-November 2001, I had the opportunity to freelance-hunt a new area. The afternoon of my arrival, I hastily headed into the woods, wearing complete scent-control armor, and cleared out a tree in the first good spot I could find. The tree was situated in a nice-looking, but somewhat wide, funnel. I worked as expediently and quietly as possible. My plan was to hunt from this tree the next morning.

True to plan, I was comfortably resting in my Ambush Saddle an hour and a half before daylight. To bring any bucks within shooting range, I set up my Carrylite decoy, positioning it broadside about fifteen yards away from the base of the tree. Just after daylight, I attempted a short rattling sequence, with no response. At noon, I left the woods, taking the decoy with me. Midday was spent in a nearby area where I thought I would find excellent deer sign. My exploratory scouting, however, did not reveal much interesting sign, so I decided to hunt the same tree that evening. Though hunting a stand twice in a row is normally counter to my usual tactics, on short-term hunts you can bend the rules a bit, as long as you practice strict scent control.

Just as the sun was beginning to set, I attempted another rattling sequence. A few minutes later, a large, tall-tined eight-point sneaked into view, looking for the two combatants. This buck was obviously a shooter. He was very cautious, however, and would not come close. He circled and remained out of range before vanishing back into the woods. For this evening hunt, I had left my decoy behind. If I had set up the decoy, the buck probably would have come into shooting range. I was a bit frustrated at my mistake but also spurred on by the sight of such a nice buck, which was the only deer I had seen to that point.

With visions of that big buck in my head, the next day I felt as if I had no choice but to do some in-season scouting. This was a new area for me, and it required a more thorough inspection. I set out to become more familiar with the layout of the land, with hopes of encountering that buck once more. Being careful with scent control, I began by walking the edge of a very open mature hardwood forest with mostly maples and beeches on one side and tall grassy growth scattered with brush and old treetops from a recent cutting on the other. The brushy weedy side was clearly the local deer herd's predominant bedding area.

Not too far down the edge, I came across the type of sign I had been looking for since my arrival in the new spot. There, in a slightly more open zone, was an active primary scrape area. This primary scrape area was much larger than what I was used to seeing. It was about seventy yards long and thirty yards wide, with about a dozen active scrapes. There were also at least that many large rubs scattered within its boundaries. This spot was different from the rest of the area. It was a little more open, with less canopy cover blocking the sunlight, allowing the undergrowth to grow a bit taller. It also had everything mature bucks look for in a primary scrape area: excellent perimeter cover, small trees to rub and make scrapes under, and good doe traffic passing through along the terrain edge. This spot was so hot that it was easy to smell the scent of rutting bucks.

Though it was a great point for bucks, I was faced with a problem: There were only two trees large enough to hunt from. The best one, from a cover standpoint, was simply out of position. It was in the middle but off to the side and did not allow a shot to both sides of the primary scrape area. The second tree provided little cover but was the only one from which any deer passing through the area would be within shooting distance, and it was on the south end of the scrape area. The choice was made. I would just have to get up in that tree at least thirty feet. I had one of my freelance packs for setting up trees with me and proceeded to set it up right then. Fortunately, there was not much brush to cut while opening up shooting lanes. This meant less disturbance for the deer to notice, and I did not have my extendable pole saw with me for heavy cutting. Since this location appeared to be better suited for morning hunting, I departed immediately after the tree was finished. That evening, I hunted a different tree in the area I had scouted the day before but did not see a single deer.

The next morning at 4:00 A.M., my alarm clock roused me from a very poor night's sleep. I was so excited to have the opportunity to hunt such a hot, active primary scrape area that all night I kept waking and looking at the clock, waiting for it to go off. I felt like a teenager about to hunt for the first time. Even with four decades of hunting experience, I still have trouble sleeping before I am about to hunt great-looking spots. I guess when the excitement fades it will be time to hang up my bow. After emerging from my blankets, the first thing I did was check the temperature and wind condition. It was going to be a very crisp morning. The temperature was slightly below 20 degrees F and there was no wind. I dressed for the cold as quickly as I could and soon was on my way to my new tree.

Even though I arrived at the tree nearly two hours before first light, I still spooked several deer from the immediate area. This bothered me, because the reason for my early arrival was to avoid spooking deer, but at least there was time for things to settle before daylight. As night gave way to morning, I could again see the scrapes. Even though it was the main rut, the scrapes were being torn up. The mere sight of them filled me with even more excitement and optimism for the hunt. I decided to attempt a rattling sequence.

Shortly after a short, aggressive roll of my rattle bag, a tall-tined yearling four-point carefully slid in to check things out. The little buck inspected a few scrapes with his nose, and then exited from the direction in which he had come. It was fun to watch the four-point, but while watching him, I began to have second thoughts about my rattling attempt. In my excitement, I had made a beginner's mistake; now I was regretting my decision. The mature buck I was pursuing had responded to a rattling sequence only two days earlier, without seeing any other deer, and cautiously moved out of the area. Now I was sitting on his home turf, taking a chance at spooking him with another rattling sequence. Not smart, especially without using a decoy for a visual attractant. I was extremely upset with myself. An active primary scrape area should always be hunted clean on the first hunt; never give the dominant buck any reason to alter his normal routine.

But the large, dominant eight-point must not have heard my rattling. At about 8:00 A.M., I was still grumbling to myself, when his antlers came into view at the north end of the scrape area. The muscular buck strutted in as if he owned the place. As he moved closer, he stopped to freshen one of the larger scrapes, not twenty-five yards in front of me. He tossed up some dirt with his front hooves and sparred with the overhanging branches, sweeping his antlers back and forth. I could clearly see that he was marking the licking branches with his forehead and preorbital glands. Though my bow was already in hand and I was concentrating on a developing shot situation, I watched the buck work the scrape, hoping to come away with new insight into deer behavior. Having a big, wild mature buck so close and completely unaware of your presence is a rare occurrence; as a hunter, you should attempt to learn as much from those rare moments as you can. The buck was obviously not in a hurry, and the show lasted several minutes. Finally contented with his work, he stepped back from the scrape and walked straight toward me. At a distance of fifteen yards, and still in cover, he stopped to survey his surroundings. He tested the air, and then lowered his head to pass under a low-hanging branch in a patch of brush. Through the brush, the buck chose a runway that would bring him broadside in a matter of steps.

I had not been paying much attention to the wind, but as the buck was standing there, I realized that he was directly downwind. But my Scent-Lok suit worked again. The buck moved a couple more steps forward. I allowed him to move a few yards, until he was quartering slightly away, before I drew my bow. At full draw, I blatted to get him to stop. I concentrated fully on the shot, and my arrow found its mark, exactly where I had aimed. The buck spun and bounded back in the direction from which he had come, right across the scrape he had just freshened. After covering about fifty yards, he suddenly stopped. All I could see was his antlers above the brush. For a few seconds, the antlers remained motionless, but then they began to sway and in a flash simply vanished in the tall weeds. That was the end.

Collecting my thoughts, emotions, and equipment, I decided to sit in my tree for about another half hour before recovering the buck. The hunt had been exciting and I wanted to savor the moment. It felt good to have a freelance hunt come together so well. Finally, with my feet on the ground, I picked up my arrow, which was at the beginning of a blood trail that any five-year-old child could have followed. I did not have to look for blood, though; I knew where the buck was lying, so I just walked to the last patch of brush. Arriving at the downed buck, I was pleasantly surprised to find that he was bigger than I had thought, in both antler and body size. He had a dressed weight of 222 pounds after hanging for two days.

This was a hunt where everything came together despite a few minor mistakes. It reinforced for me the importance of primary scrape areas in the pursuit of mature bucks during the rut phases. It was also a good example of a mature buck's vulnerability during the rut, which may be the only time of the season when it is possible to catch him moving during daylight.

After adjusting his position, John was able to take this big eight-point.

It is important to note that these pressured mature bucks remain bedded or in cover while the majority of deer activity is taking place and most bowhunters are in the woods. The exception is the midday movement. The mature bucks have learned that it is dangerous to move in the morning or evening and generally do so only when pursuing estrous does. This is often a direct reaction to hunting pressure. Mature bucks are very aware of the average bowhunter's time frame and adjust accordingly. In pressured areas, the very few that live beyond their first hunting season will begin to assume this routine by their second year. This minor adjustment in behavior is why most mature bucks in pressured areas have reached maturity in the first place.

In nonpressured areas, the major difference in mature buck activity is the amount of daytime movement. Instead of returning to bed before daylight, the buck may not return to his bedding area or staging area until well into the morning. Or he may just continue moving, searching for estrous does, throughout the midday. This buck covers exactly the same areas as the pressured buck. The nonpressured buck is also more likely to be up and moving before the onset of darkness. Bucks that live in areas with little pressure, or extremely controlled pressure, such as on large QDM properties, can live to maturity without becoming quite so nocturnal. On managed properties, until a buck reaches maturity, he experiences no negative consequences when confronted with hunters and therefore loses some of his fear of humans. He may eventually spook from a slight hint of human odor or seeing a human, but this most likely will not happen until he has totally confirmed the intrusion, whereas in pressured areas, mature bucks spook instantly at any hint of human presence.

Bowhunters should attempt to have this buck movement pattern ingrained in their hunting thought pattern and make every effort to exploit this one major weakness. Mature pressured bucks are very nocturnal, even during the rut, and this midday movement pattern is often their only point of vulnerability. Taking advantage of this pattern is a key element to success in pressured areas. Hunting this pattern naturally works very well in nonpressured areas as well.

Location is important when planning an all-day hunt. Some hunting locations just do not make the cut as all-day stands. Forget about field edges or open areas; mature bucks will remain in the thickest cover possible as they make their daily rounds, unless they are actually scent-trailing an estrous doe.

In selecting your stands, the first thing to consider is destination points. Where will a mature buck be looking for a doe? The best destination points are primary scrape areas, which are always located in high-traffic areas. As does approach estrus, they gravitate toward primary scrape areas. Since all the bucks and does in a given area know where these are, they check them or loiter near them regularly. We have witnessed this behavior often. A single mature doe shows up at a primary scrape area and just lingers. She knows a mature buck will eventually visit the area, and if she leaves her scent there, he will follow it when he shows up. If, for some reason, you cannot hunt a primary scrape area, the next best bet is the most direct travel route to it. Another good bet is staging areas. Bucks stage in the morning, scent-check during midday, and sometimes stage again in the afternoon, waiting for does to pass out of bedding areas. Another good location is along the edge of a bedding area that has some sort of travel connection to other nearby bedding areas. Bucks scent-check these edges in pursuit of estrous does. If you have none of these options available, hunt an isolated food source, such as fruit-bearing apple trees or mast-bearing oaks located in cover. Does are often up and feeding during midday and could attract a mature buck.

Successful all-day hunting also requires that you hunt at the right time of year. All-day hunting a primary scrape area before it is active is a waste of time. The time to spend some long hours in the woods is when your primary scrape areas are active. Hunting all day does not simply mean the more hours you put in, the better; it means optimizing your hunting time at your best high-traffic spots that offer cover. This will increase your chances for success. You should be in your stand at least an hour and a half before daylight to assure that you are settled before a mature buck returns to bed. During your approach and departure, you need to remain as undetected as possible by any deer feeding or moving in the immediate area. We hate to repeat ourselves, but early arrivals, midday hunting, and avoiding spooking the deer are so critical to success that they cannot be overstated.

All-day hunting requires rigorous attention to detail and preparation. The first thing to consider is comfort. If you are not comfortable, you will be miserable, and the time on stand will crawl by. Comfort begins with your clothing. Prepare for any weather situation. If there is any hint of rain in the forecast, take your raingear along, and carry extra warm underlayers in your pack in case of a sudden drop in temperature. Also carry several Grabber adhesive body, hand, and toe warmers, which will provide extra warmth to get you through.

Another item of critical importance is food. In addition to snacks such as granola bars, chocolate bars, and apples, take along some sort of lunch on all-day hunts. We're not talking about a full meal; carry just enough to get you through the day. Jerky, small sandwiches, Vienna sausages, or anything else easy to eat with good nutritional value is fine. Everything must be kept in bags both before and after you eat.

Also carry along water. Water is crucial to your overall comfort, but limit intake to an absolute minimum. Keeping water consumption low lessens nature's call. It is also important to carry a bottle to pee in so as not to leave any scent in the woods. If you need to move your bowels, you'll need to get down and go as far downwind of your location as possible. Dig a hole with a stick and cover it up when you are finished.

Hunting for us is never dull, so we tend to be on constant alert. We do not carry anything that could distract us from the activity around us. This means no magazines or books. The fact that a big mature buck could step out at any second keeps us on our toes.

Adjustment is not completely ruled out when you hunt all day, however. You are not limited to the tree you selected in the morning. Most of the time we stick it out in one spot, but not always. If the situation dictates, it is perfectly acceptable to change trees. If you have been in a tree from a couple hours before daylight until 2:00 P.M. and have not seen a deer, changing locations is probably a good idea. Or if you notice a spot where all the deer entered a bedding area in the morning, and you will be able to cut them off as they leave in the afternoon, by all means adjust. When you decide to move, do so in a manner that will cause as little disturbance as possible. Stalk though the woods if you have to.

Another trick we employ to get through the day is a little movement. In most places we hunt, there is a noticeable lull in deer movement between 2:00 and 3:30 P.M. During this time, we sometimes climb out of our trees, sneak to the area most unlikely for deer to travel through, and stretch out or even lie down for a couple minutes. Climbing down will limber up your muscles, which will be stiff from half a day on stand, and get your blood flowing again. Only a few minutes of movement will rejuvenate your sore body and help your waning concentration. This short break can make your afternoon hunt more bearable.

Midday hunting is a key element to success on mature pressured bucks. In 2003, two of the six mature bucks Chris saw while bowhunting in Michigan were seen at midday, between 11:00 A.M. and 12:30 P.M. It always feels good to see a big buck moving comfortably through the woods at midday while most of the other hunters are elsewhere eating lunch. If you give all-day hunting a serious try, you may be impressed with the results.

CHAPTER 10

Hunting on the Ground

Although we hunt primarily from trees, and this is our preferred method of bowhunting, we do not limit ourselves to this method of hunting. In fact, when John started bowhunting in the early 1960s, hunting from trees was illegal in Michigan. He spent his first ten years bowhunting from the ground. The ability to adjust to ever-changing circumstances is a virtue in bowhunting, so hunting from the ground should be included in your arsenal. Bowhunting can, without question, be more productive from the ground at times. If the area or specific location you are hunting does not offer any trees large enough to hunt from, set up a ground blind. It is better to see one deer while hunting on the ground and get a shot opportunity than to see a hundred deer and not get an opportunity from a tree because you were sitting too low and exposed.

We cannot even begin to count the number of tree stands we have walked by that were hung ten to fourteen feet high and offered absolutely no cover. Hunting from a stand that is so low in a tree is a definite disadvantage. Living and hunting in a state with bowhunter numbers hovering around 350,000 each year, we cannot imagine how a mature buck—or any mature deer, for that matter—could be taken from such exposed stands with any consistency. A whitetail's peripheral vision is very keen. A hunter in a pressured area is not likely to get away with the movement required to make a shot from such a low platform without cover. Any deer that is more than ten yards away will be able to see the hunter in its direct line of sight. In nonpressured areas, a hunter may be able to get away with this, but even on the few occasions we have traveled out of state and hunted in nonpressured areas, we could never bring ourselves to hunt that low without cover. If you are not prepared to hunt high enough in a tree to get out of the deer's peripheral vision, it is simply better to hunt on the ground where you can use cover to your advantage.

In some situations and areas, hunting from the ground is your only option. One such place is in large cattail marshes, which provide the best hunting in some of the areas we have access to. In the spring, thoroughly scout every such marsh that you have on your hunting property. You might be surprised to find small, dry islands that are secure bedding areas. Sometimes the main entry and exit points to such a marsh are quite some distance from any huntable tree, or they are on property you don't have access to. In this case, it is time to think about hunting on the ground.

Even though you found these spots in late spring, it is impossible to prepare a blind until fall. In the early fall, while practicing extreme scent control, find a spot fifteen to twenty yards off the side of the runway to which you would like to shoot, preferably on the downwind side in reference to the prevailing wind direction. In that spot, clear out a three- to four-foot-diameter circle down to the bare dirt so that you will not make any noise while on stand. From this point, clear two lanes in a V shape to the runway. One of those lanes is a spotting lane, and the other is a shooting lane. Keep in mind when you do this that deer's peripheral vision is incredible, particularly at ground level. You have to make absolutely sure that you have enough cover between yourself and the deer to remain undetected. Move some cattails around if necessary; be creative, and make sure the cover is where you need it.

When you hunt such a spot, wear a camouflage pattern designed for such cover. A lighter brown or tan pattern with high definition is best. Your normal tree-stand camouflage pattern will generally be too dark for such a spot, causing you to stick out like a sore thumb. This is also a place to consider using a pop-up blind, which can be excellent in this situation, both as general camouflage and to cover up your movements.

In pressured areas, we reserve hunting these marshy spots for prime time, during the prerut and rut, and for short-term hunts. Even while practicing extreme scent control, you will most likely be able to get away with only a few hunts before the deer notice your presence and begin avoiding that entry point into the marsh. These cattail marsh stands have to be hunted initially in the morning. It is practically impossible to sneak into such a spot in the afternoon and remain undetected. Arrive an hour and a half before daylight, and then remain on stand until at least midday, or all day if you can. This way you will not spook any deer returning to bed down just before daylight, and you will be set up in a bedding area, which can be very productive during any of the rut phases. A marsh often has so many runways that it resembles a maze, and because of their excellent cover, bucks will scour them in pursuit of estrous does during the rut phases. The actual shot procedure is simple. When the buck you want passes the spotting lane, draw and get ready to shoot. When he steps into the other lane, shoot.

Another area where it can be better to hunt on the ground is in cornfields. Some of the areas we hunt have corn in abundance. One way to hunt these fields is by stalking. To stalk the deer in corn with much hope of success, you have to wait for days with high winds, heavy rain, or both—generally the ugliest weather possible. These are days when sitting in a tree is unlikely to lead to success. It is time to change gears, adjust, and take advantage of an otherwise difficult situation. In such weather, most deer remain bedded during daylight, and depending on what the area offers in bedding areas and the size and height of the available corn, a lot of this bedding takes place in standing corn.

Deer just do not like to move in heavy wind or heavy rain. Both conditions diminish the sharpness of their most important senses. Wind causes a lot of movement in the trees, thus limiting the deer's sense of sight. Heavy wind and rain are loud, hindering their ability to hear approaching predators. And scent is either blowing by quickly or being diluted into the ground, either of which makes the scent dissipate more rapidly than normal, hindering their all-important sense of smell. In short, extreme weather conditions weaken the deer's defenses. This is an excellent opportunity for us, as predators. When the wind is howling, forget your tree stands and get into the corn. The best fields in which to stalk are the biggest ones you can find that have woods surrounding them or are bordered on several sides by travel routes or swales. When deer have destination points at opposite ends of a field, they are more likely to bed in that field than in fields that are essentially dead ends.

Cornfields are relatively easy to stalk. Starting across the rows and into the wind, slowly stick your head into the aisle between two rows and look in both directions. If you don't see anything, carefully step into that aisle, then poke your head between the next two rows and look in both directions. Scan the corn directly in front of you for deer as well. Move as silently as you can and as slowly as possible, always scanning to the sides and forward. Eventually, when you least expect it, a deer will be bedded in one of the aisles. If the deer is a shooter, step back a couple rows and silently stalk into shooting range. When you are within shooting range, draw your bow, step into the aisle the deer is in, and shoot. If the deer you spot is not a shooter, move back a couple rows and stalk away from the deer, counting your steps as you do so. When you are far enough away that you think you can safely cross the aisle with the bedded deer, do so. Move a couple rows forward, stalk back the same number of steps to the point where you left off, then continue forward in the same manner as before. Whenever you spot a deer, take a few minutes to carefully scan the area. Anywhere one deer is bedded, there will usually be others nearby. During the rut, any bedded doe could have a buck bedded nearby. After you finish passing through a field, move down the field twice as far as you could see when stalking through it, and make another pass in the opposite direction. Continue this pattern until you have covered the entire field.

Even though the bad weather conditions hamper the whitetail's senses, you must still practice diligent scent control. At some point in time, if you are seeing deer, you will be upwind of them. We prefer stalking in corn during nonrut periods for the simple reason that any mature buck should be bedded and not up pursuing does. When deer are up and moving in the standing corn, the element of surprise diminishes greatly. It is the weather, however, that ultimately determines when we attempt to stalk deer in corn.

JOHN'S STATE LAND EIGHT-POINT

In the fall of 2002, I heard about two big bucks on a piece of state land that I had stopped hunting fifteen years ago. My reason for no longer hunting that spot was simply that it was too far away from where I lived. My current job takes me all over the state, however, so I decided to scout on the land once the postseason rolled around. One very small portion of the property had changed dramatically: an area on the side of a big hill that used to be relatively open and weedy was now densely covered with ten-foot-tall autumn olive trees. The trees were so dense that the only way I could scout them was to occasionally get on my hands and knees and crawl through the maze of tunnels that the deer managed to keep open.

This new travel corridor and bedding area was about two hundred yards in diameter and was bordered on the north and south by thick, swampy bedding areas, the kind that hold water during wet years. The autumn olive area, which was always dry, was a pass-through zone from bedding area to bedding area. I would not call it a funnel because it was very wide. However, after thorough inspection, I found an area that the deer definitely gravitated to when they passed through. That small opening had, and still has, a primary scrape area in it.

It was the perfect location for a primary scrape area. About twenty-five yards long and twenty yards wide, it had scrapes all around its perimeter. The only problem was that there were no trees to hunt from. Looking over the situation, I immediately decided to use a pop-up blind. This location happened to be perfect for hunting on the ground. I immediately cleared out a very subtle area five yards back in the bushes that was just big enough for setting up my blind. After that, I cleared out two very small shooting lanes to the open area by knocking down some tall weeds. I was not concerned about anybody finding this primary scrape area because it was so well hidden, but I still did not want to make an obvious permanent ground blind. Though, if this had been private property, that is definitely what I would have done.

Once I was finished, I set out to find where the other hunters in the area were hunting. I wanted to make sure that if I happened to hunt on the same day as someone else that they would not interfere with my hunting by being too close. Their trees were very easy to find: every other hunter in the area was clearly using bait, which had left huge scars on the ground. Their locations were actually so far from mine that I felt their presence would actually help my hunting. My plan was not to even step foot into the area until the prerut or early November. I knew the other hunters would be hunting heavily during the entire month of October. I was counting on them to push any mature bucks' movement toward my less accessible spot.

A quick check of that spot in late September 2003—to open up my shooting lanes again—made me want to hunt there during the early season.

Two of the scrapes were active, but I knew that there was a lot of other scouting going on, and that more than likely the mature buck sign I was looking at was made after dark. My only opportunity to hunt that location that year was in early November on a morning hunt. Although the scrapes were very active, I saw only a six-point and two does that day. My work schedule did not allow time for another hunt in that area that season.

My next hunt there was on Halloween morning, 2004. Once again, the scrapes were active. I saw two small bucks and seven does and fawns that morning, all of which passed through between 9:00 and 10:30 A.M. My next hunt there was on November 11. It was a very crisp, clear morning. Nothing happened until 9:00 A.M., when a very respectable buck hurriedly passed through the thick autumn olive bushes directly downwind of the scrapes. The cover was way too thick to even consider taking a shot. After he was out of sight I tried a doe bleat, then a grunt call, and several minutes later a rattle sequence. He was not interested and did not immediately return.

During the next two hours a spike, a six-point, and six does and fawns passed through the area without noticing me. This I can only attribute to remaining as scent-free as possible, considering that several of the deer were at one time directly downwind of me at less than twenty yards. I was wearing activated Scent-Lok from head to toe, and my pop-up blind had been set up outside in the shade for over a month to air out any fabric or foreign odors.

At 11:00 A.M., the larger buck returned. He walked, nose to the ground, right through the middle of the opening and stopped to freshen a scrape only eight yards away. The shot was an easy one, and he covered only about a hundred yards before crashing into the brush. He was a nice two-and-a-half-year-old eight-point, which for state land in Michigan is very respectable.

This hunt was a prime example of the importance of several strategies for hunting pressured areas, including postseason scouting, finding out-of-the-way places where other hunters usually do not look, hunting from the ground, hunting primary scrape areas at the appropriate time, and staying on stand through midday.

John took this eightpoint on state land while it was walking through its primary scrape area.

Unless there is unseasonably bad weather, the conditions for stalking corn will be perfect only a few days a season. Therefore, this is a tactic that you will not be able to employ regularly. As when hunting cattail marshes, put on your light brown or tan camouflage for hunting in cornfields.

Cornfield stalking is the only type of still hunting we attempt in pressured areas. A great deal has been written about still hunting in pressured areas, but as far as we are concerned, this is mere fluff. Still hunting is spotting and stalking or just slowly moving through the area looking for a buck and then attempting to sneak within shooting distance. We are not saying that it is impossible, but other than walking corn, it is the method least likely to lead to success, especially with a bow in your hand. Late on a rainy morning in early November 1997, Chris was hunting from a large oak along a huge marsh. He had seen several deer that morning, and a button buck was feeding on acorns just inside the marsh. Suddenly the little buck looked east along the edge of the marsh and dropped to the ground. Chris thought this was a bit curious but really didn't think much of it and continued watching the deer, whose attention was squarely focused to the east. Chris kept looking in that direction, hoping a mature buck would step out. To his surprise, a hunter stepped into view, still-hunting the edge of the marsh. Arrow nocked and moving slowly, he passed within ten yards of Chris and about fifteen yards of the button buck. When the still hunter got to within thirty yards, the little buck just dropped his head lower to the ground and swiveled his ears, following the hunter's every step, even though it was raining. After the hunter disappeared, the button buck stood up and kept feeding on acorns. If a button buck reacts to still hunting in such a fashion, imagine how a mature buck with a few seasons of hunting pressure behind him would react. In pressured areas, limit your still hunting to the cornfields, when the conditions are perfect.

Another way to hunt cornfields is almost like hunting cattail marshes. Many cornfields have fencerows, small swales, overgrown rock piles, fingers of tall grass, or simply open spots. Any combination of these can create a travel route through a cornfield or along one of its edges. In most of these situations, the only common denominator is the lack of trees. Because of the increased popularity of tree-stand hunting, spots like these often go unnoticed. Imagine how secure mature bucks must feel using a travel route through the corn, perhaps waiting until dark to leave their maize sanctuary. In fact, it is common for mature bucks to take up residence in the corn, using it as their main bedding area and leaving only after dark. So while the corn is standing, you may intercept a mature buck by slipping into the security of the corn and setting up a ground blind. First obtain permission from the farmer, then prepare a spot with two lanes as described for the cattail marsh, and follow the same hunting procedure. You can use the cornstalks you cut for spotting and shooting lanes as blind material.

A spot that Chris likes to hunt is a simple strip of tall grass between two cornfields. This strip of tall grass happens to connect two draws that drop off the fields. On this property, Chris has permission to hunt only the fields; the woods on both sides belong to a neighboring landowner. The deer use this travel route regularly, but only when the corn is tall.

Whatever the situation, as you make the final touches to your stands, check all the spots that you thought might harbor deer movement in the early fall. By this time, they should show some use. Most often, by the time the rut phases start and the hunting for big bucks begins to peak, most of the corn will have been picked. Therefore, hunting the corn, whether you stalk or use a ground blind, generally should be done during the October lull. This takes pressure off your other hunting locations, which will heat up later.

There are a few more things to keep in mind any time you are hunting in areas with large cornfields. Mature bucks spend a great deal of time in the corn, more than most people are aware of. These fields are a refuge of sorts. Bucks can feed and move at ease in them, tend does, and enjoy almost total security, leaving only under the cover of darkness. Usually the most dominant buck in an area will bed in the best cornfield and attempt to keep all the subordinate bucks out as the rut phases near. That mature bucks love the corn becomes very obvious in years when the corn is still standing for the gun opener. In those years, fewer mature bucks are killed than usual. And the following year will usually produce a banner crop of mature bucks if the corn is down. It is quite clear where all the bucks were hiding.

Cornfields can also have scrape and rub lines along their edges, and sometimes even primary scrape areas. The primary scrape areas are usually found on inside corners where there is some other attraction as well. A good example is one spot Chris hunts, with an apple tree and a small opening on the inside corner of a cornfield. The farmer never seems to be able to get corn growing all the way into that corner. There are always half a dozen scrapes under that apple tree and a scrape line leading along the field edge in both directions. Setting up in a spot like this can lead to good results.

Reacting to the transition in deer movement that takes place when the corn is harvested is yet another component to hunting cornfields. Bucks simply stay in the corn until they are disturbed. The biggest disturbance is the harvest. It is always amazing to witness the yearly change: The corn comes down and the number of buck sightings goes up. Reacting to this change involves giving up on your cornfield edge stands. Quite often by the time the corn is cut, the prerut has begun, and you can move right into your main stands at primary scrape areas and staging areas. Any travel route stands near or on the edge of the now-picked corn will be used primarily after dark by the mature bucks, which now use the best bedding alternative available. Another form of cornfield disturbance that can be helpful to your bowhunting is pheasant hunting. Bucks will only tolerate a disturbance a couple times before they start looking for a new place to bed. Understanding the importance of cornfields can be vital to your bowhunting success.

Another terrain situation that can call for hunting from the ground is clear-cuts. Those that are between five and fifteen years old will always have deer activity, because the cut treetops and thick young saplings provide great cover and offer excellent browse that the deer love. You will often find deer travel routes through them but no mature tree in sight.

Setting up a makeshift ground blind or a pop-up blind can definitely lead to success. John's youngest son, Joe, shot a nice eight-point in such a location a few years ago. The clear-cut that Joe was hunting was right next to where he parked, and because it did not have any trees large enough to hunt from, he concentrated most of his hunting on the woods farther back on the property. Several times while walking in, however, only about forty yards from his parking spot, he noticed a well-used runway crossing his lane, along which more and more rubs kept showing up. With this spot in mind, Joe borrowed a pop-up blind from his dad. On his next hunt to the area, Joe set up the pop-up about twenty yards from the runway in an old pile of slash and near a big fallen tree. Barely settled into the little tent, he looked up and noticed a nice buck walking steadily right down the runway. The buck covered the remaining distance quickly and was broadside at twenty yards in a minute or two. Joe drew and then blatted to stop the buck. The instant the buck turned his head in Joe's direction, Joe let his arrow fly. His shot was just a hair high and forward but good enough. His broadhead cut through the buck's shoulder blade on the entry side and through the shoulder blade on the other. The buck dashed about forty yards before toppling into a heap. Joe's adjustment from the trees to the ground proved to be a good decision.

For ground blinds in wooded areas to work best, they should become part of the natural surroundings for some time before you hunt them. Deer have good memories, and anything that is suddenly out of place in their environment will receive extra scrutiny whenever they are near it. This makes getting a shot opportunity much more difficult. Joe's buck was obviously an exception—there are always going to be exceptions, and nothing is carved into stone.

This small patch of ungroomed apple trees in the middle of a tall weed field is a prime location for a ground blind.

When setting up ground blinds in the woods, use any natural ground cover to make them as inconspicuous as possible. Take advantage of fallen trees, their root systems, old dead branches lying around, and trees and brush from clearing shooting lanes as blind material. Don't try to use foliage as cover; it will probably be gone by the time you actually hunt that location. For added cover, you can use camouflage mesh or 3-D fabric of similar color to the surroundings. The ground inside the blind should be bare of anything that could potentially make noise when touched. Use a comfortable chair that does not squeak, preferably with a backrest, so that you are not adjusting your sitting position constantly. It is vital to remain as still as possible while hunting on the ground. There must also be at least a couple adequate areas of the blind from which you can shoot. We prefer to build up our ground blinds above head level, as we are always moving our heads while looking around for approaching deer. There is nothing worse than being out of position when a buck is within shooting distance, because you then have to move into position without his noticing your movements. This is tough to do. It is always best to be alert and notice any deer well before they move into shooting range, and it is even more critical when hunting on the ground, because you are at their level.

Scent control is another factor you need to consider. While hunting from trees, your scent is often above the deer. When hunting on the ground, your scent is at ground level, making it easier for the deer to detect you. We would not even consider hunting on the ground without a Scent-Lok suit and head cover, rubber boots, and all our other equipment being as scent-free as possible. Scent control is critical; you cannot always count on the deer coming in from upwind, no matter how well you think you know their travel patterns. It takes only one deer to smell you, snort, and totally give away your location.

Any time a good location has no adequate trees to hunt from, don't hesitate to hunt on the ground. Many mature bucks have been taken from ground blinds, in all types of terrain. Be smart in your setup location, timing, and scent control, and you may be surprised at the results. This style of bowhunting has become nearly nonexistent, and if you become proficient at it, it will open up areas that nobody else hunts, making them good mature buck locations.

CHAPTER 11

Hunting the Suburbs

When hunting mature bucks in pressured areas, do not overlook the suburbs. As sprawl continues to consume farmland and woods, hunting the suburbs will become more and more prevalent and could even be considered the face of bowhunting's future, with all its advantages and disadvantages. It is very sad to see how much hunting land is lost each year because of our economic myopia, but it is a simple fact that hunters must deal with. Changing land-use patterns and surging deer populations around towns and cities have caused us to add suburbs to our bowhunting locales in the last few years.

The positive side of hunting the suburbs is that the nature of hunting these close quarters suits bowhunting very well. And it is no secret that suburbs and towns produce some huge bucks. Every year, some of the biggest bucks taken, both nationally and regionally, come from the suburbs or within the limits of towns and cities, sometimes small ones, but particularly in zones of massive sprawl like that around Chicago, Columbus, or Detroit. The intricate nature of land consumption and use creates a situation where deer have a virtual checkerboard of safe places interspersed with areas that get hunted and ones that are uninhabitable, such as huge parking lots or dense tracts of housing. Interestingly, though, sometimes deer incorporate a parking lot into their movement patterns, if it is bordered by good cover. A friend of ours has video of bucks chasing does around a parking lot in the middle of the night; the doe even circles a couple parked cars in an attempt to elude the amorous buck. A friend of John's, a police officer and avid bowhunter, witnessed a 180-class buck fighting a 160-class on a soccer field at a local community college while he was eating lunch during his night shift.

The land development situation has a dramatic effect on deer behavior and movement patterns. With a limited amount of wooded or edge area, the home range of deer, both bucks and does, is often confined to a much smaller area than it normally would be. Travel corridors are usually squeezed between buildings in small, narrow woodlots or along creeks or ditches. Finding a hunting spot in a suburban setting, where the local deer absolutely have to pass through, is a tremendous shortcut to regular success on mature bucks. Another aspect of suburban hunting is the usual lack of gun hunting, which allows bucks—the ones that do not get hit by cars—to live to maturity. Michigan's Oakland County, which produces some of the top bucks in the state every year, is mostly suburban, with limited gun hunting. But hunting the suburbs presents a host of difficulties, some of them deer-related, but most of them people-related.

The people-related problems are the hardest, and most discouraging, to deal with. Hunting permission in good suburbs or wooded urban wasteland is not easy to obtain, making access the first and most difficult problem in suburban bowhunting. In the suburbs, hunting permission is received almost exclusively through connections. If you are fortunate, you might happen to live in a neighborhood that is teeming with deer and will be able to hunt in your backyard. Be careful, though; regulations vary from state to state about how far from a dwelling you have to be to hunt with a bow. In some instances, you have to get the permission of your neighbor or neighbors to hunt your own land. Also make sure that you do not overlook any city ordinances that make hunting in your area illegal. In some states, because game management is a state-run function, the lower forms of government cannot outright ban hunting. They can ban the use of guns, they can ban hunting on all land without written permission, they can erect some obstructions, but they cannot ban hunting itself. A problem often arises when local government officials or police tell you that hunting is illegal. Often these people don't know the rules, want to bully you into not hunting, or don't want to have to deal with citizen complaints. Check into the legality of any local hunting ordinances with the state game management agency. Such local ordinances are particularly prevalent—and controversial—in affluent areas, which generally are the best places to find mature bucks because of the large lots and interspersed woods between houses.

In some areas, suburban whitetails are becoming a nuisance, yet most of these deer are in protected areas.

It is almost impossible to get permission to hunt in suburbs by knocking on doors. The quarters are simply too tight, and most people do not allow strangers to hunt in their backyards. Some regional organizations and cities, however, organize hunting in parks and certain neighborhoods. If this sort of organization exists in your community, by all means apply for access and do what it takes to gain permission. Depending on the community, such hunting might be as simple as buying a permit or getting permission from the county clerk. In other instances, a lottery system may be in place, you might have to take a short bowhunting class, or you might have to know someone in a position to decide who receives access. In a situation like this, a history of hunting success can come in handy.

Considering how difficult it is to find a place to hunt, it is particularly important not to lose permission once it has been granted. Respect the wishes of the landowner, and don't do anything stupid. Often the people granting hunting permission in the suburbs are doing so on an experimental basis. They are usually nonhunters who are tired of all the deer eating their flowers, shrubs, or gardens. If you are inconsiderate, these people may take a negative attitude toward all hunters, closing yet another piece of land to hunting, and perhaps even shifting their attitude from nonhunting to antihunting, thus adding to the uncertainty of hunting's already precarious future.

In suburbs with numerous deer, the population is generally nonhunting and usually to some extent antihunting—or, better stated, antihunter. Most of these people don't like what they perceive as hunter behavior. This means they don't like guys in camouflage walking around or hanging around their trucks. They don't like weapons in plain sight. And they don't like public changing of clothes. Most people, though, are not opposed to hunting if the entire deer is used for food and the individual hunter is perceived as a thoughtful, ethical person who is honestly concerned with making a clean kill. True antihunting attitudes are rare. The worst enemy of a hunter seeking permission to hunt is the hunter himself.

This means that taking precautions to avoid conflict is of utmost importance. Ultimately, you are well advised to always keep a low profile while hunting suburbs. An antihunter neighbor can cause enough stress in a neighborhood to cost you your permission. Do not underestimate the importance of this point. When you hunt a small property surrounded by houses, it is best if most of the residents have no idea you are there. If the neighbors don't know you are hunting, they cannot make trouble.

Since 2001, we have had permission on two tiny pieces of property, which we gained through friends after the family had had enough of the deer eating their garden. On one property, in particular, we have instructions from the landowner not to let the neighbors see us hunting. He wants the deer controlled as much as possible on his property, a couple acres, but most of the neighbors are antihunter and would undoubtedly both harass us and cause neighborly strife. To avoid contact, we hunt this property almost exclusively in the morning, with a very early arrival; park behind the landowner's garage; and wear no camouflage while scouting, entering, or exiting. The neighbors work, so we are able to depart later in the morning unnoticed. It is also necessary that we refrain from using tree stands. Nothing gives a bowhunter away more easily than a tree stand that can be seen while walking through the woods. Because we use an Ambush Saddle, this is not a problem. We also have nothing on our cars advertising the fact that we are hunters. Though there is absolutely nothing to be ashamed of while hunting, we are not out there to insult or confront the sensibilities of the nonhunting or antihunting public. There is a time and place for the propagation of our hunting passion, and they are definitely not while trying to hunt mature bucks in the tight quarters of a suburban setting.

Keeping a low profile is absolutely paramount to suburban hunting. It is especially important before and after you shoot a deer. If shot placement is critical in rural areas and in the rain, it is even more so in tight suburban quarters. Properties are usually quite close, and a poorly shot deer will be difficult to recover from a sheer permission standpoint. Some people will not allow you on their land, no matter what, and asking a neighbor for permission to track a wounded deer could lose you permission on your existing property. Knowing this, we often limit our shots in such areas to fifteen yards or less, and broadside shots only. This gives us a higher assurance of a clean kill than our normal twenty-five-yard range. If you are not sure of a short, clean shot, do not shoot. You want the deer to collapse within sight or hearing distance, on the property on which you are hunting. Although this is somewhat out of your control, it should always be your goal. This is naturally a limitation, but since the deer in suburbs are more confined than in rural areas, you should look at this like more of a trade-off—limited shot range for good hunting and possibly another chance at the buck you just let walk. Short shots help you maintain your low profile.

Nothing is worse than tracking a deer around a subdivision. If you have to do this, remove all signs that you are a hunter, don't wear camouflage, and leave your bow in your car. Do not attract attention to yourself. When you find your deer, make sure you can get it out of the woods without being seen. In most cases, we wait until after dark to get the deer out. This might mean leaving it in the woods all day. With a morning-shot deer, we gut it and hide it until we can come back later to pick it up. It is also very important to hide the gut pile. Put it in a hollow stump, under a pile of brush, or in a hole. Make sure that it disappears. A gut pile in the woods can be like a beacon to anyone walking in the woods and could draw negative attention to your hunting. Keeping a low profile includes erasing or covering up any sign you may leave behind.

In 2003, a friend invited John to hunt with him near his home, which was close to suburban Chicago. Since gun hunting was not allowed in the area, John decided to wait until late December. He could not believe it when he was put in a tree within one hundred yards of three magnificent homes. John had hunted some suburban areas before, but none of those hunts were anywhere this close to houses. His evening hunt was uneventful, but his friend took a doe "for the freezer." One of them must have been seen that evening by one of the property owner's neighbors, because John's friend received a phone call telling him that the neighbors were complaining and that he couldn't hunt there anymore. Every aspect of that hunt went against the proper way to go about hunting in a suburban area.

Most hunters have problems with detection during parking and entry and exit. Whenever you receive permission to hunt a suburb, make sure you have a defined parking spot that both you and the landowner agree on. Often it is best to try to fit in, with your automobile parked in the landowner's driveway. Whenever we hunt in suburbs, we always wait until the coast is clear to walk in and out. It is best to remain as invisible as possible, even if this means waiting several minutes for the neighbors to leave or a car to drive by. In some instances, it might mean hunting all day to avoid being seen, using the cover of darkness to go in and come out. We have even carried street clothes in our packs to wear back out of the woods on morning hunts. This means leaving our hunting equipment in the woods until we return. Upon our return for the evening hunt, we reverse the procedure, wearing street clothes on our way into the woods and changing before hunting. These are great lengths to go through for something that you are legally undertaking, and fortunately they are not necessary in every case, but with ever-dwindling hunting land, permission in some suburban areas may be well worth all the effort.

If you can get around the people problems, suburban hunting can be spectacular. Because of the limited space that most suburban areas provide, the home ranges of deer are much smaller than normal. The tight quarters can lead to more overlap in home ranges of mature bucks. More deer often live in a single area, leading to increased deer density, and with the lack of hunting pressure, this can lead to high mature buck-to-doe ratios. Yards and brushy woods between houses create a tremendous amount of edge habitat and usually provide a diversity of food that is also responsible for the high deer densities. This situation—more deer in less space—increases your chances of seeing the local dominant buck. His travel options are far more limited than in more traditional hunting areas.

In a lot of suburban settings, the deer are forced to move through confined areas that are much narrower than in rural settings. These funnels are tremendous ambush sites, particularly if they are between large protected areas and feeding areas. Suburbs often have other places that hold deer that get overlooked, such as golf courses, wooded buffers along major highways, and parks. One of the best places we ever hunted was a sparse finger of woods that extended into a large cropfield. At the far end of the field was a suburb. There were no other woods within half a mile of this spot, other than between the houses. The tip of this finger was a primary scrape area and the center of deer activity. To the casual observer, the spot did not look as if it would hold more than a few cottontails. We had this area to ourselves for years, until the landowner sold the property and the land was developed. Most places like it hold deer. There may not be many deer, but the nature of the situation allows bucks to live to maturity, even though other factors, such as automobile collisions, dogs, and coyotes, cause a great deal of mortality in such populations.

The actual hunting on small suburban properties is essentially the same as hunting other small parcels. It is extremely important that you scout each property thoroughly and develop a plan for it. Every property is different and will have a specific time when the deer use it most. This could be early season, the rut, or even the late season. When you receive permission to hunt in a suburban location, check out the property for deer sign, no matter how small the parcel may be. Occasionally you will encounter an absolute gem, a tiny piece of land in perfect position that always holds mature bucks. It might be a small acreage surrounded by land off-limits to hunting, a sliver of land between a large swamp and the nearest crops or yards where the deer feed on the lawns, or a few trees along a creek that connects two larger woods. No matter what the property seems like at first glance, look around.

If you are offered hunting permission in the suburbs, typically the landowner is having problems with deer, meaning there is an abundance of them. During your first visit, trace the outside border of the property. Since these are small properties, this shouldn't take very long. After this is done, inspect the property. Again, while scouting on small properties, leave no stone unturned. It is extremely important to your hunting that you figure out when and how the deer are using the property. When you know what the deer are doing, you can adjust your hunting accordingly.

Chris hunts one small parcel that is good only during the early season.

When the foliage is still on the trees, the deer bed in small woods that border dense subdivisions. The deer follow a movement pattern that takes them north to a large section of crops, almost devoid of woods, where no hunting is allowed. In their daily pattern, they move through a small neck of woods leading to the crops in both the morning and evening. After the leaves drop, the woods where the deer had been bedding have very little cover. In reaction to the opening of the woods, the deer move about a mile north to a larger woods. These northern woods where no hunting is allowed provide more cover, but access to the crops is more difficult. To get to the crops, the deer have to cross through a subdivision. At this point, the deer are out of reach and only move through the huntable area during darkness, except for the errant straggler. It took Chris one full season to learn this pattern. That first year he was chomping at the bit to get in there during the prerut, but when he hunted it, the area was devoid of deer. The implications for hunting are obvious: This spot has to be hunted during the first few weeks of the season. At this time, Chris has found ample buck sign and has seen a couple really nice bucks. But by late October, the activity has dried up.

The situation when hunting the suburbs can, however, be the exact opposite. Another tiny spot that John's son Jon hunts doesn't really get good until late November and into December. This particular spot is a small cedar swamp surrounded by large homes, where gun hunting is legal but not allowed by any of the homeowners. The land surrounding the homes is a mix of agriculture and river bottom that gets gun-hunted quite heavily. As soon as gun season starts, deer seem to flock to the cedar swamp from the surrounding country. The deer population appears to double almost overnight. Usually a mature buck shows up just ahead of the shooting. In this spot, Jon concentrates his bowhunting during the late season.

Most of the time, when hunting small suburban properties, your tiny parcel will contain only a fragment of a buck's territory. If you happen to have his primary scrape area, core bedding area, or perhaps an acorn-laden oak on your spot, you are lucky. Most of the time, however, this will not be the case. Locate the best sign available and make the best of the situation. For instance, the best sign might be a portion of a rub line. Unlike pressured rural areas, where mature bucks are most likely nocturnal until the rut phases, the mature bucks in these suburban spots are more likely to move during early morning and evening hours prior to the rut phases, simply because there is less hunting pressure. There may be a lot of human activity, but it will not be threatening.

In this case, set up along that rub line. You may not be able to determine where the rub line is heading, but it is the best sign you have. Attempt to determine when the buck that made the rub line is using that travel route, and hunt accordingly.

Having access to just a fragment of a buck's core territory can have severe implications on how you hunt. Even though deer that live in suburban areas are much more tolerant of humans and human activity than those in pressured rural hunting areas, one false move and the buck that had been using your small parcel can react by altering his pattern. He only has to move slightly to be out of reach. On larger properties, you can move and still have a chance to intercept that buck someplace else. This is impossible on small parcels. Critical to a situation like this is to hunt your trees only when they are absolutely ready to be hunted.

Depending on your situation, bowhunting the suburbs may or may not be an option. If you are prepared for every eventuality, including the difficulties of dealing with people, the suburbs can sometimes provide excellent hunting for mature bucks. It can provide excellent doe-hunting opportunities as well. We hunt mature bucks because we like the challenge; the bottom line, though, is to fill the freezer with tasty venison. In a lot of areas, suburban deer populations are heavily out of balance, and extra tags are often available for does. In the suburban areas we hunt, we shoot does to fill the freezer, usually in December, after gun season has made mature bucks scarce. Though suburban hunting is somewhat new for us, we see its potential and believe this sort of bowhunting will become more prevalent in the future.

CHAPTER 12

The Baiting Problem

Baiting is one of the most controversial issues in all of hunting, both within and outside of the hunting community. The reasons for the controversy are well documented, and we will not delve into them. It is safe to say that most nonhunters view baiting as being ethically questionable, at the least, and ethically reprehensible, at most, which may negatively affect the future of hunting. We have to touch on the subject simply because it cannot be ignored. In most areas we hunt in our home state, it dramatically affects our bowhunting. We want to make it very clear that we do not hunt over bait, nor do we recommend baiting. We are not interested in the conflict surrounding the subject; there is a place and time for that discussion. Here our focus is merely on how baiting affects the pursuit of mature pressured bucks.

Baiting is clearly an effective method for killing deer with a bow. In some parts of Michigan, according to a deer biologist we spoke to, the bowhunter success rate has risen dramatically with the acceptance of baiting as a hunting method. Our biologist friend claimed that bowhunter success rates on deer, both does and bucks, before baiting became common were lower than 10 percent. That number is now nearing 40 percent. Of course, other technological advances have helped with the increase, but he claimed bait to be the major reason. Back in the late 1970s, when he worked at a local sport shop, John knew a lot of bowhunters who struggled just to kill a deer with a bow. By the mid-1980s, when baiting became prevalent, those same hunters began to experience consistent success, not just at taking deer, but at taking small bucks.

It is clear that baiting alters deer movement patterns dramatically and draws them to specific, tiny destination points, creating close shots. This fact becomes obvious if you scout from a plane in areas that are heavily baited. Runways radiate from bait piles like spokes from the center of a wheel. This is obviously an unnatural movement pattern caused by the influx of easily accessible food. The fact is, deer are feeding opportunists, and easy food on the ground will attract them, even to a point where they will ignore more normal food sources. We have witnessed this behavior change in many of our hunting spots, even to the point that deer movement has steadily shifted in the opposite direction from that of a couple years ago. Does and fawns that once took a route to and from farmers' fields now head for the nearest bait pile when they get up to feed. And bait is available on a first-come, first-served basis until it is gone, which actually forces the deer to compete for it. Hunting over bait requires little knowledge of the woods and even less woodsmanship, but it appeals to hunters because the chance of seeing deer and getting a shot is good. Regular success becomes more a question of keeping bait on the ground than of hunting skill. Put a bait pile in woods holding deer, and they will come.

In pressured areas, does and yearling bucks are the ones most likely to be interested in bait, at least during daylight. The ease of killing yearling bucks over bait is seriously detrimental to the number of bucks surviving to maturity, as the majority of bowhunters are happy with any buck and will shoot the first couple yearlings they see. Mature bucks usually have had enough experience to know to avoid bait piles during daylight. Some hunters, though, specialize in killing mature bucks over bait and do this with regular success. These hunters usually have access to a small piece of land next to a large tract where hunting is prohibited, such as a refuge, park, scout camp, or private no-hunting zone, or they hunt a single large parcel with exclusive access. Strategically placed bait piles near the border of the larger, non-hunted property initially draw does and young bucks to the bait. As long as the hunter continues to bait, does continue feeding there. Simply put, the trick for hunting a mature buck in this situation is to wait until the prerut and rut to hunt the bait, and then hunt all day. The mature bucks incorporate this spot of heavy doe activity into their routes for intercepting estrous females and may even turn the spot into a primary scrape area. Their visits usually take place during midday, when mature bucks are most vulnerable to bait hunters.

This practice has been incorporated into many video productions, though the actual bait or feeder is never shown on film. Some fairly well-known hunters employ this method, and in some places, such as Texas and some of the Canadian provinces, it is now accepted as the normal way to hunt. Baiting has become so prevalent in Michigan that it is almost synonymous with bowhunting. The situation has become so extreme in some areas that hunters feel as if they have to bait to counter the baiting taking place on the property next door or even on the same property. And the truth is, if you have permission on a property that does not contain a good bedding area, the bait piles next door will not only pull the deer from the land you hunt, but also eventually shut off all activity on your property. We prefer not to bait, so in some areas, we have had to come up with methods to counter the practice and still be successful.

How to react to baiting is a touchy subject. If you have absolute control of a piece of property, you can plant food plots and take other habitat measures to counter the baiting. This is unrealistic for most bowhunters, however, and in areas devoid of agricultural activity, it could be considered just another form of baiting. Another solution is to treat bait as a normal food source and hunt it as such. This sometimes requires that you cut off a fellow hunter. Our take on this is that the guy doing the baiting is not doing you any favors. In fact, he is making your hunting far more difficult by causing deer to change their normal movement patterns dramatically, not to mention the other problems created by baiting, including the spread of disease, such as bovine tuberculosis in Michigan and perhaps chronic wasting disease. Considering this, you should not be overly worried about doing him any favors in return. Our solution to the baiting problem is very pragmatic in nature. When we hunt a piece of property where baiting is taking place, we hunt around the bait hunter and use him to our advantage, if at all possible. We also keep a low profile, and usually the bait hunter never even knows we are around. We never take a course of confrontation. As long as baiting is legal, bait hunters have as much right to do their thing as we do. If the bait hunters mess things up for us completely, we hunt elsewhere.

In some instances, baiting can be positive to your hunting. On one piece of public land where we hunt regularly, there are several other hunters who bait heavily. These men hunt a lot. Their stands are all within a couple hundred yards of the road and very obvious. The same guys hunt these stands year after year and always kill small bucks. Anyone new who decides to check out the property immediately encounters tree stand after tree stand. This discourages most hunters from scouting any further and leaves the back half of the property to us. In this case, the bait hunters are a sort of deterrent that reduces the competition. We always see mature bucks on this piece of land and have been successful on several occasions. Interestingly, before bow season even opens, the hunters' baiting activity—which is supposed to be illegal prior to the season—has the mature bucks avoiding the front half of the property during the daytime.

In another area, we share a parcel with a hunter who sets up along the field edges and baits. As long as this hunter does not venture back into the woods, he is not a problem at all. Though his bait attracts deer, his evening departure always alarms the deer feeding in the field. After he spooks deer a couple times, the mature bucks avoid his bait until well after dark.

On other properties, bait presents more of a problem. In this case, your preparation has to begin in the spring. Baiting normally leaves scars on the ground and trails that are obvious and trampled. In your scouting logbook, mark every bait pile you find. With enough scouting, a pattern should become obvious. Most bait is less than a hundred yards from a road or path, simply because bait is heavy. You should notice gaps where no baiting is taking place. Concentrate your hunting in these areas. The deer movement in these areas will usually be toward the nearest preferred food source, usually the bait. Find the travel routes and set up just like you would with a normal food source, but remain far enough from the baited stand that the bait hunter does not know you are there. The closer to the bedding area you set up, the better. Most bait hunters are less than average in hunting ability, so their arrival time at their stands will be normal to late. You can use this to your advantage by arriving at your stand at least an hour and a half before daylight on morning hunts and very early on evening hunts. In the morning, the hunter's arrival will spook deer in your direction, and in the evening, the deer will anticipate the bait hunter's departure and hang just out of range—with luck, close to your stand. Since you are hunting mature bucks anyway, most deer will pass by unharmed and arrive at the bait as usual.

We attempt to take advantage of another hunter's baiting only when we are sure there is a mature buck in the area, and usually only during the rut phases. In pressured areas, bait hunters usually have pushed the few local mature bucks into a nocturnal routine prior to the season opener. These bucks will not move during daylight until the rut phases start.

You can also hunt these areas successfully during midday using the same hunting pattern to your advantage. Deer are aware that hunters leave their stands at midday and often feed at bait piles during this time. Even more important, during the prerut and rut, bucks cruise from bait pile to bait pile during midday searching for estrous does, since they are centers of doe activity, just as they would from one primary scrape area to another. Mature bucks, however, are aware of the potential consequences associated with visiting bait piles during daylight and will likely scent-check or visually check them from a distance. By hunting travel routes along cover that lead to baited areas, you may intercept an amorous buck during the rut phases. In early November a couple years ago, on four different occasions, Chris witnessed a buck exhibiting this behavior. The big ten-point cruised back and forth just inside the edge of a large, thick bedding area for does returning from early-morning feeding on bait. He would move back and forth and follow does, but he would not cross the threshold into the more open baited area. Unfortunately, the buck would not present Chris with a clear shot, either.

Bait piles such as this pile of sugar beets severely alter deer movements in the area. Mature deer tend to go nocturnal in pressured areas when given abundant, easy food sources such as this.

In areas of heavy baiting, also look for alternate travel routes that skirt the area through thick cover. These are likely to be little-used runways through the thickest cover possible. When you prepare your trees in spring, clear out trees along any such route you find. Mature bucks will use these routes to avoid the bait hunters, sometimes during daylight, while moving from one secure area to another. A patchwork of secure areas and heavily hunted areas is quite common these days, particularly in semiurban areas where most properties are twenty acres or less in size. Some property owners allow hunting, but others are strictly against hunting. The mature deer seem to be well aware of where it is safe and where it is not, despite the need to feed.

Bucks will skirt baited areas to counter normal bait hunter behavior, which in most instances includes overhunting their few stands. Almost every bait hunter is guilty of this hunting sin, for a couple reasons. First, they almost always see deer, which in most hunters' minds eliminates the need for more stands. Second, bait is expensive and heavy. The cost and work involved limit most hunters to just a few stands. Baited areas are normally permeated with hunter scent. Even though does and yearling bucks will still use the area, most mature bucks will skirt such places, at least until the rut. Even then, overhunting will limit their use to the cover of darkness.

Bowhunting for mature bucks in areas with heavy baiting is difficult at best. The bait hunters usually do a great job of keeping many bucks from growing to maturity. All you can do is attempt to make the best of a tough situation.

CHAPTER 13

Hunting Away from Home

All serious bowhunters who hunt in pressured areas, including both of us, like to head off to big-buck states. Getting away from your old stomping grounds is a lot of fun and can be a good measure of your hunting skill level. For some hunters, hunting out of state is a once-in-a-lifetime trip; for others, it is a yearly ritual. Some hunters have given up altogether on hunting in pressured states, such as Michigan, because of the constant frustrations of dealing with heavy competition and the lack of mature bucks, and hunt only in less pressured states.

Hunting in areas with far less hunting pressure requires slightly different tactics, though any hunting method that works well in a pressured area will work even better in a low-pressure area. This chapter sheds some light on how to hunt these areas on your own, without having to pay big dollars for a guide, who quite often will be less of a hunter than yourself. Never having been forced to deal with the problems of heavy hunting pressure, some of these guys would not be able to kill a yearling six-point under pressured conditions. Shooting a nice buck while on a guided hunt is perfectly acceptable, and depending on the property, length of your hunt, and time of season, it can sometimes be very tough. However, traveling to a new unfamiliar area, setting up on your own, and killing a mature buck with a bow on a short-term hunt is much more of a challenge. This type of hunt demonstrates your hunting prowess, requires some hard work, and is a major hunting accomplishment.

WHERE TO GO

It's no secret that some places produce more big, mature bucks than others. Some well-known big-buck states are Iowa, Wisconsin, Kansas, Illinois, Nebraska, and the Dakotas, among others. Agricultural areas in Canada are also known for their huge whitetails. There are also less publicized areas that produce notable quantities of mature bucks. Some of these sleepers include Idaho, Montana, and portions of Wyoming and Colorado, to mention just a few, along with other pockets of good hunting throughout North America. Most of these places present a stark contrast with pressured areas in the number of mature bucks running around.

The first step to hunting outside of your home state is deciding where you want to go. If you have a relative or friend in one of the big-buck areas who has property or access to property, that is where you should focus your attention; hunting permission is always easier to obtain through connections than any other way. A relative or friend also can be a big help in getting set up in a big-buck area. Locals usually have some idea where the big bucks are located, even if they do not hunt. And because they are familiar with the area, it will be easier for you to find a place to stay, as well as other facilities such as supermarkets, coin laundries, and gas stations. This reduces the time you have to spend exploring unfamiliar terrain.

If you don't have a relative or friend who can help you, the decision of where to hunt becomes a bit more complex. The first question you have to ask yourself is how far you want to travel. This is followed closely by several other important questions: What are your budget constraints? Will you be camping or staying in a motel? How much comfort do you want? How much time will you have to hunt and to scout? Is this a one-time hunt or will you be able to return in following years? What kind of terrain do you want to hunt? Where can you gain access to hunt? Can you get a license for the area? All of these questions have to be taken into consideration long in advance of any adventure afar. We usually make a single weeklong hunting trip out of state per season. A look at John's first hunt in another state will give you an idea how to get started with hunting away from home.

John hunted outside his home state of Michigan for the first time in 1997, after thirty-four hunting seasons spent entirely in the state. His main reason for checking into hunting elsewhere was to increase his bowhunting opportunities. He wanted to continue bowhunting after Michigan's gun season started on November 15. Over the years, he found himself gun hunting less and less, and by the mid-1990s, he had basically given it up altogether. With the massive influx of more than 750,000 gun hunters in late November, bowhunting became nearly impossible, especially since he did not own his own property. He wanted to exhaust every opportunity at a mature buck in Michigan before heading elsewhere, so he looked for a state where bow season was open during the second half of November and gun season did not open until Thanksgiving or later. He also wanted a place that had low hunter numbers, produced good bucks, and was within a ten-hour drive from home. After a bit of research, he came up with a few possibilities: Ohio, Illinois, and Iowa all fit his selection criteria. He chose Iowa because of its overall lower hunter numbers.

His next step was to apply for a license. Iowa has a permit lottery for nonresidents, and the state is broken down into ten zones, with each zone allowing a different quantity of permits. John called the Iowa DNR and had them send him all pertinent information for nonresident applicants. The paperwork he received listed the number of permits available for each zone, along with the number of applicants that had applied the previous year. John chose the zone with the best odds of receiving a permit, even though it was the zone with the lowest population of deer. While waiting for the results of his permit application, he purchased a state map book. Since he would not be hunting until late November, he looked for places where the deer would be found after the crops, corn in particular, were cut, so he chose counties with the most rivers running through them. As luck would have it, he received a license on his first attempt. He now needed to decide on a specific place to hunt. After selecting the three counties that looked the most promising, he called the county clerk of each and ordered plat books.

His plat books arrived by midsummer. Plat books show the size and shape of each property, listing the owner's name and sometimes even phone number. The next step is something most hunters from heavily hunted states, such as Pennsylvania, West Virginia, or New York, can hardly imagine: John simply started calling landowners in the areas he had selected to hunt and asked them for permission. These landowners had no idea he would be calling, nor did they know him. It took him only a couple hours on a single afternoon to gain permission to hunt three properties, consisting of just over two thousand acres total. Considering how difficult it is to land hunting permission in Michigan, even on small tracts, this was almost unbelievable.

This also shows the drastic difference in hunter densities between pressured areas and nonpressured areas and reveals how seldom landowners in nonpressured states are approached for hunting permission, or at least how seldom they were approached in 1997.

The next step was simply to follow up on the permission with a couple confirmation phone calls in October to tell the landowners the exact dates he would be hunting. Upon arrival, John visited each of the landowners to introduce himself and solidify his permission. This took up most of the first day of his hunt. He then began with his scouting and hunting. An initial quick run through portions of the three properties revealed that one of the properties was less than spectacular, consisting mostly of pasture field, without any good terrain to hold deer. The other two, though, were excellent. John has permission to hunt all three of those properties to this day, and he has been fortunate enough to hunt them five times, taking five good bucks.

JOHN'S IOWA TWELVE-POINT

A prime example of a postrut hunt in a nonpressured area took place in Iowa in 2003. It was November 21, the fifth day of John's seven-day Iowa bowhunt, and the late phase of the main rut. The bucks were up and moving. The previous four days had been very eventful. He had already seen two very big bucks, a 140-class eight-point and a 150-class ten-point, during his first two hunts and had passed on a borderline Pope and Young eight-point that paid a visit to his decoy on day three. Though his time was running short, John was optimistic as he settled into his Ambush Saddle a couple hours before daylight. He was sitting in the same tree the big ten-point had run directly underneath earlier in the week. The ten-point was the buck John was hoping to get a shot at.

Just as the eastern horizon began to lighten, John reached for his rattle bag. Within minutes after completing an aggressive rattling sequence, he could hear a deer approaching through the timber. The deer that emerged out of the still, gray woods was a handsome eight-point. It was a good buck, even by Iowa standards. With its ears laid back, the buck long-necked to smell the tail end of the decoy that John had placed a mere fifteen yards from his tree. The buck provided a couple good shot opportunities that John passed on, determined to arrow one of the bigger bucks from earlier in the week. As the buck meandered out of sight, John hoped he had not made a mistake and spent the remainder of the morning thinking about the situation. Each time he hunted this spot in the evening, several deer would pass through about a hundred yards on either side of his tree on their way to the crops to the north. All the deer seemed to emerge, though, from about the same general area farther back in the timber. Not convinced that he was in the best location, John decided to investigate after the morning hunt was over.

By 8:30 the deer activity ceased, and although there was a buck movement phase later in the morning, John climbed out of his tree. After a quick change of clothes at his van, replacing his hunting Scent-Lok with his lightweight scouting Scent-Lok, he was back in the woods with his scouting equipment. If he had been hunting a pressured area, he would have been reluctant to scout on a dry day in a transition area, but time was short and this was Iowa. John covered about a hundred yards before finding some better sign, and about another 150 yards farther, he found what he had hoped for: six large scrapes in a small area, with four well-used runways converging close by. That the rut was in full swing was obvious by how the scrapes had been used. The ground scrapes had not been scraped recently, but the licking branches were well used and the scrapes had been urinated in, which was obvious by their pungent odor and large tracks. John could have kicked himself for not having investigated the area more fully earlier in his hunt. Being accustomed to hunting a highly pressured area, he had been overly careful not to disturb anything.

The primary scrape area was located at the convergence of three separate types of terrain: a large river system 150 yards to the south, bordered by 50 yards of extremely thick red willow; heavy, mature timber with waist-high undergrowth to the west; and sparse select-harvest timber with thick undergrowth to the east. The scrapes were positioned right in the middle of it all, in a narrow buffer of mature trees with very little undergrowth. About a quarter mile to the north was a steep bluff. Beyond that were picked cropfields as far as the eye could see. This was the spot!

Inspecting the scrapes a bit closer, John noticed that every available branch above the main scrape had been used as a licking branch. The scrape also had fresh droppings in it, which were so tightly clumped that he had to get close to identify them as deer droppings rather than coyote or dog dung. Upon close inspection, he could see the large pellets bonded closely together, an indication of buck dung. The droppings were also of large diameter and relatively long compared with typical buck droppings, a sign of a larger-than-normal animal. Utterly convinced that he was in the right spot, John set to work getting a tree set up for his saddle.

There were three trees that would put him in position for a shot to the scrapes. The first was a huge, rough-barked poplar. After climbing about ten feet up that tree, John climbed back down. The tree was too large to get a safety climbing strap around, and since he was hunting alone, it was not worth the risk. The second tree was a prickly locust covered with six- to ten-inch needlelike thorns. Again, John climbed only a few feet up the tree before returning to the ground. There were just too many thorns that had to be cut to allow his climbing harness to slide up and down the opposite side of the trunk. John was now down to his last tree, the one he dreaded. This tree was smaller in diameter than the other two, was located in an excellent spot, and had a nice crotch about thirty-five feet up. The major drawback to this tree, however, was that it was covered with poison ivy all the way to the top. John was wary of trying his luck with the treacherous vine. Another quick glance at those hot scrapes, though, and the decision was made. After two hours of carefully cutting poison ivy, removing rough bark, and placing steps, John had reached the desired position in the tree. While he was working on this tree, the same eight-point from the morning hunt walked within five yards of him.

As soon as the tree was finished, John left the woods. Arriving at his van, he removed his scouting Scent-Lok and stowed it in a plastic bag. The suit would have to be washed to remove the poison ivy oil before he wore it again. He sped to his motel and showered as a precaution against getting the dreaded rash. By 2:00 P.M., he was perched in his new spot. An hour later, the action started.

Two fawns sped out of the bedding area and chased each other in circles for about twenty minutes. Right on their heels followed a yearling four-point. The little buck approached from the southwest and marked the licking branches over the main scrape with his forehead and preorbital glands. As the buck was working the licking branches, a doe and her fawns sauntered onto the scene. As soon as the four-point noticed the doe, he attempted to give chase. The doe, however, stood her ground and would not be intimidated into running. These deer then slowly moved north. Right after they had disappeared from sight, another small four-point and a yearling eight-point walked out of the brush along the river. The eight-point stopped at one of the secondary scrapes and scent-marked several of the licking branches. They then followed the path the other deer had taken to the north, toward the fields.

As soon as the two young bucks were out of sight, two very large, mature does materialized out of the timber to the west. Both of them walked directly to the scrapes. One of the does proceeded to work the licking branches over the main scrape. She then turned and urinated in the center of it. Both does then just loitered in the area for about twenty minutes, as if they were waiting for the dominant buck to show up. Then they, too, slowly moved to the north. The way the does acted convinced John that he was sitting over the primary scrape area of the local dominant buck. When does approach their estrous cycle, they seek out the primary scrape areas of the local dominant buck.

At 4:30 P.M. John's attention was drawn to the northeast by the sound of yet another approaching deer. Glancing in that direction, he noticed a very large set of antlers. As the buck closed the distance to the scrapes, it became apparent that he would not present a close shot. John had left his laser rangefinder behind and guessed the position of his shot opportunity to be forty-five yards. He was already at full draw when the buck stepped into the opening. He blatted to stop the buck. Holding his thirty-five-yard pin on the top of the buck's back, he opened his fingers. John watched the arrow as it disappeared into the top of the buck's back, above the spine. It was obviously a nonfatal shot. The buck was clearly much closer than he had estimated. In an instant, the buck was gone.

John was sick with himself for what had just happened. Never before had he attempted a shot at such a distance, and he was now kicking himself for it. He nearly decided to end his hunt, head back to his motel, and return later to attempt to track the buck—an attempt that he knew would be futile. On second thought, he decided to stick it out until dark. Perhaps that big ten-point from earlier in the week would show himself, and besides, moping in a motel room never accomplishes anything. The remaining time on stand, however, crept past torturously slowly. John kept replaying the shot in his mind. Perhaps a grunt or a doe bleat would have brought the buck closer. Or perhaps a grunt would have spooked the buck. Perhaps…

As the sun was setting, John decided to attempt a short, aggressive rattling sequence, about thirty seconds of rolling the sticks of his rattle bag together. Within minutes, a large buck appeared, approaching from the direction in which the wounded buck had fled. As the buck moved closer, John could hardly believe his eyes. This was the same buck he had just shot at. This time, though, the buck walked straight to the main scrape. John drew his bow and waited for the buck to stop on its own at the scrape. The buck was quartering away at twelve yards, urinating in his scrape in the exact spot the doe had stood earlier that afternoon. John let his arrow loose. This time, the arrow found its mark. The buck dashed about forty yards, stopped, stood for about ten seconds, then fell and expired.

This typical twelve-point carried seven points on its right antler and five points on its left antler. Five of the tines were longer than ten inches. The buck eventually earned a gross score of a little over 180.

Hunting the postrut becomes much easier in less pressured states. In late November of 2003, John took this twelve-point in Iowa.

While this hunt is a great example of how luck can sometimes play an important part in the outcome, it also shows that later in the rut, big bucks can become more vulnerable because most of the does have been bred. They have to search more for receptive does toward the end of the rut and during the postrut, making tactics such as rattling more effective.

Attempting to gain permission on private property like this is one way to find a place to hunt out of state. Another possibility is hunting public land. Just about every state has some form of public hunting land, whether it is state land, federal land, parkland, or wildlife management areas. These areas can be worth the effort to hunt. In some states, public hunting opportunity is vast; in others, it is quite small. Some public land hunting in states with low hunter densities will be better than the best hunting you have ever experienced hunting private property in pressured states.

This fact was hammered home for Chris in 2000. That spring, Chris knew he would be in Montana for a few weeks in September, so he applied for a deer permit and, in what was probably a stroke of luck, received one on his first attempt. From maps, he located a couple tracts of public land that looked promising in the area he was going to visit. Such land is abundant in Montana. These were not out-of-the-way places; access was very easy, and hunting was taking place. He spent a couple days scouting, set up a few trees, and then hunted. In three days of hunting, in 90-plus-degree weather, Chris saw more mature bucks than he had ever seen in an entire season in Michigan, and he arrowed a mature ten-point.

In states with low hunter densities, local hunters often ignore public land for the simple fact that they have great places to hunt all to themselves. This allows bucks on public land to grow to maturity and gives out-of-state hunters who are willing to make the extra effort the opportunity to kill these bucks. Any large tract of public land where access is somewhat difficult will fall into this category, particularly if access involves using a boat or mountain bike.

Public land and hunting areas have become quite easy to locate on the Internet. Almost every state has lists and maps available online. With this initial information, you can expand your search by ordering map books and plat maps. By looking at and printing aerial photos off the Internet, you can also cut down on your scouting time after your arrival. You do not have to stick to the state land after you arrive at your destination. When you are in an area that you plan to hunt again, always be on the lookout for hunting property. Knocking on a few doors can land you permission, though you should never rely solely on this method. Always have a huntable destination in mind before any trip.

Timing is important for out-of-state hunting. You have to be aware of deer activity during the time you plan to hunt. Most hunters plan out-of-state hunts for prime time—that is, during the prerut, the rut, and, in states where gun season opens in December, the postrut. Throughout most of the Midwest, the prerut usually starts around the first week of November, the peak of the rut is generally during the middle of the month, and the postrut is usually the last week of the month. John likes to hunt his best spots around home during the first half of November, trying to catch a wary pressured buck off guard, and then travels out of state after the fifteenth. Chris, on the other hand, because of different time constraints, hunts out of state whenever the opportunity arises.

Early-season hunting is an often overlooked aspect of out-of-state hunting trips. Hunting seasons begin at different times in different states, and in several states, mostly west of Michigan, bow season begins in September. Some states and provinces begin their bow seasons as early as late August in some years. The early start in some states is an excellent opportunity to get in some hunting before your season at home even begins and gives you a chance to score on a mature buck still leisurely moving in a summer routine. In some less hunted states, the local hunters have a tendency to wait for the rut periods to hunt, and often, even though the season is open, the deer experience little, if any, hunting pressure. Early-season bucks in nonpressured areas are very huntable. The lack of scouting pressure in such areas means the bucks have no reason to change their late-summer habits of moving during daylight. Bowhunters from pressured areas, though, have to hunt a little more aggressively. If you normally hunt a pressured area, you may find it difficult to change your normal hunting tactics; in these situations, it is not necessary to avoid spooking deer during the early season or save your best spots for the rut phases.

On one occasion, Chris went to another state during the first week of that state's season to scout and set up some trees for later in the season. He had not planned on hunting then, but after finding a well-used travel route lined with large rubs leading into a hayfield, he decided to set up a tree and hunt that afternoon. Chris took an eleven-point that evening.

There is another benefit to early-season hunting trips. If you plan two trips in a year, you can hunt and scout during the first trip, and set up for the second. This will increase your odds at tagging a mature buck. Whatever time of year you plan to hunt, scouting and preparation should be your first step.

SETTING UP

Whenever you enter a new area, your first goal is to gain an overview of the area. On a short-term hunt, though, this task has limits and requires a compromise. You have to scout just enough to find good places to hunt, while taking every precaution not to spook the deer. In areas with little or no hunting pressure, however, you can get away with much more aggressive scouting. We do things on out-of-state hunts that we would never consider doing in our home state. Scouting should be done aggressively, without fear of spooking deer, on your initial scouting and tree setup day.

When you arrive at a new hunting area, you should be armed with topographical maps and aerial photos. These can direct you to funnels without your having to fully explore the area. Along with these maps, we normally take four freelance fanny packs, each containing twenty tree steps and reflective tacks. We carry these together with our regular scouting packs, which contain a saw, rope, screw-in bow holder, quiver holder, compass or GPS, Ambush Saddle, and some other important gear. Since you will be hunting immediately after scouting, it is vital to practice extreme scent control. This means wearing an entire Scent-Lok suit, including head cover, along with gloves and rubber boots. Stepping into the woods, make your way directly toward the points you have marked as interesting on your maps and photos. When you come across a spot that looks good, clear out the tree immediately and then move on to the next, leaving the steps in the tree. For short-term hunts, there is really no time for secondary stands. Look for those superlative spots: primary scrape areas, staging areas, and funnels between bedding areas. Although in Michigan we do not place as much emphasis on travel routes between bedding areas and feeding areas or rub lines, in nonpressured areas we consider them primary locations.

A freelance pack with contents for quickly setting up a tree. The extension saw in the foreground will reach branches otherwise out of reach.

This scouting and stand preparation should take the entire first day of a hunt. Sacrificing a day of hunting time on a short-term hunt is difficult. Most hunters want to walk out into the woods and simply start hunting. The sacrifice of the first day is worth it, however. Rather than walking blindly into the woods and hoping for the best, you are now set up in four separate good locations. When all four of your freelance packs are empty, get out of the woods. With only a single day of scouting, it is possible that you did not select the perfect spots or trees, but your stand selections should have put you in a position to observe deer activity. You can adjust according to the activity you encounter.

Pictured here, a Game Tracker versa-cart in an Otter ice sled, and a target. These are essential items for bringing deer out of the woods and practicing on hunts away from home.

John loading a buck into his van with the aid of an ice sled and a homemade ramp.

The next morning should be your first hunt. Of the four spots you cleared out, select the one you feel is best. Be situated in your tree a minimum of an hour and a half before daylight. Even though undisturbed bucks are not nearly as nocturnal as their pressured brethren, your hunting habits should not slacken while away from home. If anything, you should be more motivated than ever by the increased opportunity that a mature buck will cross your path. Stick to the motto: Anything that works in a difficult situation will work even better in an easier situation.

We drive minivans, and when their back seats are out, their "payload" areas are large and comfortable. They also draw less attention from both hunters and nonhunters. For getting deer out of the field, we always carry a Game Tracker versa-cart and an Otter ice sled. The versa-cart is by far the best cart on the market. The deer rides just over the axle. With a low center of gravity and tires that are angled outward, the cart can pull a deer over logs and uneven ground without tipping over. (John has owned several other carts and had problems with all of them tipping over.) We dump the deer from the cart into the ice sled once we are at the vehicle, then slide it into the van through the back hatch. The sled keeps all of the blood contained; when there's snow on the ground, we also use it to drag the deer out.

HUNTING NONPRESSURED BUCKS

The main differences between pressured and nonpressured mature bucks are daytime movement and rut competition. Nonpressured areas generally have a deer population structure that is more natural, meaning a higher percentage of mature bucks. The more mature bucks, the more competition among bucks during the rut. This means that the bucks are more susceptible to scent use, rattling, calling, decoys, and other tactics. Because the competition for breeding rights among mature bucks is so intense, it is common for those bucks in nonpressured areas to move during daylight. And since the bucks were not pressured in the first place, they may not enter a forced nocturnal routine due to hunting pressure at all. In nonpressured areas, mature bucks often continue daytime movement patterns throughout the entire fall, not only during the rut. This is why early- and midseason rub lines are such effective spots in nonpressured areas but not so effective in pressured areas. This daytime movement and heavy breeding competition make nonpressured bucks more susceptible to aggressive hunting tactics, and therefore easier to hunt. Bucks that experience little hunting pressure also tolerate disturbances that are unacceptable in pressured areas.

THE BOWHUNTER'S ATTITUDE

PUTTING IT ALL TOGETHER

We have somewhat quantified the amount of work and time involved in hunting mature pressured bucks and described the bowhunting system that works for us. This system may not be for everyone. Some hunters do not want to hunt from trees; others do not like to get up three hours before daylight to go hunting; still others seem to be afraid of going out into the woods in the dark. We have heard these things from some of our own hunting friends, most of whom are very good hunters. The point is to develop your own hunting style, one that works for you.

Whatever your method, probably the most important key to bowhunting success with mature pressured bucks is your attitude. The bowhunter should be humble yet determined. These two attributes don't always fit well together. If you hunt pressured areas long enough, though, the deer will teach you humility. The minute you think you have a buck figured out, the situation can, and usually will, change. When you're hunting pressured areas, even the best hunting plans overwhelmingly end without bringing home that big buck. Deer are far better equipped at detecting predators than we are at being predators, softened as we are from civilization.

The important thing is to actually spend as much time as possible hunting and becoming familiar with the environment in which deer live. Attention to every event that happens while hunting is critical to success. How the deer move and react to their changing environment and how they react to both hunters and other deer are both very important pieces of the puzzle. The more knowledgeable you are about natural behavior and responses, the better hunter you could become. This knowledge is best gained through actual experience. Nothing beats hunting time to make you a better hunter. Books and magazines can provide you some theoretical base information, but this information means nothing unless you can apply it to your personal hunting situation. Every bowhunter should be a student of nature.

If you take this attitude toward bowhunting, you will never suffer boredom while hunting, some of your most memorable and cherished moments will be those when no deer was killed, and you will become more proficient at bowhunting. You may never forget that little chickadee landing on your arrow, that red fox sneaking up the edge of the swamp, or that glimpse of a black bear in an area where they are not supposed to be. So many things happen while bowhunting; the wonder of the natural world is endless. The experience, and not the big buck, is the true reward of bowhunting. Being able to bowhunt and get away from our fast-paced world is a real gift.

The most important aspect of a bowhunter's attitude is patience. Bowhunting pressured whitetails successfully takes time. Even if you do everything exactly as we have outlined in this book you probably will not meet with instant success. Instant gratification is a part of our modern culture that is not very compatible with real bowhunting. We use the term "real bowhunting" because instant gratification can indeed be purchased at a game farm, ranch, or high fence operation, which is ethically questionable. Success at hunting mature bucks can take years. Even though we have a combined hunting experience of more than sixty years, we sometimes go entire seasons without killing a mature buck. We have gone entire seasons without even seeing a mature buck in Michigan. Considering the amount of work we put into our hunting, this is somewhat frustrating, but we know eventually things will come together. When those dry spells come, we push through them and continually ask ourselves what the problem is.

Hunting, like everything else, is in a constant state of change, and you have to be willing to adjust. Years of hunting experience alone do not necessarily make a good hunter. Keeping an open mind to the changing situation is critical. We have often encountered hunters with decades of experience who complain of a lack of deer in areas we know are crawling with them. Further questioning usually reveals hunting stagnation. Some of these guys have been hunting from the same stand for the last ten years.

There is also no guarantee in bowhunting, no matter how good you become. Sometimes even when you do everything right, things simply do not fall into place. For instance, the huge buck that passed well within range but stuck to the brush and would not come any closer, no matter what call you used. Or the buck that you saw several times but somehow always managed to slip by unharmed. Or the missed shot. Situations like these are all part of the challenge that makes bowhunting so much fun. If you could kill a mature buck every time out, it would not be worth hunting.

John with Fred Bear in 1978. Fred embodied the sport of archery and was a major influence on bowhunting being what it is today.

Patience involves not only spending time in the woods, but also developing your skills as a hunter. This means building on your strengths and knowing your weaknesses. It also involves taking all the steps that lead up to seriously pursuing mature bucks. For novice hunters, we do not recommend starting out strictly trying to kill big bucks. Of course, big bucks fill the dreams of every hunter, and even a beginner should attempt a good shot if it is presented, but we recommend killing as many deer as possible in the beginning. Kill does, yearlings, or whatever you can, until you are proficient at simply killing deer. After you gain experience at killing deer, you can begin to concentrate on bucks. Only then, after killing bucks becomes less of a challenge, should you take the step to mature animals. Skipping a step in this progression can be detrimental to your hunting enjoyment and can lead to extreme frustration.

Both of us hunted for close to ten years before killing our first mature bucks in Michigan. John began seriously pursuing mature bucks only after twenty years' experience, and Chris took up the challenge after fifteen years. We often encounter younger hunters, and even some older hunters, who tell us they target mature bucks only. Often these guys have taken less than a handful of deer total, and no mature bucks to that point. They have been caught up in the popular big-buck mania and have seen all the videos and television shows, which fill young hunters with false expectations. You don't have to wait as long as we did to seriously pursue mature bucks— bowhunting is a lot different today than it was when we started—but you should at least be proficient at filling the freezer before you take up the big-buck challenge.

85050034R00150